CHRIST TRIUMPHANT

Christ Triumphant

Biblical Perspectives on His
Church and Kingdom

RAYMOND O. ZORN

THE BANNER OF TRUTH TRUST

THE BANNER OF TRUTH TRUST
3 Murrayfield Road, Edinburgh EH12 6EL
P.O. Box 621, Carlisle, Pennsylvania 17013, USA

*

© Raymond O. Zorn 1997
First published as *Church and Kingdom*, 1962
Revised edition, 1997
ISBN 0 85151 696 3

*

Scripture quotations are taken from
the New King James Version
© 1982 by Thomas Nelson, Inc.

*

Typeset in 11/12pt Plantin
by Gardner Graphics, Grand Rapids, Michigan, USA

*

Printed in Great Britain by
The Bath Press, Bath

CONTENTS

[v]

PART II
CHURCH AND KINGDOM IN
ESCHATOLOGICAL FULFILMENT

PART III
THE TASK OF THE CHURCH IN THE
KINGDOM OF GOD

TO MY LOVING WIFE, EDITH

*Who together with me for almost fifty years
has been a co-labourer in Christ's church and kingdom.*

INTRODUCTION

The subject of this book is one of continuing interest, as the wealth of literature written about it both in the past and in the present testifies. However, the last word on the subject has not yet been said, as is witnessed by the differing conceptions of the relationship between Christ's church and the kingdom of God. This book's purpose, therefore, is to examine the Scriptures anew to determine what they teach with respect to the church and the kingdom and their relation to one another. In doing so, it will be necessary to evaluate various conceptions on this continuingly intriguing subject.

For example, are church and kingdom to be thought of as without significant distinction, as is the position of Roman Catholicism and some branches of Protestantism? Or, should church and kingdom be thought of as being in sharp disjunction from one another, as modern Dispensationalism teaches?[1]

A more recent trend in some circles has been a de-emphasis of the eschatological concepts of kingdom and church as these concepts would pertain to eventual historical realization. Eschatology on this view, if not already realized, has been lifted above the historical plane to become a supra-historical ideal and is, therefore, not to be seen as future. Karl Barth, for instance, serves as a representative spokesman when he says concerning the first mission of Christ, "It became clear that the disciples would not have gone over the cities of Israel till the Son of Man came (*Matt.* 10:23). Now he had come, now 'everything had happened'."[2] What was not, therefore, fulfilled by Christ in his first mission to earth will not be fulfilled.

---

[1] *The Scofield Bible* has been one of the most influential exponents of Dispensationalism, together with Dallas Theological Seminary.

[2] Quoted by H.N. Ridderbos, *The Coming of the Kingdom* (Philadelphia: Presbyterian and Reformed Publishing Co., 1962), p.455.

This view has arisen against the background of a higher criticism which adherents of this view feel has discredited both the historical and the supernatural aspects of the Bible. Prophecies of events yet future are thus likewise discredited. This approach nevertheless assumes that where biblical historicity, both past and future, must be sacrificed, an attempt should be made to maintain, in some measure at least, the import of the Bible's message. The exegetical labours of proponents of this view are, therefore, to be taken much more seriously than those of the older theological liberalism, which arbitrarily rejected whole portions of the Bible, such as the eschatological, as practically meaningless and hence of little exegetical worth. Some benefit can, therefore, be derived from a discerning study of their efforts.

However, the inadequacy of their collective views lies in their failure to recognize objective truth and final authority. For, according to them, biblical history is primarily a fallible record of man's varied religious experience, and only secondarily a record of God's acts in human history. But if the Bible is not an inerrant revelation of the *magnalia Dei* ("the great deeds of God", *Acts* 2:11), not only with respect to the past but also in connection with the future, then the control of man's destiny has shifted from divine to human hands or to pure chance, as the case may be. For then man has in the Bible not a revelation from God to which, as a trustworthy chart and compass, he is bound, but only a fallible human document with subjectively interpreted ideals and norms of truth. As such, it can be no more than a limited guide to be either followed or selectively disregarded as man by this self-established autonomy decrees. This is a frightening weakness in this view, which, if fully pursued, can only lead to the tragedy of disillusion and despair because man, being cast on himself alone, is powerless either to chart properly or to fulfil his course as he should.[1]

----

[1] The writer has in mind here the Neo-Orthodox school of theology, though he has two reasons for not singling out specific representatives: 1) he has already pointed out the logical end rather than stating the *de facto* position as it may be held with greater or lesser degree by its various advocates; and 2) the variations in this view are such as to make it almost too elastic for any particular exponent to

The writer holds to theological orthodoxy as it is defined by such Reformed confessions as the *Belgic Confession*, the *Heidelberg Catechism*, the *Canons of Dort*, and the *Westminster Confession of Faith*. He believes in the trustworthiness of the full corpus of Scripture as an inerrant account of God's acts in the stream of human history and as an infallible revelation of what God will yet bring to pass in the ultimate destiny of mankind.

This book is, therefore, a humble attempt to set forth the relationship between church and kingdom, while at the same time interacting with differing viewpoints and evaluating them with the necessary criticism and correction furnished by the light of Scripture.

This book is divided into three parts. The first two parts present aspects of church and kingdom as they are developed by Scripture from the beginning of history to its end. The third part is an attempt to apply the biblical data about church and kingdom to the people of God and the society in which they find themselves today.

Now for a brief synopsis of the book's contents. The first chapter gives an introductory presentation of the scope and manifestation of the kingdom as a setting for what follows.

Chapter Two sets forth the significance of Old Testament Israel, whose calling and function as the covenant people of God must first be understood before their oneness with the people of God in the new dispensation can be seen. The oneness of the people of God is an *a priori* consideration for the relationship between church and kingdom.

Chapter Three sets forth in detail the reasons why Old Testament Israel has given way to New Testament Israel as the people of God. Moreover, an added exegetical *excursus* gives the relevant New Testament texts which speak of the relationship

---

be singled out as a consistent representative of it. It is, therefore, against this school with its inherent weaknesses of subjectivism and lack of final authority, rather than against its exponents, who may be either wholly or partly identified with it, that the writer would seek to expound a more biblical view.

that exists between the kingdom of Christ and the kingdom of God. We do this because too often confusion arises from a failure to associate properly the one with the other or to see their separate significance when reference is made in Scripture to these similar and yet differing concepts.

Chapter Four is a deductive summary of the previous development of the church in relationship to the kingdom. The way in which the two are allied and yet to be differentiated is restated with the addition of such new material as will most clearly set forth the necessary and vital relationship existing between the two. This chapter also serves as a transition to Part II, where the church and the kingdom in their eschatological fulfilment are dealt with.

Part II traces to their eschatological fulfilment those aspects of the church and kingdom which, though yet future, will nevertheless come to fulfilment in this present age, culminating in the age to come. With the exception of the question of the millennial rule, these aspects are not something completely different from those previously dealt with in Part I. But the treatment in this division is rather a tracing out to their proper conclusion of those aspects of church and kingdom already operative in this age, along with a viewing, in so far as is possible from Scripture, of the setting up of the final order or eternal kingdom.

In Part III, a practical application is made of the principles set forth in Parts I and II as those principles apply to the task of the church in the kingdom, or the programme which she is to fulfil in society, which she recognizes is under the dominion of the Lord her God. That programme includes a battle against all foes, visible and invisible, as they make up the opposing kingdom of darkness; a programme which turns in loving attention to the individual to provide him with spiritual life and adequate nurture in the means of grace; and a programme which in ever-expanding fashion includes the needs of the social unit, whether in its most basic form, the family, or in the broader aspects of state and society at large. For, as the church properly recognizes, the programme of God will not be complete until God's kingdom has come in the fullest sense, and his will is done on earth as it is in heaven. Part III, therefore, while introducing

new scriptural data and fresh material where relevant, is nevertheless basically the logical outworking of biblical principles
established in the two previous parts.

The writer's aim has been to be selective rather than exhaustive. By the concentration on relevant Scriptures, along with
quotations where necessary of the pertinent scholarly works in
this field, it is hoped that sufficient evidence has been marshalled
to prove the position that the writer has sought to establish.
Where, at certain points, some repetition occurs in the development of particular subjects, it is hoped that this will prove
clarifying rather than redundant. Not only is some repetition
desirable as a pedagogical device but in certain places it is
unavoidable. Again, the aim in this case has been to set forth a
logical classification of subjects, with exposition where it was
felt that it would be most effective.

This second edition preserves the main contours of the first,
though some parts have been changed where it was considered
that the wording, together with the outline of the book's contents,
could be improved. The title of the book has been modified to
bring to the reader's attention the fact that, while the book's
theme is the relationship between the church and the kingdom
of God, the one who brings his triumphant cause to pass in church
and kingdom, yes, and the world at large, is none other than
the triumphant Christ, who, since completing his redemptive
work with his death and resurrection almost two thousand years
ago, now rules at the right hand of God the Father, exercising a
present mediatorial sovereignty that will accomplish all his
purposes so that, ultimately, "God may be all in all" (*I Cor*. 15:29).

A number of new footnotes have been added where it was
thought that they might be helpful. A new *excursus* on theonomy
has been included, since it concerns the relation of God's law to
the state. The *excursus* is in the nature of a critique, especially of
this movement's advocacy of the maintenance for today of the
Mosaic law-code, including its penal sanctions. Biblical quotations have been changed from the Authorised Version to the
New King James Version. A commonly agreed-on choice of a
version which is acceptable to all today is still an unachieved
desideratum. The writer has chosen the NKJV because, like its

renowned predecessor, it has sought to be both literally and idiomatically faithful to the original languages, while at the same time giving a translation that is in modern English. The reader of this version, with its alternative footnote renderings, has the advantage of the Greek behind the Authorised Version and the Greek behind virtually all modern translations. Moreover, the translation of the Old Testament is based on up-to-date studies of the Hebrew and cognate languages and research using the latest manuscript findings, including the Dead Sea Scrolls.

The writer freely acknowledges his debt to many authors, and he has warmed himself at the fires of various schools of thought with which he is either not necessarily in accord or at variance. Where this is the case, he trusts that the particular context will make clear the point of agreement or disagreement, as the case may be. I also wish to express my appreciation to the Rev. Iain H. Murray and the staff of Banner of Truth Trust publishers who have given me valuable assistance in the preparation of the revised manuscript of this book.

The aim in writing this book has been to present a clearer picture of Christ's church and the kingdom of God as distinct entities, their relationship to one another and the scope of the activity they encompass. If the writer's labour opens up to the reader new areas of thought or avenues of further exploration, or gives a basis for more confident Christian daily living, he will deem his efforts as more than repaid and will have been given the satisfaction of knowing that others, as well as he, have found the study of the relationship of the church to the kingdom a subject of fruitful doctrinal and practical value.

RAYMOND O. ZORN
Newtown, Victoria, Australia
31 July 1996

PART I

The Church in Relation to the Kingdom

I: THE KINGDOM OF GOD DEFINED

1. Its etymological definition

In the broadest sense God's kingdom refers to the furthest reaches of his sovereignty. As Psalm 103:19 puts it, "The Lord has prepared his throne in the heavens; and his kingdom rules over all." God is sovereign and therefore he exercises control over everything he has created. As the heathen monarch Nebuchadnezzar was forced to confess after experiencing God's power, "All the inhabitants of the earth are reputed as nothing; he does according to his will in the army of heaven, and among the inhabitants of the earth. No one can restrain his hand or say to him, What have you done?" (*Dan.* 4:35).

Scholars today are generally agreed that the biblical concept of God's kingdom, whether the Hebrew, *malkut,* or the Greek, *basileia,* refers to his reign or rule rather than the sphere or domain of his rule.[1]

God is sovereign, but not all his creation acknowledges or acquiesces in that sovereignty. This is due to the presence of sin in the universe which God has made. A part of his creation, with mankind as its crown, has dared, under the instigation of previously-fallen angels, to rebel against their maker. And God, in consistence with all the attributes of his nature, has taken steps to counteract and overcome this evil with the effects it

---

[1] K.L. Schmidt, "Basileia", *Theologisches Wörterbuch zum neuen Testament,* ed. Gerhard Kittel (Stuttgart: Verlag von W. Kohlhammer, 1933), vol. 1 (cf. the entire article).

has brought on his world. Being sovereign, God is free to deal in judgment or in mercy to manifest his sovereignty to the acknowledgment of all. Ultimately, every knee shall bow, of things in heaven, or on earth, or under the earth, and confess to his lordship and glory (*Phil.* 2:10-11).

God's kingdom, therefore, takes specific form where this process of conquest comes to concrete expression. Its beginning is with his chosen people whom he redeems and makes his by grace, though its end will only be completely realized when all things shall have been subdued to him and God shall be all in all (*I Cor.* 15:28).

Basic to the thought of the kingdom of God, therefore, is its divine origin and operation, though it comes to earthly and visible expression in the world. In redemption, God may choose a people, subdue them to himself, rule over them as their king, call them to the privileges of his rule and the duties of their high calling (*Exod.* 19:5-6, *I Pet.* 2:9-10). But it is just because of this that the divine operation and the emphasis of his activity in it can never be minimized or disregarded. Quite fittingly it can be referred to as the kingdom of heaven. As Schmidt says: "And it therewith follows that such heavenly rule cannot have its nature set forth as a kingdom that comes into being by either a natural development of earthly relationship or through human efforts, but rather through an intrusion of God from heaven itself."[1]

2. Is it only future?

The question may now be asked, in what way are we to think of the kingdom? May it be thought of as already present? Or is it solely future? This question arises because some interpret the kingdom of God only in the idealistic sense of a goal or fulfilment towards which history is progressively moving. Oscar Cullmann, for example, maintains this and attributes the same to Schmidt.[2]

[1] Schmidt, "Basileia," pp.582-583.

[2] "The Kingdom of God is a purely future concept". Cf. Schmidt, "Basileia;" Oscar Cullmann, "Königsherrschaft Christi und Kirche im Neuen Testament", *Theologischen Studien*, herausgegeben von Karl Barth, Heft 10 (Zurich: Evangelischer Verlag U-G Zollikon, 1941), p.11.

According to this interpretation, the kingdom of God is an eschatological concept that is to be limited solely to the future.

Our theology, however, should be the result of scriptural exegesis rather than of the superimposition of the interpretations of a philosophy which is thereby made more basic than it. That the Scriptures teach a present aspect of God's kingdom can be seen by scholars of various theological backgrounds. For instance, Minear says, "God and Satan are battling for the souls of men, and the place of battle is creation-wide and history-long."[1] Wendland agrees, "It [the kingdom of God] is not a metaphysical realm behind or above this world, lying behind the things of this world or hovering over them. God comes; that is the direct and simple import of the New Testament message of the kingdom of God."[2] And, in the words of Braun, "The present kingdom is not separate from that of the future; however it first manifests itself in its whole power after a time of testings, persecutions and severe conflicts. Whether 'present' or 'future,' it is nevertheless unitary: in all of its stages of development it relates itself always unto the endtime, and always it is grounded, sustained and permeated by the spiritual power of the messianic times."[3]

We must therefore be fully aware of the fact that written large, especially in the prophetic portions of the Old Testament, was the future day of the Lord when he would strike a decisive blow in the full manifestation of his kingdom. God himself would come and dwell among his people, bringing with him deliverance from the bondage of sin. With him also would come the full blessings of salvation in the kingdom of God, for God would come bringing his salvation with him. The Old Testament foreshadowed the experience of this grace. It awaited the New Testament time for its incipient realization. In unmatched

---

[1] Paul S. Minear, *The Kingdom and the Power* (Philadelphia: The Westminster Press, 1950), p.220.

[2] H.D. Wendland, "The Kingdom of God and History", *The Kingdom of God and History: A Symposium* (Chicago, New York: Willett, Clark & Co., 1930), p.146.

[3] F.M. Braun, O.F., *Neues Licht auf die Kirche* (Koln: Benziger and Co., A.G. Einsideln, 1946), pp.154-155.

eloquence, the prophet Isaiah, speaking of God's promised dominion and glory, foretold how it would be ushered in by the coming of God's anointed servant, the Messiah, himself Immanuel whose fittingly descriptive names are: Wonderful Counsellor, the Mighty God, the Everlasting Father, the Prince of Peace. His birth would mean the establishment of God's kingdom and the increase of his government and peace without end (*Isa.* 9:6-7).

Daniel also speaks of the kingdom as a mountain filling the whole earth (*Dan.* 2:35, 44). And he, too, sets forth the role of God's anointed in this, coming as the Son of Man with the clouds of heaven to the Ancient of Days. To him is given glory and a kingdom consisting of all people, nations and languages who serve him in a dominion which is everlasting (*Dan.* 7:13-14). Attending the establishment of this kingdom would be super-natural wonders and signs in the realms of both nature and grace. Wonders would appear in the heavens and in the earth (*Joel* 2:30), and God's people will perform great deeds under the stimulus of the Holy Spirit's effusion (*Joel* 2:28-29). The time will be unprecedented as a day of salvation (*Joel* 2:32). The Lord whom his people sought would suddenly come to his temple, even the Messenger of the Covenant (*Mal.* 3:1). But before the Sun of Righteousness would arise with healing in his wings, the Lord would send a herald before him in the spirit and power of Elijah to turn the people to the Lord in repentance and expec-tation of his advent (*Mal.* 4:5-6; cf. *Luke* 1:17, *Matt.* 17:12).

3. Its present aspect

We are therefore prepared to understand the present aspect as it was ushered in by the advent, message and ministry of Jesus, the divinely promised and long-awaited Messiah, or Christ. As the Gospels record, the ministry of John the Baptist begins that dispensation in which the kingdom of God may be proclaimed as "at hand". For here in John is the herald who was foreseen in the Old Testament as the way-preparer for the Lord. Not surprising therefore is the fact that Jesus begins his ministry by preaching the good news of the kingdom of God, for by his advent the time previously awaited has now been fulfilled

(Mark 1:14-15). In him the kingdom of God exercises force and the forceful lay hold of it *(Matt.* 11:12).[1] Because he has bound "the strong man", he is able to divide his spoils by freeing his people from Satan's power. By his exorcism of demons there can be no doubt that the kingdom of God has arrived [*ephthasen*, Aorist, or past tense].[2] People can therefore no longer be indifferent or careless about the coming of the kingdom, for in the presence of Jesus Christ, the kingdom is in the people's very midst *(Luke* 17:21).[3] People must now, above all else, seek the kingdom of God and his righteousness, subordinating all else to this highest good and supreme goal of life *(Matt.* 6:33).

What began with the message and ministry of Christ continues throughout this present dispensation, for in him the messianic times, or "last days", have come *(Heb.* 1:2). Pentecost is therefore merely a new aspect of Christ's continuing reign *(Acts* 2:33-36), by which Old Testament prophecy concerning the messianic age is fulfilled *(Acts* 2:16-21), and by which the kingdom of God can continue to be proclaimed *(Acts* 8:12; 19:8; 20:25; 28:23, 31), with the promise of the risen Lord that he shall ever remain with his own in this task, even to the end of the age *(Matt.* 28:20). Only then shall he send forth his angels who shall gather out of his kingdom all things that offend, and those who have practised lawlessness, and having judged and punished them, will enjoy

[1] The verb, *biazomai,* is used in only one other place in the New Testament *(Luke* 16:16) where it is given the middle voice (active sense) by the AV, ASRV, RSV, Luther's German, the Dutch (1953) and French versions. The NIV therefore correctly renders it in the active sense, "[the kingdom] has been forcefully advancing". To adopt the active sense is therefore not only a properly consistent rendering of the verb, but also fits in better with the context of the kingdom's presence from the days of John's preaching as Jesus here teaches. It was present whether "exercising force" or "suffering violence" (NKJV). But the gospel proclamation can more easily be understood as a part of the kingdom's manifestation of power rather than that it creates forceful activity that becomes a part of it. The latter meaning is true enough but it is secondary to the former meaning which is primary. A realm of power first exercises force and in so doing may or may not create forceful activity that becomes part of it.

[2] Luke 11:19-22.

[3] Translations beside the RSV and the footnote of the NIV which support this rendering are: the 1953 Dutch *(Want Zie, het Koninkrijk Gods is bij u)* and the 1874 French translation of David Martin *(Car voici, le regne de Dieu est au milieu de vous).*

with his own, the righteous, the kingdom of the Father when it will have attained its ultimate goal.

The kingdom, therefore, has a present as well as a future aspect. The two are not to be confused or identified, but are to be seen in their respective significance. The Old Testament, with only the perspective of the distant future, looked on the kingdom as an undivided whole. The task of distinguishing between the several stages of fulfilment lay with the ministry of Christ and the interpretation to be furnished by subsequent New Testament revelation. The kingdom of God has come in Christ. But it will have come in the fullest sense when Christ, having subdued all things to himself, delivers the kingdom to the Father, that God may be all in all (*I Cor.* 15:24-28). To this end we continue to pray, "Thy kingdom come".

4. May the kingdom be identified with the church?

A question which now engages our attention is: may the kingdom for all practical intents and purposes be identified with the church? May we agree with the statement of Bannerman: "It may be enough to say that practically the kingdom of God in this world is just the church at work. It denotes 'all those throughout the world who profess the true religion, together with their children,' — that is according to the *Westminster Confession,* 'the catholic Church visible,' (XXV 2) — regarded especially in their life and work, their influence direct and indirect in the world."[1]

This statement has much to commend it, for as Bannerman recognizes, the Westminster divines framed this article of the *Confession* with scriptural references as their foundation, the strongest of which is Colossians 1:13 where in speaking of the redemption given by the Father to his people, we read, "He has delivered us from the power of darkness and translated us into the kingdom of the Son of his love." Here, the church is spoken of as the kingdom of Christ. And who would deny this truth

---

[1] D. Douglas Bannerman, *The Scripture Doctrine of the Church* (Grand Rapids: Eerdmans, 1955), pp.249-250.

since the redemption of God's kingdom as announced in its gospel was purchased by the atoning death of Christ for sin and is applied to his people in their salvation (*Col.* 1:14, *Acts* 20:28, *Eph.* 1:17, etc.)? The unsatisfactoriness of Bannerman's statement, however, lies in its not sufficiently taking into account all the data concerning this truth. The statement is an oversimplification.

But at the other extreme, Bright's statement would also appear to be an oversimplification: "There is no tendency in the New Testament to identify the visible church with the kingdom of God."[1] This statement can only be made if the kingdom of Christ and the kingdom of God be rigidly kept apart, identifying the former with the present and the latter with the future alone. But besides the previous argument against such an interpretation (headings 2 and 3), we have a clear linking together of the kingdom of Christ and the kingdom of God in Ephesians 5:5.[2]

What, then, is the relationship between the church and the kingdom of God? Hort puts it aptly when he says: "We may speak of the Ecclesia as the visible representative of the kingdom of God, or as the primary instrument of its sway, or under some other analogous forms of language. But we are not justified in identifying the one with the other, so as to be able to apply directly to the Ecclesia whatever is said in the Gospels about the kingdom of heaven or of God." And again: "Through the apostle's guarded words [especially in Ephesians 4] we may probably gather that the Ecclesia...was to him likewise a kind of pledge for the complete fulfilment of God's purpose in the dim future."[3]

5.   The demand of the kingdom of God

There is a further consideration under this subdivision; namely, the demand of the kingdom. "God's kingdom manifests itself as

---

[1] John Bright, *The Kingdom of God* (New York/Nashville: Abingdon/Cokesbury Press, 1953), p.236.

[2] "For this you know, that no fornicator, unclean person, nor covetous man, who is an idolater, has any inheritance in the kingdom of Christ and of God."

[3] F.J.A. Hort, *The Christian Ecclesia* (London: MacMillan, 1900), pp.19 and 142.

judgment and *salvation*."[1] Judgment appears in that the perfect embodiment of God's righteousness has come in the person of his Messiah against whom the best man is exposed in his complete moral and spiritual destitution (*John* 9:39, *Rom.* 3:23). In the light of the kingdom demand for righteousness (*Matt.* 6:33) as made by him, all who previously thought that they saw must now confess their blindness and utter inability to fulfil that demand. The wages of sin being death (*Rom.* 6:23), God has appointed a day in which he will judge the world in righteousness by the Messiah whom he has ordained to this end (*Acts* 17:31, *John* 5:28-30). Judgment, with respect to both the present insufficiency of the sinner's works and his future condemnation, is a stark reality of kingdom manifestation.

Over against this negative manifestation of the kingdom comes the positive manifestation as the sphere of salvation. The righteousness of which man himself is destitute may be received as a gift of God's grace since it has been vicariously provided by Christ on behalf of his people (*Rom.* 5:18). As in Adam all men die because, as their federal head, his sin became theirs, even so in Christ shall all his people be made alive because of the salvation he earned on their behalf as the second Adam (*I Cor.* 15:22). His death was an atonement for sin (*Mark* 10:45, *I Pet.* 2:24) and his righteousness is the ground of his people's favour with God (*Rom.* 3:22).

How is kingdom salvation made the portion of God's people? Here the necessity of repentance is made clear. The sinner must change his mind (the literal meaning of the Greek, *metanoia*) in the light of the kingdom manifestation and its demand. He must learn of his blindness, recognize the illusion of his self-sufficiency, learn of God as he truly is in the manifestation of his holiness, justice and mercy. In short, the sinner must do a complete turn-about. We can therefore understand the integral part the preaching of repentance played in the ministry of John the Baptist, the Lord Jesus Christ, the apostles — yes, and in the prophets of the old dispensation. God offers the blessings of

---

[1] Wendland, *The Kingdom of God and History*, p.146.

kingdom salvation by grace. But they are received on his terms alone through repentance and faith. A sinner must first see himself as lost before he will be willing to trust in Christ and be found.

But though the kingdom salvation comes as the gift of God's grace, "Righteousness is to be sought from the pure desire of satisfying him who is the supreme end of all moral existence... Jesus emphasized that in the pursuit of righteousness the satisfaction of God should be man's supreme concern."[1]

Man can do nothing to cleanse himself from either moral defilement or the penalty of sin. He is as spiritually dead as a corpse is devoid of physical life. But having experienced the grace of God in salvation, the regenerated individual is to walk in the way of new-found obedience to his Saviour God. "[Be] as obedient children, not fashioning yourselves according to the former lusts in your ignorance: but as he who has called you is holy, so be holy in all your conduct: because it is written, 'Be holy, for I am holy'" (*I Pet.* 1:14-16). This obedience must be more than mere external conformity; it must pervade the whole individual who is a part of God's kingdom, for as Christ made plain, "Unless your righteousness exceeds the righteousness of the scribes and Pharisees, you will by no means enter into the kingdom of heaven" (*Matt.* 5:20).

"Jesus' doctrine of the kingdom as both inward and outward, coming first in the heart of man and afterwards in the external world, upholds the *primacy of the spiritual and ethical* over the physical. The invisible world of the inner religious life, the righteousness of the disposition, the sonship of God are in it made supreme, the essence of the kingdom, the ultimate realities to which everything else is subordinate."[2] God's people, as members of his kingdom, will love him who has first loved them and made them his own, with all their hearts and souls and minds and strength and will seek in every way to glorify him who is the object of their love, the source of their salvation, and the goal of their life (*Matt.* 22:37, *I Cor.* 10:31, *Col.* 3:1-4).

---

[1] G. Vos, *The Kingdom and the Church* (Grand Rapids: Eerdmans, 1951), pp.60-65.

[2] *Ibid.*, p.103.

II: OLD TESTAMENT ISRAEL

1. Israel's place in the world

We are now prepared to deal with the relationship of the kingdom of God to the Old Testament nation of Israel. Israel, as a nation redeemed from Egypt's bondage, was constituted by God as his people (*Exod.* 19:4-6). With the outstretched arm of his power he delivered them from the slavery of an imperial world-power that they might become his possession and serve him as a kingdom of priests. As a people they were to be the firstfruits of a larger treasure the Lord would redeem from the nations of the earth,[1] serving the Lord and representing him

---

[1] This statement is based upon the covenant of grace as God established it with Abraham in Genesis 12:3, "In you all the families of the earth shall be blessed", and as interpreted in Galatians 3:8, God deliberately narrowed the redemptive line to Abraham and his seed in Isaac (of whom through Jacob the nation of Israel was established) that he might ultimately broaden his redemption of men to include people from all nations of the world. Israel may not have been properly aware of this role which they were to play in God's comprehensive plan, and may even have misinterpreted in a jealously exclusivistic sense such revelation of God's redemption of them to fulfil promises made to their forefathers as is found in Deuteronomy 7:8. But as seen on the background of this Old Testament aspect of the covenant of grace and its New Testament interpretation, the oath which God had sworn to their fathers and would keep by bringing them out of Egypt by a mighty hand of redemption (*Deut.* 7:8) cannot be so construed. Israel's redemption fulfilled God's promises to the fathers, to be sure, but these promises had for their goal the salvation of the nations. Israel may have lacked the perspective that we must not fail to see. As Cullmann puts it, "This sacred history runs in two directions: the one goes from the many to the One [Christ]. That is the old covenant. The other goes from the One to the many. That is the new covenant" ("Königsherrschaft Christi", p.36).

before the world.[1] And at Mt. Sinai, God formally bound himself in covenant agreement with Israel. "Now therefore, if you will indeed obey my voice and keep my covenant, then you will be a special treasure to me above all people; for all the earth is mine. And you shall be to me a kingdom of priests and a holy nation" (*Exod.* 19:5-6).

Israel was therefore a congregation of the Lord (*qehal Yahweh,* Mic. 2:5, *Num.* 16:3, 20:4, *I Chron.* 28:8). The word, *qahal,* i.e., assembly, comes from a root meaning to call or to summon. At first, when reference was made to Israel as the assembly of the Lord, it was used interchangeably with another Hebrew word, *'edah,* i.e., congregation, which was taken from the root which in another voice (i.e., the Niph'al stem) means "to meet at an appointed place." In passages such as Leviticus 4:13 and Numbers 16:3, *'edah* and *qahal* even appear as synonymous. Both meant the gathering together of the people as an assembly, whether for counsel, civil affairs, or religious purposes. In later usage, however, *qahal* gained the ascendancy so as to be used almost exclusively as a desigation for Israel as an assembly of the Lord by the time of the nation's return from exile.[2] Though it was later translated as *ekklesia,* i.e., assembly or church, by the translators of the Greek Old Testament (LXX), a noun coming from *ekkaleo,* to call out, its original concept was different in that the people of God had been called out of the world. Even the Greek in its root meaning does not bear out this idea, *ekkalein* originally meaning, "the calling of the citizens of a Greek town out of their houses by the herald's trumpet to summon them to the assembly."[3]

While being called out of the world is a legitimate biblical teaching for the people of God, the emphasis of the original is that they have been called into fellowship as a united assembly or congregation of the Lord. *Qahal* should therefore be our starting point in the definition of *ekklesia* (or *ecclesia*) rather

---

[1] As deduced from the basic functions of the priestly office to which Israel was broadly assigned as a "kingdom of priests".

[2] "*qahal* abounds in Chronicles, Ezra, and Nehemiah". Hort, *The Christian Ecclesia,* p.7.

[3] *Ibid.,* pp.5-6.

than vice versa. Identified as it was with *ecclesia* by the LXX translators, a ready-made word was at hand in the New Testament dispensation to designate the people of God when they should arise as the people of the Messiah, or the new Israel. Hence, already from etymological definition we learn that the people of God, while a separate entity from the world, were not, however, to be in isolation from it. For they were to be in the world's midst to serve and represent their King, and bring it under obedience to his rule.

2. Its king

The Lord God was Israel's king.[1] True, there was already provision made in the law for the appointment of an earthly king (*Deut.* 17:14-20), but the king would exercise his office only as his vicegerent in conjunction with the law of the Lord. He would not be able arbitrarily to make his own laws, set his own standards of conduct and worship. He was ever to be in subordination to the law of God. And his whole reign would be judged in the light of faithfulness or unfaithfulness to that law. King David was a man after God's own heart because he walked in the way of his commandments, whereas Jeroboam and his successors gained Scripture's unmitigated opprobrium for bringing Israel low in sin for their faithlessness to and rebellion against the Lord and his law.

As this was true for the king, so it was also for every other office among the people of God. It was the Lord who made provision for the Levitical order and constituted the Aaronic priesthood among the people of God as those who would perform the services in the rites of worship, represent the people before God and act as mediators between him and the people.[2] In the same way, as revelation became necessary in addition to that of the law, at such a time the Lord would raise up a prophet to

---

[1] Some New Testament passages which refer to God's kingship over Israel are Matthew 5:35; 8:12; 21:43.

[2] See the entire book of Leviticus, but especially chapter 8. Also the epistle to the Hebrews, chapters 7, 8, 9.

declare his will (*Deut.* 18:15-22). Israel was not therefore to learn the abominations of the nations whose land the Lord was giving them, for these nations worshipped idols and were in league with the powers of darkness (*Deut.* 18:9-12). Israel was to be perfect before the Lord and be guided by him. The means of identifying a true prophet would be twofold; he must speak in the name of the Lord only (*Deut.* 18:20), and the thing which he prophesied must come to pass (*Deut.* 18:22). And Israel must ever remember the anticipatory and unfulfilled character of its present covenant as made by the Lord through his servant Moses, for the Lord would yet raise up another prophet like Moses, but greater than he, and to him they were to give heed (*Deut.* 18:15, 18; cf. *Acts* 3:20-22, *John* 1:45).

We may conclude, therefore, that every office among the people of God was no more than a vicegerency of his designation and in subordination to him who was Israel's true king.

3. Its role as the people of God

Israel's role as the people of God was to be a kingdom of priests and a holy nation. That is to say, it was to reflect God's glory and embody his grace and truth, not only to preserve it as a witness, but to perpetuate it among the nations as well (*I Kings* 8:41-43). Only in preliminary fashion was this role ever realized to any degree. During the reign of Solomon the Queen of the South came from the far country of Sheba to learn if the reports she had heard concerning Solomon's divinely-bestowed wisdom were true. And so evident was the blessing of God on the words and deeds of Solomon that her praise took the form of a benediction on Solomon's God, the covenant God of Israel (*I Kings* 10:9).

But this centripetal role of Israel in attracting the nations of the world to the city of its great king and to a proper knowledge concerning him was short-lived. The sinful breach of the theocracy by Jeroboam and the ten tribes in their renunciation of the Davidic dynasty was a repudiation of the Lord and their relationship to him as a covenant people. Their consequent idolatry and apostasy soon made this all too evident in the course of their sin-checkered history, whose end was finally made necessary by the Lord's judgment through the Assyrian captivity.

[13]

It is true that flashes of Israel's true role as the people of God were here and there seen on the generally dark canvas of sin caused by a wayward people. The conversion of the Gentile widow of Zarephath to the Lord[1] under the ministry of the prophet Elijah may be cited as an example. So also is the healing of the Syrian general Naaman's leprosy through the ministry of Elisha (*II Kings* 5).[2] Here were Gentiles who were blessed by Israel's God.

But though this might reflect upon what could well have been, we cannot plead these as examples of the norm. As a matter of fact they rather reveal the continuing grace of God to his people and through them to others even though Israel had made itself unworthy and had forfeited every claim to it. In this sense, the ministry of Jonah to the Ninevites proves instructive. Israel, having repudiated its loyalty to God and denied its responsibilities to the covenant he had made with them, was ripe for judgment. Instead therefore of being an embodiment of the grace and truth of God from which the nations should be savingly instructed, Israel was to forfeit that grace and truth, which would proceed to find lodging among her enemies, and who would be preserved to become a scourge in the Lord's hands on his faithless people. That Jonah understood this is made obvious by his extreme reluctance to preach at all to Nineveh, though the burden of his message was impending doom.[3] He realized that, in the grace of God shown in the message given him by the delay of judgment, the desired effect of repentance would be aroused in the Ninevites (*Jon.* 4:2), so that they would

---

[1] I Kings 17:9-24. My conclusion as to her conversion is based on the significance of Christ's reference to her in Luke 4:26 where he cites her case as an example of the mercy God in the salvation Christ was making real by means of his ministry. Israel as a whole during the time of Elijah was unworthy of the salvation of God. He therefore showed it to a Gentile widow. In the same way Israel of Christ's day was showing its unworthiness to receive God's salvation by their rejection of his anointed one. But God's salvation would nevertheless be shown though it would mean bestowing it upon the Gentiles as it had been in the case of the widow of Zarephath in Elijah's day.

[2] Christ used the healing of Naaman as an example in the same way as he did for the widow of Zarephath (cf. *Luke* 4:27).

[3] "Yet forty days, and Nineveh shall be overthrown!" (*Jon.* 3:4).

be spared to become the ravagers of his people. The thought was too much to bear for a patriot of Jonah's calibre, but the truth nevertheless remains clear. Israel had denied, repudiated and forfeited its role as the people of God. Judgment was inevitable.

4. Its promises and expectation

In the south, the kingdom of Judah inconsistently perpetuated the role of the theocracy. It is true that here the temple with its rites of worship, the law of God in whose path of obedience the people were to walk and the Davidic dynasty as the continuing succession of the divinely appointed monarchy were still to be found. But apart from the breach made by the ten tribes which seriously weakened the testimony and influence of the southern kingdom because of this powerful rival to the north posing as a more or less constant threat to Judah's existence, the internal weakness of Judah itself was present as the result of sin. Though the ox might know his owner, and the ass his master's crib, the inhabitants of Judah too often did not know their Lord (*Isa.* 1:3). Furthermore, though they had possession of the law of God, its denial through disobedience was more often the norm. Isaiah's round indictment of them is, "Alas, sinful nation, a people laden with iniquity, a brood of evil-doers, children who are corrupters! They have forsaken the Lord, they have provoked to anger the Holy One of Israel, they have turned away backward" (*Isa.* 1:4).

And though the Davidic dynasty continued in their midst, a rather steady degeneration of its kings led the people away from rather than towards obedience to the Lord. A king such as Jehoshaphat, though a godly man, could nevertheless lead Judah into sinful alliance with the northern kingdom and allow the marriage of his son Jehoram, the crown prince, to Ahab's wicked daughter Athaliah. That the Davidic dynasty was not shortly afterwards extinguished by Athaliah's treachery and the nation polluted by idolatry during her brief reign, can be attributed only to the providential action of God in bringing her diabolical efforts to nought. Again, a king such as Uzziah, though also God-fearing, could nevertheless attempt to usurp the prerogatives of the priesthood to himself in pride and scornful disdain of the bounds of divine official appointment. Even a godly

[15]

Hezekiah could be guilty of such folly as to set the stage for Judah's later conquest by Babylon when with a proud heart he showed her ambassadors all Judah's treasures. We are hardly surprised therefore when by Manasseh's time Judah too was ripe for judgment, which descended shortly afterwards in the form of the Babylonian captivity.

More than ever it became apparent that the old dispensation must give way to the fulfilment of the promises of God for something new and better. "Behold, the days are coming, says the Lord, when I will make a new covenant with the house of Israel and with the house of Judah — not according to the covenant that I made with their fathers in the day that I took them by the hand to bring them out of the land of Egypt, my covenant which they broke, though I was a husband to them, says the Lord. But this is the covenant that I will make with the house of Israel: after those days, says the Lord, I will put my law in their minds, and write it on their hearts; and I will be their God, and they shall be my people. No more shall every man teach his neighbour, and every man his brother, saying, know the Lord, for they all shall know me, from the least of them to the greatest of them, says the Lord. For I will forgive their iniquity, and their sin I will remember no more" (*Jer.* 31:31-34).

That this prophecy finds fulfilment historically in the present Christian era is made plain by the inspired interpretation of these verses found in Hebrews 8:7-13: "For if that first covenant had been faultless, then no place would have been sought for a second. Because finding fault with them, he says: Behold, the days are coming, says the Lord, when I will make a new covenant with the house of Israel and with the house of Judah: not according to the covenant... In that he says a new covenant, he has made the first obsolete. Now what is becoming obsolete and growing old is ready to vanish away."

Again, in Hebrews 10:14-18 we learn, "For by one offering he [Christ] has perfected forever those who are being sanctified. And the Holy Spirit also witnesses to us; for after he had said, This is the covenant that I will make with them after those days, says the Lord, I will put my laws into their hearts and in their minds I will write them. Then he adds, Their sins and their lawless deeds I will remember no more. Now where there is remission of these, there is no longer an offering for sin." The old order not only looked forward to fulfilment by the new, but itself was of such typical construction and shadowy grace that it needed the new for its proper realization. God's people had the law but not the power to keep it. "With Israel, as a nation taken in its whole, one can say that the Word of God was present but not the power. The oracles of God were entrusted to Israel, and it possessed the law of the Lord upon stone tablets. But there was no talk of Israel — we are not speaking of individual believers but of fleshly Israel as a nation — that it had the law of the Lord in its heart."[1] The people had the presence of God in their midst, but they needed him to dwell in their hearts. The people had an earthly king but they needed to become the citizens of heaven with the king of that domain exercising his rule over their whole being.

What advantage, then, had Old Testament Israel over the nations? The apostle Paul answers, "Much in every way: chiefly because to them were committed the oracles of God" (*Rom.* 3:2). Israel had the Word of God, in which were not only God's covenant and law but also the promises of better things to come. And though Israel might prove faithless to his covenant and disobedient to his laws, God in grace had bound himself in covenant relation to this people through their forefathers; the gifts and calling of God are apart from his repudiation of them (*Rom.* 11:29). From them would come Zion's deliverer. Yes, and from their number, for election's sake, a remnant would be saved (*Rom.* 11:28) to form a part of the true spiritual Israel.

5. True Israel

a. As alone the people of God

This brings us to consider true spiritual Israel as over against Israel after the flesh. In the life of Israel as the people of God, this differentiating concept was not prominent in the Old Testament, though it was nevertheless present from the very beginning. The apostle Paul shows how this was the case as he proves in Romans 9

---

[1] A. Kuyper, Jr., *Van het Koninkrijk der Hemelen* (Kampen: J.H. Kok, 1932), p.221.

that it was necessary for God to save only this remnant in order to bring to fulfilment the promises of God concerning Israel. "That is, those who are the children of the flesh, these are not the children of God: but the children of the promise are counted as the seed" (*Rom*. 9:8). Israel existed as a theocracy with its national, political and religious life bound together in covenant relationship with the Lord. But they were not all Israel which were of Israel, as the history of their proneness to idolatry and apostasy made all too evident. This truth of the remnant as being alone the people of God, as Paul further shows, emerges in such prophetic writings as Isaiah 1:9, 10:20 ff., and Hosea 1:9-10, 2:23, which he quotes in the development of his theodicy on how God can fulfil his promises to Israel by saving only this elect remnant (cf. *Rom*. 9:25-29). These Old Testament verses bear closer scrutiny in their original context in order to determine their full significance for the teaching concerning true spiritual Israel as alone the people of God.

In the first chapter of Isaiah, the prophet, after indicting Israel for its sins, goes on to prophesy of the desolation that God's judgment would bring over the people and their land. Then he notes that so terrible would be that desolation that, were not God to preserve a remnant, their destruction would be as complete as it was for Sodom and Gomorrah,[1] cities totally destroyed by God in judgment on their wickedness. In other words, only a remnant would be saved from the fires of judgment. That remnant alone would be considered his true people out of the greater mass of those who were only nominally his.

In Isaiah 10:20 ff., the truth of the remnant as being alone the people of God is further made explicit. There, in the context of the Assyrian captivity which put into effect the judgment of God after the Babylonian captivity so that the prophet often views both as an undivided whole, (cf. 14:24-27),[2] the remnant

---

[1] "Unless the Lord of hosts had left to us a very small remnant, we would have become like Sodom, we would have been made like Gomorrah" (*Isa*. 1:9).

[2] "At the time when the prophecy against Assyria had actually been fulfilled, the prophet attached it to the still unfulfilled prophecy against Babylon, to give a pledge of the fulfilment of the latter. This was the pedestal upon which the *Massah Babel* was raised." Franz Delitzsch, *Biblical Commentary on the Prophecies of Isaiah* (Grand Rapids: Eerdmans, vol. 1, 1954), p.317.

as the people of God are encouraged to endure through the oppression of the enemy, for though Israel should be reduced from number as the sand of the sea to a mere remnant (*v.* 22), that remnant would be preserved, even those who returned "to the mighty God"(*v.* 21). They are therefore given the Lord's own encouragement in verse 24 and are there referred to as his people.

These are but two contexts in a prophecy whose broad theme may be described as "a remnant shall return", the name given to the oldest of Isaiah's sons, *Shear-Jashub* (*Isa.* 7:3), for in keeping with the prophet's commission, he is to prophesy "until the cities are laid waste and without inhabitant, the houses are without a man, the land is utterly desolate" (6:11). But a remnant, the holy seed who are truly the Lord's people, shall return, though their reduced number be only a tenth (6:3).

Hosea's prophecy concerning the remnant is much along the same vein as that of Isaiah. In fact, we might expect as much for, being a contemporary of Isaiah (*Hos.* 1:1; cf. *Isa.* 1:1), the Lord's prophetic message delivered through him arose from the same bleak background of Israel's history. Hosea, by symbolical action in the naming of his son, teaches by divine instruction the truth of Israel's rejection by God as his people. They are "not my people" (*lo ammi* – *Hos.* 1:9). But then Hosea gives further light, for this remnant, contrary to our expectation of its being small, would be as numerous as the sand of the sea, thus fulfilling the promise of God already given to Abraham (*Gen.* 22:17).

This prediction of a numerous remnant is not in contradiction to Isaiah but rather supplemental to it, as the apostle Paul makes clear in Romans 9:24-25. The remnant would be numerous because true Israel would include, not only the natural seed of Abraham in which would be found the spiritual seed among the reunited tribes of Israel (*Hos.* 1:11), but also spiritual seed. It would include the Gentiles also (*Rom.* 9:24) who exhibit the same faith as did Abraham (*Rom.* 4:11). From Israel's rejection and judgment at Jezreel (*Hos.* 1:4), the seeds of her renovation would be sown so that the remnant, or true Israel, would number its members from the northern and southern kingdoms and from the nations of the Gentiles. Great indeed would be the day of Jezreel (*Hos.* 1:11), for judgment would be turned by the

Lord into blessing! And as Paul shows by his linking of this prophecy with God's calling of the Gentiles (*Rom.* 9:24-26), the re-adoption of the Israelites as the people of God would be practical proof that God could make the Gentile world his people in the same way.[1]

Hosea 2:23 need not be examined in detail because it is but a reiteration of the truth that God would once more show mercy and salvation to Israel presently experiencing his rejection and judgment. That the remnant is here meant is made clear by the previous context.

b. *As a church*

These Old Testament prophecies are sufficient to show clearly the emergence of the truth concerning spiritual Israel as alone the people of God. National Israel might suffer judgment so as to lose her political identity and social independence. National Israel might even cease to exist as a nation. No matter, for the bond of the covenant as finding continuing relevance among those who were truly God's people would perpetuate the community so that it would remain as the organism through which the prophetic promises would be realized. From this prophetic and historical development the concept of Israel as a church arose. As Rieker puts it, "This prophetical distinction between Israel after the flesh and Israel after the Spirit...is the root of the church concept...only Israel as 'church' is the people of God."[2] That is to say, the concept of the *qehal Yahweh* (assembly of the Lord) continued into the exile and beyond into the restoration but now the community as a religious entity gained the ascendancy.

It is true that this had been the case when the theocracy was originally founded[3] and that it had suffered subsequent eclipse

---

[1] For a more detailed exposition, cf. C.F. Keil, *The Twelve Minor Prophets, Biblical Commentary on the Old Testament,* vol. 1, (Grand Rapids: Eerdmans, 1954), pp.45-50.

[2] Karl Rieker, quoted in a footnote by Olof Linton, *Das Problem der Urkirche in der neueren Forschung* (Uppsala, 1932), p.147.

[3] Cf. Acts 7:38 where Stephen calls the wilderness congregation a church, i.e., *ecclesia.*

because of Israel's apostasy. Even after Israel's restoration, the concept would again lose its purity; witness the Sadducees, the religious naturalists and the Pharisees,[1] the blind leaders of the blind, in Jesus' day! Nevertheless, the prophetic revelation and historic fact did serve to bring into focus this concept of Israel as the church. The congregation of the Lord may still have engendered false doctrine (*Mark* 12:27), nursed false expectations of a purely nationalistic Messiah (hence their rejection of Jesus), and become once more the superfluous husk within which true spiritual Israel was to be found, but the truth of the remnant alone as the true people of God had made its appearance in history and in its impact on the experience of God's people. Israel, though in a sense still a nation, had rather become a church or religious community. With the establishment of this truth, the groundwork was laid for New Testament revelation with its further implications for the kingdom of God and the church.

---

[1] This sect arising out of the religious life of post-exilic Israel reinforces the conclusion that Israel conceived of herself as a church. At the apex of this conception were the Pharisees (*pharash*, the separated ones), who in painstaking manner, "aimed at a conscientious fulfilment of the law and guarded against all foreign influences. It was their ideal that Israel should live as a 'separated' people with God as their only king... While observing outward provisions of the law very painstakingly, they violated the real spirit of God's laws in many instances and fell into hypocrisy. This was the case especially in the time of the Lord when they had already for a long time been the 'people's party' and had in various ways become degenerate." Norval Geldenhuys, *Commentary on the Gospel of Luke* (Grand Rapids: Eerdmans, 1952), pp.190-191, in a special note on "Pharisees and Doctors of the Law".

III. THE NEW TESTAMENT CHURCH
(successor and embodiment of true Israel)

1. Because the Lord's Messiah is her king

a. The New Testament interpretation of Psalm 110:1

The kingship of Christ as a teaching of the New Testament is plainly in evidence. We find a reference to it as a fulfilment of Psalm 110 in Acts 2:34-36, where Peter tells his Jerusalem audience at Pentecost, "For David did not ascend into the heavens, but he says himself, The Lord said to my Lord, Sit at my right hand, till I make your enemies your footstool. Therefore let all the house of Israel know assuredly that God has made this Jesus, whom you crucified, both Lord and Christ." In addition to this reference, the thought of Psalm 110:1[1] is embodied in a number of other New Testament passages.

In Acts 5:31, Peter's word again is, "Him God has exalted to his right hand to be Prince and a Saviour, to give repentance to Israel, and forgiveness of sins." In Acts 7:55, we read that Stephen, "being full of the Holy Spirit, gazed into heaven and saw the glory of God, and Jesus standing at the right hand of God." In Romans 8:34, we find, "Who is he who condemns? It is Christ who died, and furthermore is also risen, who is even at the right hand of God, who also makes intercession for us." In I Corinthians 15:25, the statement is made, "For he [Christ]

---

[1] "The Lord said to my Lord, Sit at my right hand till I make your enemies your footstool."

must reign till he has put all enemies under his feet." And Ephesians 1:20-23 states, "which he wrought in Christ when he raised him from the dead and seated him at his right hand in the heavenly places, far above all principality and power and might and dominion, and every name that is named, not only in this age but also in that which is to come. And he put all things under his feet, and gave him to be the head over all things to the church, which is his body, the fulness of him who fills all in all." In Colossians 3:1 we are told, "If then you are raised with Christ, seek those things which are above, where Christ is, sitting at the right hand of God." The Epistle to the Hebrews has several references to Psalm 110:1. In 1:3 we read, "Who [Christ] being the brightness of his glory and the express image of his person, and upholding all things by the word of his power, when he had by himself purged our sins, sat down at the right hand of the Majesty on high." Again, in 8:1 we read, "Now this is the main point of the things we are saying: we have such a high priest, who is seated at the right hand of the throne of the Majesty in the heavens." And in 10:12-13, we read, "But this man, after he had offered one sacrifice for sins forever, sat down at the right hand of God: from that time waiting till his enemies are made his footstool."

There are yet two further references. In I Peter 3:22, we read, "Who [Christ] has gone into heaven and is at the right hand of God, angels and authorities and powers having been made subject unto him." And lastly, in Revelation 3:21, we read, "To him who overcomes I will grant to sit with me on my throne, as I also overcame and sat down with my Father on his throne."

As the original thought of Psalm 110 expresses and as we see from the New Testament's interpretation of it, the reference is to the rule of the Messiah. And the Messiah is Jesus Christ. His reign after its beginning was to continue until all his enemies were subdued. This is what Psalm 110 teaches and this is also what the New Testament avers for Christ.

b. *Christ's present reign*

When, however, does this reign of Christ begin? In the Psalm itself, the time is left indefinite, though it would be in association with the advent of the Messiah, for the Lord would send the rod of his strength out of Zion (*v.* 2), Messiah's people will be willing in the day of his power (*v.* 3), he shall execute kings in the day of his wrath (*v.* 5), and judge among the nations (*v.* 6). Now, though the sovereign rule of the Messiah is associated with his advent, which advent is here meant? There are thoughts which express both salvation and judgment.

By reviewing the New Testament references to this psalm, we learn that they make it refer to Christ's present reign. Perhaps I Corinthians 15:25, if considered in isolation, might be relegated to a yet future reign, but in connection with Acts 2:34-36, a clearly present reference must be seen, for two important reasons: In the first place, Peter's arguments about the Holy Spirit's effusion (*v.* 33), the fulfilment of the prophetic import of Psalm 110 (*vv.* 34-35), and Israel's need to repent and accept the salvation of God as offered in Christ, are all based on the exaltation of Christ which, having just previously occurred, gave conclusive proof that Jesus was the Messiah. And, as the exalted Messiah, he now possessed a sovereignty to which the obedience of repentance and faith was a present imperative. Hence the strength of Peter's exhortation. Would his hearers willingly submit to Messiah's saving rule or would they remain among his enemies to suffer the ultimate defeat of his judgment when he makes them his footstool?

In the second place, Peter refers to Jesus, not only as the Messiah, but as the Lord also (*v.* 36). "To a Jew, there was only one name 'above every name' — the ineffable name of the God of Israel represented in synagogue reading and in the LXX text by the title 'Lord'."[1] Peter therefore ascribes to Jesus the covenant name, *kurios,* or Lord (the Old Testament equivalent being *Yahweh*), which is the Lord God's alone. This is further seen in his exhortation to have his repentant hearers call on Jesus as Lord in order to be saved (compare *v.* 38 with *v.* 21), a reference to Old Testament Scripture which, in its original context, referred to the covenant God of Israel alone (*Joel* 2:32). In this he is supported by other passages in the New Testament where Old

[1] F.F. Bruce, *Commentary on the Book of Acts* (Grand Rapids: Eerdmans, 1954), p.74.

Testament references to *Yahweh* are made to refer to Jesus (e.g., *Phil.* 2:10 with *Isa.* 45:23; *I Pet.* 3:15 with *Isa.* 8:13; *Rom.* 10:13 with *Joel* 2:32, etc.). "The first apostolic sermon leads up to the first apostolic creed; 'Jesus is Lord' (cf. *Rom.* 10:9, *I Cor.* 12:3, *Phil.* 2:11)."[1] Since the Lord God alone is sovereign, we may therefore understand from the designation, "Jesus is Lord", the delegation by the Father of kingly authority and sovereign power to the Son on his ascension and exaltation.

In this light, Psalm 110:1 becomes fraught with deepest messianic significance and highest relevance for Christ's present reign. Cullmann, in commenting on this stupendous designation which became the most ancient creed, says, "For the first Christians this meant that Christ is not only the true sovereign over men, as the Roman emperor claimed to be, but also that he is sovereign over the whole visible and invisible creation."[2]

When we examine Hebrews 10:12-13, where the reference to his enemies becoming his footstool is also made, we further see its relevance to the present reign of Christ. By his once-for-all efficacious sacrifice, the work he wrought for the salvation of his people is complete, the victory has been won and now, "Only the fruits of it remain to be gathered,"[3] a process presently being carried out, the end of which will come only when his enemies will have heen subjected to him.

The references of Ephesians 1:20-23, I Peter 3:22, and Revelation 3:21 clinch the argument. Ephesians and I Peter make Christ's victory a reality which includes sovereignty over all principality, power, dominion and name, not only in this world, but also in the world to come. This sovereignty is already being realized, but its climactic completion will take place at his second advent.[4] And to this Revelation 3:21 lends agreement when it speaks of Christ presently seated on the throne of dominion with the Father, or, as Psalm 110 puts it, seated at the Father's

[1] Bruce, *Commentary on the Book of Acts*, p.73.

[2] "Königsherrschaft Christi", p.6.

[3] B.F. Westcott, *The Epistle to the Hebrews* (Grand Rapids: Eerdmans, 1952), p.315.

[4] As Cullmann puts it, "Christ already exercises his lordship over all subdued powers", "Königsherrschaft Christi", p.12.

right hand where he exercises mediatorial sovereignty culminating in judgment and victory over his foes at his second advent.

The present aspect of Christ's rule may not exhaust all the prophetic significance of Psalm 110 in which the aspects of Christ's two advents are blended into a unified whole. But this means merely that Old Testament prophecy, seeing future events on the distant horizon where their differing aspects were indistinguishable, needs the additional revelation of the New Testament for its proper clarification and interpretation. That the New Testament teaches the present kingship of Christ must be our inevitable conclusion.

(1) Over the cosmos

The kingship of Christ includes all the created cosmos. This fact he himself announced to his disciples prior to his ascension. In Matthew 28:18, the evangelist gives record of him saying, "All authority (*exousia*) has been given to me in heaven and on earth." The meaning of this short statement is tremendous in scope. Christ has not been given some authority or even much authority, but *all* authority. The stretch of this unlimited authority is not simply over the heaven or the earth alone, but over both heaven and earth. In a word, his authority is unlimited. The implications of this universal sovereignty immediately begin to unfold in the verses following which have come to be known as the great commission, "Go therefore and make disciples of all the nations, baptizing them into the name of the Father and of the Son and of the Holy Spirit, teaching them to observe all things that I have commanded you; and lo, I am with you always, even to the end of the age" (*Matt.* 28:19-20).

Because of Christ's sovereignty, he is able to commission his disciples with the world-wide preaching of the gospel of God's redeeming grace. Because of Christ's all-embracing sovereignty, they may go to make disciples of all nations, for no nation lies beyond the sphere of his dominion or the pale of his redemption. For the same reason, he is able to ensure the success of his disciples, for through their efforts in the preaching of the gospel, he brings peoples of the world into the obedience of the faith ("teaching them to observe all things that I have commanded you") and a right relationship with the triune God ("baptizing them into (*eis*) the name of the Father and of the Son and of the Holy Spirit").

World-wide conversion, or the winning of all men to Christ, is not necessary for the recognition of Christ's sovereignty. Christ is Lord. This confession is both the willing acknowledgment and glory of Christ's people. But it is a truth that shall one day be acknowledged by the whole of the created cosmos, whether willingly or unwillingly, for he must reign until he has made all his enemies the footstool of his feet. The destiny of all creation, therefore, whether of heaven, earth, or hell, is one day to pay Christ homage on bended knee and give assent to his universal sovereignty *(Phil.* 2:10-11). The culmination of that sovereignty's purpose will have been completed only after Christ has fashioned the full salvation of his people, the full subjection of all his foes and the full removal of every vestige of sin's curse from the inhabited world.

With regard to the first, this will involve the deliverance of all his people from the curse of sin and wrath of God, bondage to Satan and full conformity of his people into his own image, a conformity which will be complete only when both soul and body shall have been transformed into his likeness *(II Cor.* 3:18, *Phil.* 3:20-21).

With regard to the second, this will involve the bringing to nothing of all his enemies' opposition, their just judgment and condemnation and their eternal punishment according to the gravity of their misdeeds *(Matt.* 25:41-46, *II Thess.* 1:7-9, *Rev.* 19:19-21; 20:12-15).

With respect to the third, this will involve the complete renovation of heaven and earth *(II Pet.* 3:13), a goal toward which creation or nature[1] already longingly looks, awaiting deliverance from the bondage of corruption, having been unwillingly subjected to physical frailty on account of man, its crown, until he himself, represented by the redeemed, shall experience the glorious liberty of Christ's full salvation *(Rom.* 8:19-22). All this can and will be accomplished because Christ is king of the cosmos.

---

[1] For a full defence of this interpretation of *ktisis* as "nature", see Charles Hodge, *Commentary on the Epistle to the Romans* (Grand Rapids: Eerdmans, 1950), pp.269-273.

(2) Over the powers of darkness

A further word needs to be said about Christ's sovereignty over the powers of darkness, for they, with the devil as their prince (*Luke* 4:5-6, *John* 14:30, *Matt.* 12:24-26, *Eph.* 2:2), are the animating force which has opposed the sovereignty of God from the beginning, and which remains the diabolical counterpart of the kingdom of light against which it wages ceaseless conflict. As Kuyper, Jr. puts it, "The goal of Satan is and remains the disrupting of the kingdom of God... Satan first tried this in paradise. In paradise God the Lord was king... But the evil one came and he carried the poison of sin into the heart of man, and over against the kingdom of God, yes rather, in its place, founded his kingdom, the kingdom of lies and deceit, the kingdom of sin and unrighteousness, the kingdom of death and darkness; in a word, *the kingdom of the evil one*. It is this kingdom that we also fittingly term 'the world'."[1] Obviously, therefore, if Jesus is to be sovereign in any sense of the word, that sovereignty must extend over the powers of darkness.

"For this purpose the Son of God was manifested, that he might destroy the works of the devil" (*I John* 3:8). That dominion was to include the ability to rescue his people from thraldom to Satan (*Matt.* 12:28) and membership in his kingdom (*Col.* 1:13). It would include, furthermore, the despoliation of Satan's realm of dominion and the stripping from him of his power. Though it is still true that the whole world "lies under the sway of the wicked one" (*I John* 5:19); this describes only the sphere of his kingdom's manifestation which is an ever-shrinking sphere under retreat from the advance of Christ's kingdom. As John has expressed it, "The darkness is passing away, and the true light is already shining" (*I John* 2:8).[2] Since Calvary, the prince of this world has been cast out (*John* 12:31), and though, on the

---

[1] *Van het Koninkrijk*, pp.198-199.

[2] "Over against this liar in whom there is no truth, who, as he speaks lies speaks that which is his own, appears the Christ of God. He is the truth, the king of truth, and over against the kingdom of lies and deceit in this world, He founds the kingdom of heaven that is the kingdom of truth; that over against the kingdom of darkness is the kingdom of wonderful light; that over against the kingdom of death is the kingdom of everlasting life." A. Kuyper, Jr., *Van het Koninkrijk*, p.195.

one hand, he may rage as a roaring lion seeking whom he may
devour (*I Pet.* 5:8), or on the other hand, transform himself into
an angel of light (*II Cor.* 11:14) by which, if possible, to deceive
the very elect, he is nevertheless a defeated foe whose evil
machinations can go no further than the chain of his binding
by Christ allows (*Matt.* 12:29).

Because Christ is now "far above all principality and power
and might and dominion, and every name that is named" (*Eph.*
1:21), his people, who have been liberated from the domain of
the "prince of the power of the air" (*Eph.* 2:2), can stand in the
full panoply of God (*Eph.* 6:11), and wage successful battle "against
principalities, against powers, against the rulers of the darkness
of this age, against spiritual hosts of wickedness in the heavenly
places" (*Eph.* 6:12). True, the powers of darkness's opposition
still comes to expression in manifestations of worldly conflict,
but this conflict is basically a spiritual one for which spiritual
weapons have been provided. And the outcome of that conflict
can never be in doubt (*James* 4:7), for the victory already belongs
to the exalted Christ. And "having disarmed principalities and
powers, he made a public spectacle of them, triumphing over
them in it" (*Col.* 2:15). Christ is king and his sovereignty includes
present dominion over the powers of darkness.

(3) Over God's people

The fact that Jesus Christ is king over his people is obvious.
If he is king over the cosmos and sovereign even over the powers
of darkness, then certainly he is his people's king and rules over
them in his kingdom. In the words of Kuyper, "A kingdom is
present where a king appears who, invested with the power to
rule, is seated upon his throne, and rules over a people who live
in his kingdom and are obedient unto his sovereignty."[1] The
point in question, however, is, are his people now the successor
and embodiment of true Israel? Two considerations evoke a
positive answer to this question:

In the first place, Jesus is the Lord's anointed to whom all
the prophets of the old dispensation gave witness (*Acts* 10:43).

[1] *Van het Koninkrijk*, p.222.

In Jesus Christ is to be found the One whom prophecy foretold as he who would "rebuild the tabernacle of David which has fallen down" (*Acts* 15:16, cf. *Amos* 9:11); i.e., restore the theocracy once more as an institution of God's salvation. The prophets, as well as David (*Psa.* 110), foresaw this as coming to pass in David's greater son, and that son, the New Testament makes clear, is Jesus Christ.

In the second place, "The concept of a Messiah without a people is unthinkable."[1] When national Israel, in spiritual blindness, rejected him, they clearly revealed themselves as not really the people of God, or true Israel. Spiritual Israel was yet to be found within Israel after the flesh in Jesus' day, but the line of demarcation was at the point of acceptance or rejection of Jesus as the Messiah. And the day was soon to come when the kingdom of God would no longer be the sole possession of national Israel. As a matter of fact, Israel having rejected its king, the kingdom of God would therefore be taken from it and be given to a nation bearing its appropriate fruits (*Matt.* 21:43). For this eventuality Jesus made provision by the establishment of his church, the new Israel and the true people of God.

2. Because the church has become possessor of Israel's promises and status

Under the previous major heading, we have considered how the New Testament church has become the successor and embodiment of true Israel *because the Lord's Messiah is her king.* Let us next see how this is true in that the New Testament church has replaced Old Testament Israel by becoming the possessor of Israel's promises and status. The following quotations eloquently express this truth:

"The historical root of the church is in the covenant which Abraham and his children entered into with Yahweh their God. As Mary sings in her 'Magnificat,' when she knows that she is to give birth to the Messiah, who is to be the fulfilment of the hope of Israel, 'He has helped Israel his servant, that he might

---

[1] Herman Ridderbos, *The Coming of the Kingdom* (Philadelphia: The Presbyterian & Reformed Pub. Co., 1962), p.348.

remember mercy (as he spoke unto our fathers), toward Abraham and his seed forever'."[1]

"Christ is the promised Messiah who has come to establish his kingdom among men; in him and in his church is all the hope of Israel for a true remnant and a new covenant made actual."[2]

"According to their own understanding Christians were 'the true Israel.' They had not stepped into a new religion, but rather the new age had *come*... The matter does not concern itself with an exchange of religions by men, but of a new creation of God (in the new world-age)."[3]

"The church is not a general society for the promotion of religion, nor is it a device for giving dignity and idealism to the nation on its own secular assumptions. It arose only because Jesus Christ inaugurated a new Israel as a judgment upon and fulfilment of the old, and it continues in being only because his life is still present in the midst as the Spirit. Its faith is that he will sustain his people until all things reach their ultimate fulfilment in him."[4]

The scripturalness of the above quotations can be seen from the following:

a. Jesus' own teaching

We have already noted Jesus' conclusion to the parable of the Labourers in the Vineyard (*Matt.* 21:43). This parable finds an Old Testament parallel in Isaiah 5:1-7, where the prophet's interpretation identified the vineyard with the house of Israel, the owner was the Lord himself, and its worthless fruits the disobedience and apostasy of Israel which made them ripe for the judgment of the exile. In Jesus' parable (*Matt.* 21:33-46) the identification runs along similar, though not identical lines. The owner is God, to be sure, but the vineyard is the kingdom of God rather than Israel. And in Jesus' parable, the cause of

[1] Daniel Jenkins, *The Strangeness of the Church* (Garden City: Doubleday and Co., 1955), p.25.

[2] Bright, *The Kingdom of God*, p.230.

[3] Linton, *Das Problem der Urkirche*, pp.147-148.

[4] Jenkins, *The Strangeness of the Church*, p.62.

the vineyard's fruitlessness to the owner is made specific in the wickedness of the husbandmen from whom the vineyard would subsequently be taken to be given to others who shall bring forth its proper fruits.

The chief priests and Pharisees may not have understood the full implications of Jesus' correction of their statement; namely, that the vineyard would not simply be transferred to more worthy hands within the nation itself (*v.* 41), but would go rather to another nation (*v.* 43). But they did perceive, at least, that the parable made clear their culpability (*vv.* 45-46). Concerning the interpretation of this parable Ridderbos says, "By this 'people' [*ethnos*] is not meant some particular 'nation,' but the new people of God to whom, in passing over the old Israel, he will give the salvation of the kingdom. Here we find in the same context the concepts kingdom of God and God's people as the new people of God to be gathered by the Messiah. It is evident that the revelation of the kingdom is directed to the formation of a people that will replace Israel in the history of salvation. At the same time it is evident that this other, this new people of God, is spoken of not only in future-eschatological terms, but also in a future historical sense. It is about a people who yield the fruits (of the kingdom) i.e., who are converted by the preaching (of the kingdom) and thus reveal themselves already in the present as the new people of God."[1]

This becomes all the more meaningful when we recall that at a point prior to this Jesus had in revelational disclosure, at least, already made plain the fact that he would build his church (*Matt.* 16:18). In connection with Peter's confession of him as the Messiah coming on the background of the multitude's unbelief, though perhaps couched in flattering form (he might be John the Baptist, Elijah, Jeremiah, or one of the prophets); "'My church' can mean nothing else than 'the church which by recognizing me as Messiah will take the place of the present Jewish church.'"[2]

---

[1] *The Coming of the Kingdom,* pp.352-353.

[2] Vos, *The Kingdom and the Church,* p.78.

When Jesus therefore came preaching the kingdom of God
as gospel (*Matt.* 4:23; 9:35, etc.), it was that message of salvation at
whose centre he himself was to be found which separated the
wheat from the chaff and disclosed true Israel who would continue as God's people to make known the salvation already
proclaimed and soon to be purchased by their Messiah. Hence,
the continuity of that preaching of the church in Acts 8:12;
20:25; 28:31, etc., with the message set forth by the evangelists
in the Gospels as the preaching of Jesus. For that message was
not only perpetuated by, but also found embodiment in the new
Israel of God, the church of Jesus Christ.

b. *Jesus' choice of twelve apostles*

The significance of Jesus' choice of twelve apostles becomes
clear as we see them in relationship to Old Testament Israel in
its composition of twelve tribes. This twelve tribe sum was basic
to the idea of the theocracy as viewed in its totality. Even the
loss of one tribe in ancient Israel, therefore, was an intolerable
thought, not so much because it would be a decimation of God's
people, as it would mean a breach in the theocracy so constituted
as the people of God. Consequently, as a result of civil war when
the tribe of Benjamin was almost wiped out (*Judg.* 20), Israel
was acutely distressed over the loss, rightly considering it a breach
in the theocracy (*Judg.* 21:15). Hence, also, the strenuous efforts
that were afterwards employed to make certain "that a tribe
may not be destroyed from Israel" (*Judg.* 21:17). Secret approval
was given to the illicit means the remaining sons of Benjamin
employed to procure wives for themselves (*Judg.* 21:16-23).

The later reprehensible act of Jeroboam and the northern
tribes in severing themselves from theocratic unity becomes all
the more heinous a crime when seen in this light. No wonder,
therefore, that a basic aspect of prophecy was the envisaging of
the restoration of the twelve tribes of Israel in their theocratic
unity (*Jer.* 31:9; 31-34; 50:4, *Ezek.* 37:21-28., *Hos.* 3:4-5, etc.).
And when John in the book of Revelation would set forth the
picture of the messianic community in its elect totality, he does
so in terms of the theocratic unity as expressed in the twelve
tribes of Israel (*Rev.* 7:4-8).

That Christian modification has taken place here, however, may be seen in several aspects. For instance, neither Reuben, Jacob's first-born, nor Ephraim, the most prominent son of Joseph whose name became synonymous with the northern kingdom, are mentioned first. Judah heads the listing, the reason of course being that from Judah had come the Messiah who gave ultimate unitary significance to the theocracy. Furthermore, the substitution of Joseph for Ephraim (though Manasseh continues to stand) and the omission of Dan with his replacement by Levi (not ordinarily listed in Israel's tribal composition because Levi received no inheritance in the land) make clear a further de-emphasis upon literalness in the interests of Christian symbolic meaning which this listing is intended to convey. The Christian community in the sum total of its election has become the true theocracy.[1] This interpretation rests on the presupposition that the message of Revelation is not something new or radically different from that presented by the New Testament as a whole.

When Jesus, therefore, chose apostles with whom to entrust the preaching of the kingdom of God and upon whom to build his church (*Matt.* 16:18-19), he significantly chose twelve as their number, because they were to be the representatives and nucleus of the new theocracy, the true Israel, the messianic community, the church of Jesus Christ. This is the place Paul assigns to the apostles when, in Ephesians 2:20, he says of the church, "[You have] been built on the foundation of the apostles and prophets [prophets here defining a New Testament charismatic office rather than referring to that of the old dispensation, cf. 3:5; 4:11], Jesus Christ himself being the chief corner-stone." As Ridderbos puts it, "The original apostles received this charge

---

[1] "[This view that the whole number of the faithful is here meant] is supported by a) the tendency of the Apocalypse to regard the church as the true Israel (cf. e.g., 2:9; 3:9), b) the use of the same number in 14:1 for the followers of the Lamb whose foreheads bear the names of God and Christ, and c) the circumstance that none are sealed but the 144,000 of Israel. Had it been the purpose of the Apocalyptist to distinguish between the two bodies of the elect, he would surely have represented both as alike receiving the seal which was to mark the 'servants of God'; but the sealing is expressly limited to the twelve tribes. It follows that the Israel of the first vision is coextensive with the whole church" H.B. Swete, *The Apocalypse of St. John* (London: Macmillan and Co., Ltd., 1911), p.99.

as the foundation of the church, their number of twelve signifying that they were to be the representatives of the new Israel."[1]

We can therefore see the significance of Jesus's statement in Luke 12:32, "Do not fear, little flock; for it is your Father's good pleasure to give you the kingdom." True it is that true Israel is ever but a "little flock" in a hostile world. True it is also that this "little flock" is Jesus's church which receives the gift of the kingdom. But most basically, as found in its historical setting, this statement applied directly to the original "little flock," the saved remnant, the new Israel, the twelve apostles to whom these comforting words of their Lord were originally spoken (*Luke* 12:41).[2]

If the twelve were indeed the representatives of the new theocracy, then we can understand their concern to restore their number to its proper complement after the defection and demise of Judas. Under Peter's initiative as spokesman of the group, they selected Matthias by lot and he was thereafter "numbered with the eleven apostles" (*Acts* 1:26). Thus the significant number twelve was re-established as the basis upon which new Israel was subsequently built. Again, as John pictures the new Jerusalem, in the perfection of the fulness of the final state of God's people (*Rev.* 21), he represents its continuity with the Old Testament people of God in the names of the twelve tribes inscribed upon its gates (*Rev.* 21:12). But the whole, with the book's characteristic emphasis upon the New Testament dispensation as the age of fulfilment, rests on the twelve foundations of the new theocracy, and in these foundations are to be found "the names of the twelve apostles of the Lamb" (*Rev.* 21:14).

Here then are the representatives of new Israel on whom Jesus was to build his church as the new theocracy. Their witness would form the basis of its confession (*Matt.* 16:16-18). Their preaching would become the gospel of "the faith which was once for all delivered to the saints", (*Jude* 3) in which the church would find its life and in which it was to abide (*II John* 9). Much of Karl Barth's theology is questionable but he is surely

[1] *The Coming of the Kingdom*, p.374.
[2] Cf. Flew, *Jesus and His Church* (London: Epworth Press, 1938), pp.53-54.

right when he says of Jesus's charge to the apostles in Matthew 28:20, "*They* and *only* they are to teach in the church. For there is no question of any other object of this teaching than that which Jesus has commanded *them*. But of what has been commanded them, the church has to teach nothing less than everything, the entire compass of this order of service. This is the New Testament foundation of the scriptural principle with which we must turn our backs on the Romanist church. Every teaching in the church can only consist in a repetition of the apostolic teaching.[1]

c. The establishment of the new covenant

The old covenant that God made with his people was ratified by blood. As Hebrews 9:22 puts it, "And according to the law almost all things are purged with blood, and without shedding of blood there is no remission." This truth we see demonstrated in the Passover when God spared the first-born of his people because of the blood of the lamb sprinkled on the doorposts, but slew Egypt's first-born who had not been ransomed by the blood of the covenant lamb. The blood of the animal sacrifice therefore signified atonement made for the soul guilty of death because of sin (*Lev.* 17:11). Consequently, we would expect the old covenant into which God entered with his people to be ratified with blood. For atonement was the only basis whereby God could yet be just and the justifier of the ungodly with whom, because of his gracious love and mercy, he had entered into a covenant relationship. So we see at the time of the old covenant's establishment at Mt. Sinai that, "Moses took the blood, sprinkled it on the people, and said, Behold the blood of the covenant, which the Lord has made with you according to all these words" (*Exod.* 24:8).

We have, however, already noted the inherent defect of the old covenant. Its grace was of a shadowy and preliminary nature. The law had been given by Moses, it is true. Grace and truth yet needed to come by Jesus Christ (*John* 1:17), for the people had the law upon tablets of stone but they were powerless to keep it.

---

[1] As quoted in a footnote by Ridderbos, *The Coming of the Kingdom*, p.395.

They needed the law to be written upon the tablets of their hearts. And the day would come, Jeremiah prophesied, when this would take place. It would be in the day when the Lord made a new covenant with his people (*Jer.* 31:31-34). What a glorious promise of grace! What a dispensation to await with eagerness!

But the new covenant would be with Israel after the spirit. Israel after the flesh thought so little of the promise of it that they refused to abide by it when God fashioned it and, moreover, rejected him who was its perfecter. That rejection, as far as they were concerned, meant the cross for Christ. But by the inscrutable counsel of God by which all things work to the accomplishment of his predestined plan, that rejection which occasioned the cross and led to the fall of natural Israel brought to pass the salvation of spiritual Israel. For on the night of the betrayal which led to his death Jesus inaugurated the new covenant with the representatives of his church on the basis of his blood which would be "shed for many for the remission of sins" (*Matt.* 26:28).

Here then was the one whose sacrifice could truly atone for sin, fulfilling the role of the suffering servant prophesied of him so long before by the prophet Isaiah. He would justify many, for he would bear their iniquities as he poured out his soul unto death (*Isa.* 53:11-12); "for he made him who knew no sin to be sin for us, that we might become the righteousness of God in him" (*II Cor.* 5:21). There could be no remission of sin without the shedding of blood. But the blood of bulls and goats of the old covenant could never take away sin (*Heb.* 10:4). Jesus Christ, the Son of God in the flesh, offered himself once-for-all for sin that he might forever perfect those being sanctified by that offering (*Heb.* 10:14). Here then was a covenant that could truly save from death, deliver its beneficiaries from sin's power as its precepts became the indwelling force and drive of its people (*II Cor.* 3:3, cf. *Jer.* 31:33), and ultimately perfect them in full conformity to the image of God's glory as revealed in the face of Jesus Christ (*II Cor.* 3:18).

The new covenant, the promise of Old Testament Israel, has become the glory of New Testament Israel, because Jesus Christ celebrated it with his people on the night before he would suffer to bring it to realization. And his church ever proclaims this truth as often as she eats of the bread and drinks of the cup in the sacrament of its memorialization.

3. Because the church is her Lord's redemptive instrument (gospel preaching and kingdom membership)

The following quotations set forth in brief form the church as her Lord's redemptive instrument for a lost and needy world:

Bannerman says, "The chief end of the church is to be in this world what Christ himself was, to do in it what he did, to carry on to final success the great work for which he came from heaven."[1]

Prenter adds, "The apostolic gospel is specifically the glad tidings that the king who brings to realization the covenant between God and a people raised up is now here, and that his new people on that account are now being gathered."[2]

Bright answers the question, "What, then is the church?", in the following way, "The New Testament understood her simply as the true Israel, God's covenant and servant people, called to exhibit the righteousness of his kingdom before the world, charged with proclaiming the kingdom in the world and summoning men into its covenant fellowship... The church, then, is called to be a people over whom God rules, who exhibit the righteousness of his kingdom before the world."[3]

Kuyper, Jr., makes the following observation, "God brings to realization through Christ the kingdom of heaven upon earth. It began small but ultimately it shall be like the fully grown mustard seed, the greatest of the herbs. The kingdom of God comes in a process of ages, and the kingdom of Satan is slowly but surely forced to retreat. And the church of the Lord, the people of God, has the enduring vocation concerning that coming of the kingdom of God both to be and to remain under her king the church militant."[4]

---

[1] *The Scripture Doctrine of the Church*, p.246.

[2] R. Prenter, "Die Systematische Theologie und das Problem der Bibelauslegung", *Theologische Literaturzeitung* (Berlin: Halle, October 1956), p.582.

[3] *The Kingdom of God*, pp.259, 261.

[4] *Van het Koninkrijk*, p.290.

The church, consequently, is both a trophy and instrument of the saving work Christ himself began in the flesh. To that end she has a gospel to proclaim, a gospel that announces to men the saving power of God, the provision of his righteousness and the blessedness into which the recipients of the kingdom enter by way of a right relationship with God. For the success of her ministry, she is empowered by the Holy Spirit, bestowed on her in fulfilment of the promise given her king by the Father at his ascension. From the Spirit is her life. Through the Spirit comes her enabling. By the Spirit is made manifest the spiritual character of the kingdom she proclaims and manifests. To understand more completely the significance of this truth with its implications, it will be necessary for us to examine it in greater detail.

a. *Christ as the personification of the kingdom*

The kingdom of God has come in Jesus Christ. He is its personification. How can this be, and what is its significance?

We learn from Luke 4:18-19 that Christ's messianic role was the unique fulfilment of that predicated by Isaiah for the suffering servant (cf. *Isa.* 61:1-2). When Jesus therefore quoted this prophecy as finding fulfilment in himself (*Luke* 4:21), he was not only giving the messianic programme of his work in broad outline, but he was asserting claims for himself that would only be true of the new age of God's kingdom in its arrival. The new dispensation was to be the age of the Spirit. The Spirit of the Lord had come upon the Messiah (*Luke* 4:18) and that without measure (*John* 3:34)[1] in order for him to exercise all the necessary powers of the coming age in the salvation of God's people. He could therefore preach the gospel to the poor and declare

---

[1] "It is uncertain whether the subject of John 3:34 is 'God' or 'Messiah'. The object in any case must be general. If, as in the common interpretation, God be taken as the subject, the sense appears to be; 'Christ speaks the words of God, for God does not give the Spirit by measure – only in a definite degree – to all, but he gives it completely.' If, on the other hand, Messiah is the subject (as Cyril takes it), the sense will be: 'Christ speaks the words of God, for his words are attested by his works, in that he gives the Spirit to his disciples as dispensing in its fulness that which is its own'." B.F. Westcott, *The Gospel According to John* (Grand Rapids: Eerdmans, 1954), vol. 1, p.134. On either interpretation according to this verse the Messiah had received the fulness of the Spirit.

that the kingdom of God was theirs (*Luke* 6:20), he could set at liberty the captives of sin and Satan; in a word, he could make his people whole. They would receive the benefits of the kingdom and enter into its blessedness, but only because it had come in his own person.

This is further illustrated by the fact that entrance into the kingdom was only by spiritual rebirth (*John* 3:3-5), a sovereign action brought about by the Spirit as he regenerated those dead in trespasses and sins so that, in repentance and faith, they were united to the Messiah (*John* 3:16) and became recipients of all his saving benefits. Yes, the kingdom of God was present and in the midst of the people. Because of this the blind received their sight, the lame walked, the lepers were cleansed, the deaf heard again and even the dead were given life! (*Matt.* 11:5). Evil spirits were exorcised as an irrefutable evidence of the kingdom's arrival (*Matt.* 12:28). But only Messiah's people were members of that kingdom. And this because they were indissolubly linked by faith to him (*John* 10:27-28) in whose hand is all the power to give them the blessings of the kingdom. To summarize, the kingdom is centred in Jesus Christ as its focal point because, as the Father's promised Messiah, he is the divinely appointed administrator of God's sovereignty (*John* 5:22-23) – even to the point of forgiving sin, the prerogative of God alone (*Luke 5:21-25*).

Why then did the kingdom not return into heaven with Christ at the time of his ascension? The question is only academic because the presence and power of the kingdom came almost immediately to embodiment in Christ's church on the day of Pentecost when she received the effusion of his Spirit. Christ had ascended to heaven to be seated at the right hand of the Father until his reign has been consummated in the fulfilment of every purpose of his rule. But his work on earth would be continued by the Spirit, coming to expression in the church and going progressively forward until the eternal state would be created, maintained and pervaded by the supernatural power of the Spirit.[1] The power of God's kingdom therefore continues to

[1] For a full discussion, cf. G. Vos, *The Pauline Eschatology* (Grand Rapids: Eerdmans, 1952), pp.298-303.

be active in the world, centred in the exalted reign of Christ, but furthered by his Spirit who makes the church the locus of his operation.[1]

b. *The kingdom of God and the kingdom of Christ*

The kingdom of God and the kingdom of Christ are not synonymous. We have seen that the term, kingdom of God, expresses the final state when Christ will have delivered the kingdom to the Father, that God may be all in all (*I Cor.* 15:24, 28). But the relationship between the kingdom of God and the kingdom of Christ must be our concern now because Scripture speaks of the presence of both existing in this current dispensation. What then is the relationship between the two and how may they be distinguished?

We must first of all remember the truth pointed out by Schmidt: "Scripture not only speaks of the presence of the kingdom of God in the same way as the kingdom of Christ, but also in specific places equally mentions the kingdom of God and of Christ."[2] He then gives several examples. For instance, when Mark 10:29, Matthew 19:20, and Luke 18:29 are compared, it is found that Luke makes the leaving of earthly possessions *for the kingdom of God's sake*, whereas Matthew makes them *for my name's sake*, and Mark makes them *for my sake, and the gospel's*. Obviously, Christ is speaking of the kingdom of God as Luke expresses it. But the parallels of Matthew and Mark must also be doing the same, while giving the added insight that the kingdom of God concerns itself with the gospel and sake of Christ. That is to say, the kingdom concerns itself with a distinct message (gospel) and Christ's sovereign cause (his sake). This could be true of this age only if he were ruling, so that full devotion to him could take place for his sake.

To cite another example, if it be conceded that there is valid association of thought between the parable of the Virgins

---

[1] Cf. Floyd V. Filson, *Jesus Christ the Risen Lord* (Nashville: Abingdon Press, 1956), pp.156-180, for a full discussion of the Spirit's presence, gifts, and activity in the church as the body of Christ.

[2] "Basileia", p.590.

(*Matt.* 25:1 ff.) and that of the Watchful Servants (*Luke* 12:35 ff.), it will be seen that Matthew places his parable within the setting of the kingdom of heaven (i.e., kingdom of God), which Luke identifies with this age by making the watchful servant's activity fall within the realm of Christ's present reign (i.e., kingdom of Christ) prior to his second advent.

A third example may be found in Revelation 12:10. Here the kingdom of God and the authority (*exousia*) of Christ are directly linked. "Then I heard a loud voice saying in heaven, Now salvation and strength, and the kingdom of our God, and the power of his Christ have come, for the accuser of our brethren, who accused them before our God day and night, has been cast down." Even on a futurist interpretation, the synonymous occurrence of the two cannot be denied.

The plainest connection of the two is made in Ephesians 5:5, "For this you know, that no fornicator, unclean person, nor covetous man, who is an idolater, has any inheritance *in the kingdom of Christ and of God.*"

The relationship and yet distinction between the two become clear when we remember that *basileia* means primarily rule or dominion rather than kingdom. Christ as the exalted Messiah and Lord has been given dominion by the Father (*Luke* 22:29)[1] which shall continue until all has been subdued under him (*Phil.* 2:9-11, *I Cor.* 15:25, etc.). In that Christ is the Son of God, this dominion is his by virtue of his being a person of the Godhead, and shall be eternal in the sense that God's sovereignty never ends (*Luke* 1:33, *Dan.* 7:13, etc.). But as the exalted Messiah, he has been given a dominion by the Father which presently holds sway until it has fulfilled all its designated temporal purposes. Then it will end by being delivered up to the Father. Over all, therefore, is the kingdom of God, and from this divine sovereignty all messianic dominion has come and to it will ultimately again

---

[1] "And I bestow upon you a kingdom, just as my Father bestowed one upon me." As in Luke 1:33, *basileia* is here 'dominion' rather than 'a kingdom' (cf. *Luke* 23:42, *Rev.* 17:12, *I Thess.* 2:12). A. Plummer, *A Critical and Exegetical Commentary on the Gospel According to St. Luke* (Edinburgh: I.C.C. Series, T. & T. Clark, 4th ed., 1913), p.502.

be surrendered. Hence, the present outworking of a dominion whose ultimate end is complete and universal sovereignty which, until it is surrendered to the Father at the end, belongs to the Lord's anointed, i.e., the Lord Jesus Christ. Consequently, there is a close relationship and yet distinction between the kingdom of God and the kingdom of Christ.

As Bright puts it, "The Bible is *one book*. Had we to give that book a title, we might with justice call it 'The Book of the Coming Kingdom of God.' That is, indeed, its central theme everywhere. In the New Testament, however, there is this difference: the kingdom of God has become also the kingdom of Christ, and that kingdom is actually at hand."[1]

c. Christ as head of his church

In I Corinthians 15:47, Adam is referred to as, "the first man of the earth", whereas Christ is referred to as, "the second man the Lord from heaven". The Scripture makes clear in this chapter — as elsewhere, notably Romans 5:12-21 — that the first man was the federal head of the whole human race, with the result that by his sin all humanity fell in him and shares with him the curse and penalty due to that sin. As the first Adam was a federal head, so also was the second Adam a federal head. What Adam brought on his posterity by way of sin, condemnation and death, Christ came to undo for his people to procure their right-eousness, justification and life. If Adam is therefore the head of humanity as a whole, Christ as the second Adam is the head of redeemed humanity. He is therefore the head of his church, that community which embodies humanity which he has redeemed.

In what way are we to understand Christ's being the head of his church, especially since he is in heaven and the members of his body are on earth? Can the following statements help us?

Hort says, "That headship of the human race which was implied in the Christ's being called the second Adam carried with it *a fortiori* his headship of the Ecclesia, that chosen portion of the human race, representative of the whole, which is brought into close relation to himself, and is the immediate object of his

[1] *The Kingdom of God,* pp.197-198.

saving and cherishing and purifying love, attested once for all by his willing self-sacrifice."[1] This statement, while true enough, does not reveal the complete significance of Christ's headship of his church.

Does Nygren tell us more? "Christ is not the head pure and simple, but he is the head of his church. Similarly, the church is not a body in itself, viewed apart from the head, but it is just the body of Christ... *The church is Christ as he is present among and meets us upon earth after his resurrection.* This is the New Testament conception of the church (*John* 14:18, *Matt.* 28:20)."[2]

While Scripture speaks of Christ as the head and the church as his body, is the church now to be equated with Christ as Nygren claims? Does the fact that he promised his church his continuing presence in the person of the Holy Spirit (*John* 14:18) make Nygren's conclusion legitimate?

Christ is in heaven. From there he sends the Spirit in fulfilment of the Father's promise (*Acts* 2:33). Now, though the Spirit represents Christ and does his work, he is nevertheless a distinct person of the Godhead and is not to be identified with Christ. And if such be true of the Spirit, how much more so must this be true of the church. The church is Christ's body but it is not Christ. There is consequently in Nygren's statement a perilous tendency, in theory if not in fact, towards a sacramentalism that exalts the church until she is virtually an extension of her Lord (i.e., Rome's incarnationalist view of the church).

A better statement of the significance of Christ's headship in relation to his church is given by Cullmann: "The concentration upon a specific point of creation, the earthly world, and within this world upon a human fellowship signifies...that the church, as the focal point, is the very heart of the reign of Christ."[3] Christ as head of his church brings his redemptive power to bear on the world by means of his members in the world, much as the head determines the functions of the body.

[1] *The Christian Ecclesia*, p.151.

[2] A. Nygren, *Christ and His Church* (Philadelphia: Westminster Press, 1956), p.96.

[3] "Königsherrschaft Christi", p.28.

There are two significant references in the New Testament to the headship of Christ over his church and the function he fulfils in this capacity. The first is found in Ephesians 1:20-23 where we read, "Which he worked in Christ when he raised him from the dead and seated him at his right hand in the heavenly places, far above all principality and power and might and dominion, and every name that is named, not only in this age but also in that which is to come. And he put all things under his feet, and gave him to be head over all things to the church, which is his body, the fulness of him who fills all in all."

In this verse Paul describes the matchless power of God in raising Christ from the dead and making him head over all things. The universality of Christ's headship is stressed by the mention of many powers which must include the heavenly as well as the earthly since the height and extent of Christ's exaltation is here the dominant theme. This total sovereignty is viewed in its perfection; the means of its progressive realization is Christ's association with the church. As head of all things he has been given to the church that, as he sustains and directs her by his power, she might become the instrument through which he works towards the full realization of his sovereignty.

Thus an internal and external working out of his sovereignty is here indicated. Inwardly, the body grows into the fulness of the head (*Eph.* 4:13). Outwardly, the body is the instrument by which the head's sovereignty is increasingly expressed in the lives of its members in the world. The final outcome of this process is guaranteed because he is already head over all things both heavenly and earthly.

The importance of the church in relation to the headship of Christ can hardly be overemphasized. Cullmann goes so far as to say, "She is not simply a separate segment on its own, as it were, but rather, the focal point from whose source the whole reign of Christ becomes visible, and what occurs here comes to decisive expression in the reign of Christ."[1] While in a way we are critical of this statement in that its focus seems to be somewhat

[1] *Ibid.,* p.28.

too narrow, it is nevertheless commendable in that it lays proper stress on the relationship between Christ as the head and his church as his body by which he is bringing his sovereignty to full realization.

The other reference to the headship of Christ is found in Colossians 1:15-18 where we read, "He is the image of the invisible God, the first-born over all creation. For by him all things were created that are in heaven and that are on earth, visible and invisible, whether thrones or dominions or principalities or powers. All things were created through him and for him. And he is before all things, and in him all things consist. And he is the head of the body, the church, who is the beginning, the first-born from the dead, that in all things he might have the pre-eminence."

In these verses the universal sovereignty of Christ is again stressed. In fact, "As all creation passed out from Him, so does it all converge again towards Him."[1] Being sovereign of the universe, he also is fittingly head of that new creation, the church, whose inheritance rights he purchased along with those of the whole of creation (*v.* 15). For all is under his sovereign disposal, whether in salvation and renewal (his body the church) or in conquest and judgment (the unbelieving world).

But in the context of his creating and sustaining activity in the universe, *kephale* (head) takes on additional significance as descriptive of his relation to the church. It makes clear to us that Christ is "the inspiring, ruling, guiding, combining, sustaining power, the mainspring of its activity, the centre of its unity, and the seat of its life... And this absolute supremacy is his, because it was the Father's good pleasure that in him all the plenitude of Deity should have its home; because he willed through him to reconcile the universe once more unto himself."[2]

We see how these verses lay stress on Christ's headship of the church. As a body is an instrument which a head uses to accomplish its purposes, the church is Christ's instrument by which his universal sovereignty comes to increasing expression and

[1] J.B. Lightfoot, *Saint Paul's Epistle to the Colossians and to Philemon* (Grand Rapids: Zondervan, n.d. reprint of 1879 edition), p.154.

[2] *Ibid.*, pp.157, 158.

full realization. What he already is will one day be universally acknowledged, whether willingly (by his church) or unwillingly (by the unbelieving world). For the present, the focal point of his dominion is concentrated in his church as "from Christ life flows out through his body to all the members",[1] to empower and direct them in the implementation of his ruling activity. All the effects of his reign will not however have been accomplished until his fulness, which begins in the church, has filled all things in every way (*Eph.* 1:23), and in all things he has attained pre-eminence (*Col.* 1:18).

d. The church as the body of Christ

The church as the body of Christ stands in antithesis to the world, for she is the congregation of the Lord, pledged to him in the obedience of faith to be the instrument of his redemptive power. By her very definition she is antithetical to the world which in its rebellion is at enmity with her Lord and therefore alienated from his family.

Since Old Testament Israel was formerly the family of God, how does this relate to the present status of the church as the body of Christ? In the second chapter of Ephesians, Paul makes clear that ancient Israel and new Israel have been made one as the body of Christ. "But now in Christ Jesus you who once were far off have been made near by the blood of Christ. For he himself is our peace, who has made both one, and has broken down the middle wall of division between us, having abolished in his flesh the enmity, that is, the law of commandments contained in ordinances, so as to create in himself one new man from the two, thus making peace, and that he might reconcile them both unto God in one body through the cross, thereby putting to death the enmity" (*Eph.* 2:13-16).

In Christ the wall of separation has been broken down, a wall that existed before primarily to separate the people of God from the people of the world (*v.* 12) but which now because of its removal has created a new Israel composed both of old Israel and

---

[1] Nygren, *Christ and His Church*, p.107.

Gentiles in the one body of Christ (*v.* 16). In the church, there-fore, as the body of Christ, is to be found "God's primary agent in his ever-expanding counsels towards mankind."[1]

The church is faced with a two-fold task during the time that her head's reign progresses to complete realization. She is first of all to grow into the measure of her head's fulness. "Holding fast to the head, from whom all the body, nourished and knit together by joints and ligaments, grows with the increase which is from God" (*Col.* 2:19). To this end her exalted head has bestowed on her all the necessary gifts for its accomplishment (*Eph.* 4:7-13), and the ministry of the offices in the church is to be discharged with a view to the realization of this goal.

In the second place the church's task is to be a living witness to the reign of Christ. That which Old Testament Israel was to be for the Lord God has now become the task of New Testament Israel. In her gospel she proclaims the reign of her king and invites others into that heavenly citizenship in which membership means, not only the increase, but the complementation of the body of Christ by her putting into use those gifts which the head has given her.

In this two-fold manner the church as the body of Christ grows. Her goal will have been reached only when one day Christ presents her to himself, "a glorious church, not having spot or wrinkle or any such thing, but that it should be holy and without blemish" (*Eph.* 5:27). Then, in language deep with symbolical meaning, we are told that she will enjoy the consum-mate bliss of the wedding feast of eternity with him as his bride (*Rev.* 19:7-8; 21:2).

The two concepts of the church as body and bride are not to be considered confusing. They are seen in closest association with each other by the apostle Paul in Ephesians 5:23-33. There, in analogy with the matrimonial bond that exists between hus-band and wife, he speaks of the church both as the bride (*vv.* 25-27) and as the body of Christ (*v.* 30). Paul makes clear why the two concepts can be so closely associated when in verse 31

[1] Hort, *The Christian Ecclesia*, p.228.

he says, "For this reason a man shall leave his father and mother and be joined to his wife, and the two shall become one flesh."

By means of the marriage relationship husband and wife become one flesh; so the church and Christ become one body: his body by reason of her connection with him who is her head, his bride by virtue of her destiny as recipient from him of all the glories of eternal felicity. The two concepts must therefore be kept in closest association though not chronologically. The church is not first bride and then body. She is already body because of Christ as her head. But in a sense she is also already bride because of that intimacy which exists between her and her Lord (*John* 3:29, *James* 4:4), though this latter relationship by its very nature is a more fitting symbol for eschatological fulfilment and is so most frequently employed in Scripture (cf. *Matt.* 25:1-13, *II Cor.* 11:2, *Eph.* 5:27, *Rev.* 19:7; 21:2, 9; 22:17).

Here we are given another instance where the New Testament applies a relationship found in the Old Testament to describe the union that existed between the Lord God and his people (cf. *Exod.* 30:15, *Ezek.* 16, *Hos.* 2:19 ff., *Mal.* 2:11). The church, therefore, as body and bride, growing into Christ's fulness as she is bound to him in loving obedience, awaits the day of her complete eschatological fulfilment when both in number and collective maturity she reaches the goal toward which her Lord is now progressively directing and conforming her. In the meantime her function is that of new Israel, the people of God under the banner of Jesus Christ her king, holding forth the gospel of redemption committed to her, herself being a living organism of its transforming power and offering the same status to all who will enrol themselves under the ensign of her king's love.

Exegetical Excursus on Texts which Relate the Kingdom of Christ and of God

Herman Ridderbos' book, *The Coming of the Kingdom*[1], may be considered a landmark in the interpretation of Scripture's teaching about the subject of the kingdom of God. Since in it he deals with the data of the Gospels on this subject, which include the kingdom of Christ and the church, we do not feel it is necessary to retrace his exegetical steps through this part of Scripture. However, we do feel that it would be helpful to the reader if we were to present a brief study of those texts in the book of Acts and the rest of the New Testament which relate the kingdom of Christ and the kingdom of God. Moreover, Acts is a good place to begin, for here the history of salvation proceeds from the ascension and exaltation of Christ as an accomplished fact and thus clearly sets forth his dominion as already present. This is not to overlook the future significance of Christ's kingdom where it may be referred to, but we will have to let text and context be our guide in determining whether the present or the future is meant.

The first reference to the kingdom of God in Acts is found at 1:3, "To whom [the apostles] he also presented himself alive after his suffering by many infallible proofs, being seen by them during forty days, and speaking of the things pertaining to the kingdom of God." Here we see the kingdom of God equated with the gospel — the events of the life, death, resurrection of Jesus and the salvation and entrance into the kingdom which faith in him brings. This has relevance for the present dispensation and the dominion of Christ by which his followers are empowered to carry out the commission of its proclamation.

The next reference is found in 1:6 where the last flicker on the apostles' part is seen concerning their hope that national Israel would once again be a political theocracy. "Therefore, when they had come together, they asked him saying, Lord, will you at this time restore the kingdom to Israel?" Jesus' answer

---

[1] Philadelphia: Presbyterian and Reformed Publishing Company, 1962.

directs their attention away from national Israel and God's purposes for it. "These were not the concern of the messengers of Christ. The kingdom of God which they were commissioned to proclaim was the good news of God's grace in Christ."[1]

In Acts 8:12, the equation of the kingdom with the gospel is again made. "But when they believed Philip as he preached the things concerning the kingdom of God and the name of Jesus Christ, both men and women were baptized." "'The things concerning the kingdom of God' at the beginning of Acts are identical with 'the things concerning the Lord Jesus Christ' at the end of the book (28:31; cf. 8:12; 20:24-25; 28:23).[2]

In Acts 14:22, the present relevance of the kingdom of God is seen in that membership in it (i.e., being "in the faith") is equated with the sufferings and tribulations of this life. "Strengthening the souls of the disciples, exhorting them to continue in the faith, and saying, We must through many tribulations enter the kingdom of God."

In Acts 19:8, "the things of the kingdom of God" is simply the gospel of Jesus Christ: "And he [Paul] went into the synagogue and spoke boldly for three months, reasoning and persuading concerning the things of the kingdom of God."

The remaining references in Acts to the kingdom of God pertain also to the things concerning Christ, or the gospel. In 20:24-25 we read, "But none of these things move me; nor do I count my life dear to myself, so that I may finish my race with joy, and the ministry which I received from the Lord Jesus, to testify to the gospel of the grace of God. And indeed, now I know that you all, among whom I have gone preaching the kingdom of God, will see my face no more." Then, in 28:23 we read, "So when they had appointed him a day, many came to him at his lodging, to whom he explained and solemnly testified of the kingdom of God, persuading them concerning Jesus from both the Law of Moses and the Prophets, from morning till evening." And in 28:31 we read, "Preaching the kingdom of

[1] Bruce, *Commentary on the Book of Acts*, p.38.
[2] *Ibid.*, p.34.

God and teaching the things which concern the Lord Jesus Christ with all confidence, no one forbidding him." These three references make the kingdom of God synonymous with the rule of Christ now begun and yet to be consummated only at his second advent when this event "will coincide with the final and complete manifestation of the kingdom, when every knee will bow in his name and every tongue confess him as Lord (*Phil.* 2:10 f.) when God's will is to be done on earth as it is in heaven (*Matt.* 6:10)."[1]

The epistle to the Romans has one reference to the kingdom of God. It is found at 14:17. "For the kingdom of God is not food and drink, but righteousness and peace and joy in the Holy Spirit." From the context in which it is found, its relevance to the present reign of Christ may be seen, for Paul in this chapter speaks of Christian liberty and the manner in which those who are strong in the faith should use it. The kingdom of God, therefore, is here a synonym for the kingdom of Christ, the spiritual theocracy. "The theocracy of the Old Testament was ceremonial and ritual; that of the New is inward and spiritual."[2]

In I Corinthians 4:20 yet another reference to the kingdom of God is equated with the reign of the Messiah. "For the kingdom of God is not in word but in power." The kingdom proclamation as well as the Corinthian believers' entrance into it had not come in words only but with the necessary power (2:4) by which the Messiah made his reign effective. Therefore Paul would not give attention to words merely but to the works by which the power of the kingdom's presence was manifested.

In I Corinthians 6:9-10 we have what may be the first reference so far to the yet future manifestation of the kingdom of God. "Do you not know that the unrighteous will not inherit the kingdom of God? Do not be deceived. Neither fornicators, nor idolaters, nor adulterers, nor homosexuals, nor sodomites, nor thieves, nor covetous, nor drunkards, nor revilers, nor extortioners, will inherit the kingdom of God." Paul's warning is here intended to reveal the inconsistency of sinfulness with inheriting the kingdom of

---

[1] *Ibid.*, p.35.

[2] Hodge, *Commentary on the Epistle to the Romans*, p.425.

God. Now conceivably Paul could mean that the Corinthian believers' profession of faith and membership in Christ's kingdom were only so much hypocrisy if the sins he enumerates were present in their lives. In this case Paul would be saying, "You may think that you are members of Christ's kingdom but this is not true if you continue to commit the following sins, for those who do so will never inherit the kingdom!"

This interpretation makes good sense and, if correct, would make this text another reference to the present rule of Christ. But it is more natural to give the full future force to the verb "will inherit" appearing in both verses 9 and 10. In this case Paul would be saying, "You have been cleansed from your sins and have been given membership in Christ's kingdom. But remember, to be members of his kingdom and yet continue the practice of sin is contrary to that membership. If you are doing this, beware! Your hypocrisy may continue now but it will be manifested to your shame and loss when at the revelation of the future kingdom of God in all its glory you find yourselves excluded from it." "He who thinks of himself as a king (4:8) runs the risk of standing outside the kingdom of God."[1] On either interpretation we have an example of the elasticity of the term, "kingdom of God", since it is able to stand both for the present kingdom of Christ and the future kingdom of glory. We may not therefore be able always to assert dogmatically which phase of the kingdom is meant by a given text. The kingdom of Christ is within the kingdom of God. And the end of the former is ultimately to merge with the latter. Hence, both or either may be meant in one context, depending upon whether the sense be general or specific.

I Corinthians 15:24 refers to a future act but is related to the kingdom of Christ. "Then comes the end, when he delivers the kingdom to God the Father, when he puts an end to all rule and all authority and power." Under chiliastic interpretation this kingdom of Christ would refer to his millennial rule. A more natural interpretation would be to associate this kingdom of

[1] F. W. Grosheide, *Commentary on the First Epistle to the Corinthians* (Grand Rapids: Eerdmans, 1953), p.140.

[53]

Christ with his present rule. However, both interpretations agree that the kingdom of Christ is here dealt with and that, at a future time, when all his foes will have been subdued and all the fruits of his victorious reign will have been gathered in, he will then return his mediatorial sovereignty to the Father.

I Corinthians 15:50 again illustrates the elasticity of the term, "kingdom of God". "Now this I say, brethren, that flesh and blood cannot inherit the kingdom of God; nor does corruption inherit incorruption." This statement is as true for the present kingdom of Christ as it is for the future kingdom of God. Flesh and blood are earthbound and temporal, the kingdom is heavenly and eternal. Hence the stress already in Christ's teaching of the kingdom being of heaven, of the necessity of the spiritual rebirth for entrance into it and of the fact that his kingdom is not of this world. Corruption cannot inherit incorruption. A man must even now become a new creature in Christ if he is to be a member of his kingdom.

But in its more immediate context it is better to take this text as referring to the yet future final kingdom. For Paul goes on to speak of the resurrection and the final victory over death. In verse 26 we are told that the last enemy of Christ's reign to be destroyed will be death. Then he will deliver the kingdom up to the Father (v. 28). In other words, the resurrection and victory over death come at the end of Christ's reign. And at that time this corruptible body will have put on incorruption (v. 53) so as to inherit the final kingdom of God since it will no longer be made of flesh and blood.

In Galatians 5:21 we read, "Envy, murders, drunkenness, revels, and the like: of the which I tell you beforehand, just as I also told you in time past, that those who practise such things will not inherit the kingdom of God." The similarity of this verse with I Corinthians 6:9-10 makes it clear that it can also be interpreted in the same twofold manner. We will not therefore go into any further detail with this verse since our conclusions for I Corinthians 6:9-10 apply here as well.

In Ephesians 5:5 we read, "For this you know, that no fornicator, unclean person, nor covetous man, who is an idolater, has any inheritance in the kingdom of Christ and of God." Despite the similarity of this verse with Galatians 5:21 and I Corinthians 6:9-10, our conclusion that the aspect of Christ's present rule rather than the future kingdom is here meant follows, for two reasons:

In the first place the verb tense here is present ["has inheritance"] whereas in I Corinthians 6:9-10 and Galatians 5:21, the tense of "inherit" is future. If the inheritance is a present reality, then so also must the kingdom of that inheritance be a present reality. And the present kingdom is Christ's kingdom.

In the second place, it is here specified as the kingdom of Christ. But does Paul say that the kingdom is Christ's who is also God, or does he say that the kingdom is both Christ's and God's? The grammar is inconclusive, i.e., *basileia tou Christou kai Theou,* for an article is not needed before *Theos* (God) to make this a reference to the Father. "*Theou* has the same climactic force here as in I Corinthians 3:22-23."[1] Now, if it is correct to say that Paul is affirming deity for Christ, no problem presents itself to prevent us from ascribing the meaning of this verse to the present reign of Christ. But if the reference is to the Father's kingdom as well as that of his anointed, there is still no difficulty because of the nature of the two kingdoms. The kingdom is Christ's, committed to him now, but to be delivered up at last to God, who is to be sole and absolute sovereign. While we note the similarity of this verse with I Corinthians 6:9-10 and Galatians 5:21, we differ in our conclusion. For here the present kingdom of Christ is meant while in those two the future final kingdom of God is taught. This once again reinforces what we have previously noted about the elasticity of the kingdom of God concept as it is used in different contexts.

In Colossians 1:13 we have a clear reference to the kingdom of Christ as a present entity. "He has delivered us from the power of darkness and translated us into the kingdom of the Son of his love." God's people are now members of Christ's kingdom. Where a kingdom exists, there a king exercises rule. This is therefore true of Christ at present. "The reign of Christ has already begun. His kingdom is a present kingdom. Whatever therefore is *essential*

[1] S.D.F. Salmond, *The Epistle to the Ephesians*, E.G.T. Series (Grand Rapids: Eerdmans, 1951), vol. 3 p.354.

in the kingdom of Christ must be capable of realization now. There may be some exceptional manifestation in the world to come, but this cannot alter its inherent character. In other words, the sovereignty of Christ is essentially a moral and spiritual sovereignty, which has begun now and will only be perfected hereafter."[1]

In Colossians 4:11, essentially the same meaning is to be applied as to the earlier reference in the epistle to the kingdom of God (i.e., *Col.* 1:13). "And Jesus who is called Justus. These are my only fellow workers for the kingdom of God who are of the circumcision; they have proved to be a comfort to me." "Fellow workers for the kingdom of God" denote the presence of that kingdom. Paul and his fellow workers laboured that the kingdom might come, to be sure, but in the sense that its already-present power might come to increasing manifestation in the community of the faithful through obedience to the one whose gospel they proclaimed. The kingdom of God is here synonymous, for all practical purposes, with the kingdom of Christ for whom Paul and his companions laboured.

More complex is the reference to the kingdom which is found in I Thessalonians 2:12, "That you would live a life worthy of God who calls you into his own kingdom and glory." One interpretation would be Schmidt's who equates *doxa* (glory) with *basileia*. "To the kingdom of God came the *doxa* as the glory of God (*I Thess.* 2:12); indeed, *basileia* and *doxa* may be exchanged with each other, as *en te doxe sou* (in thy glory, *Mark* 10:37), shows, where the parallel passage, Matthew 20:21, has *en te basileia sou* (in thy kingdom)."[2]

It may be questioned however, whether Schmidt's appeal to the parallel Gospel passages establishes his position. Was not Salome, after all, labouring under the popular misconceptions which were current among the Jews of Jesus' day, misconceptions which equated Messiah's reign with the splendour of Solomon's kingdom and which might well be referred to also as "glory"?

---

[1] Lightfoot, *Saint Paul's Epistle to the Colossians and to Philemon*, p.142.

[2] "Basileia", p.584.

This notion died hard even among the disciples, as we have seen from Acts 1:6. But as Jesus there made clear, the kingdom of this dispensation was spiritual and would come to expression in the proclamation of the good news of God's grace in Christ.

More accurate, therefore, is Milligan's comment, "The two expressions, *basileia* and *doxa*, must not...be united as if they equal 'his own kingdom of glory,' or even 'his own kingdom culminating in his glory,' but point rather to two manifestations of God's power, the first of His *rule*, the second of His *glory*."[1] In other words, Paul makes both a present and future reference to the kingdom of God in this verse: the present in that he *has called (kalountos)* us into his kingdom which must therefore be a reference to Christ's present kingdom; the future in that "through the influence of the LXX, where *doxa* is commonly used to translate the Hebrew *cabhod* (honour, glory), it came to be applied in the New Testament to the full manifestation of God's glory... the future bliss or glory that awaits God's people."[2] Since this latter has not yet taken place, the future aspect is embodied in this verse along with the present.

Of course there is the possibility that the future alone may be the actual reference of this verse. "Kingdom" would then be the kingdom of God in its final form, of which Christians are already members as they await its glory. But because the New Testament clearly teaches that the present aspect of God's kingdom is the rule of Christ, and since it is here stated that Christians are already members of that kingdom, it is therefore a more natural interpretation to assign the kingdom of God to the reign of Christ and the glory to its future aspect.

On first consideration, it might be concluded that the present aspect of the kingdom is being taught in II Thessalonians 1:5, "Which is manifest evidence of the righteous judgment of God, that you may be counted worthy of the kingdom of God, for which you also suffer." If suffering for the kingdom was then already being experienced, a logical deduction would be that

[1] George Milligan, *St. Paul's Epistles to the Thessalonians* (London: Macmillan and Co., Ltd., 1908), p.27.

[2] *Ibid.*

the kingdom too, was present for which (*hyper hes*), the suffering was being endured (cf. *Acts* 14:22). In other words, upon this interpretation, the suffering was an evidence of kingdom membership.

But in the larger context we find that Paul is speaking of retribution which God is righteously to dispense on behalf of his people at the time of the final judgment which is yet future (*vv.* 6-9). Their divinely-bestowed patience and faith being manifested during their present affliction, served as a token (*endeigma*) that God would yet vindicate his honour by judgment on their enemies at the return of Christ. Their suffering in the meantime was an indication that they are God's people against whom his enemies' wrath is being directed. By that suffering for God, they may be sure that in the future kingdom they shall be fully vindicated by him and enjoy the final glory of that age.

The reference to the kingdom in II Timothy 4:1 is clearly future: "I charge you therefore before God and the Lord Jesus Christ, who will judge the living and the dead at his appearing and his kingdom." This aspect of Christ's kingdom is future because it is associated with his second advent. But what phase of his yet future kingdom is here meant? Chiliasts would say that this is a reference to the millennium which is to begin at the return of Christ.[1] We may set to one side, however, this understanding of the verse, for Paul is speaking of the inevitable judgment of Christ which is to occur at his second coming. This awesome fact brings with it the solemn obligation to his herald to carry on faithfully proclaiming the truth despite the development of widespread apostasy from it (*vv.* 2-3). For the basis of that judgment and separation of Christ's people into one camp and his enemies into the other will be according to that self-same truth (*Rom.* 2:16) whether accepted or rejected.

Now, since his kingdom is linked with his appearing, the reference need mean no more than that its consummation in final victory and judgment will occur at the time of his second advent.

[1] See, for instance, both at this passage and Revelation 20, Jamieson, Fausset, and Brown, *Commentary on the Whole Bible* (Grand Rapids: Zondervan reprint of 8th edition, n.d.), pp.428, 598.

The next reference is II Timothy 4:18: "And the Lord will deliver me from every evil work and preserve me for his heavenly kingdom. To him be glory forever and ever. Amen!" Here Paul is speaking of the Son's kingdom, as his appellative "Lord" makes clear. And the reference to his present rule can be seen when verse 18 is seen in connection with verse 17 whose thought it supplements. "The stress falls on the divine rescuing activity. *In the past* there had been danger. Now, too, there was that which men would consider danger. But in the past the Lord had intervened; now again he will *intervene decisively for deliverance...* In the past Paul had been rescued *from* death. Now he will be rescued by means of death... The Lord is going to bring Paul to heaven, that is, to that kingdom which, though seen on earth in shadow, has its seat in heaven, and belongs to heaven as to its essence and fulness."[1] Quite properly, therefore, Paul refers to the Son's dominion as a heavenly kingdom in whose glory in the presence of Christ he would shortly be found (*II Cor.* 5:8). This verse cannot refer to a future kingdom of Christ on earth after the manner of a millennarian construction because it is specifically referred to as a *heavenly kingdom (ten basileian ten epouranion)*. Its spiritual character is more emphatically expressed in the original than in translation and must therefore refer to the present dominion of Christ.

In the Epistle to the Hebrews the first reference to the kingdom is found in 1:8-9. "But to the Son he says, Your throne, O God, is forever and ever; a sceptre of righteousness is the sceptre of your kingdom. You have loved righteousness and hated lawlessness; therefore, God, your God, has anointed you with the oil of gladness more than your companions." This text is a quotation of Psalm 45:6-7. That the writer of the Hebrews considered it messianic is clear from his application of it to Christ to whom he ascribed its fulfilment. By virtue of the work Christ fulfilled in his humanity (loving righteousness and hating iniquity) he has been given the position of pre-eminence by the Father,

[1] William Hendriksen, *Exposition of the Pastoral Epistles*, N.T.C. (Grand Rapids: Baker, 1957), p.327.

anointed with the oil of gladness above any other who might be classed as a companion.

The rise of higher criticism, however, with its effect on translations (notably the RSV) has affected the ascription of deity in verse 8 to Christ because of the way that the Hebrew has been translated from its original setting. There (*Psa.* 45:6), the text of the RSV has made "Your throne, O God", "your divine throne", though retaining the proper translation of the Hebrew *kise'qa 'Elohim* in a footnote with another variant. This brings about a contradiction at Hebrews 1:8 where, "Thy throne, O God", is left to stand in the text of the RSV though a footnote gives, "God is thy throne". All these variants from the Hebrew and Greek must be regarded as arising from presuppositional Arian bias because they do not fit the sense of the text. "God is thy throne" might be a possible translation of both the Hebrew and Greek words but the sense is meaningless because God is neither the throne nor can the throne be considered as a part of God.

The weight of this difficulty has been felt by the RSV translators. Their paraphrase in the psalm of the phrase, "Thy divine throne", which is not made in Hebrews 1:8 to correspond, leaves a jarring contradiction. Despite this Arianising attack on the deity of Christ, a reference to the present rule remains the clear teaching of this text. That it is viewed as continuing forever is an oblique testimony to his deity, for since Christ is truly God, then of course his kingdom will never end as he enjoys its perpetuation together with the Father and the Holy Spirit. This is the meaning of this text.

This brings us to the other reference in Hebrews to the kingdom, which is found at 12:28-29: "Therefore, since we are receiving a kingdom which cannot be shaken, let us have grace, by which we may serve God acceptably with reverence and godly fear. For our God is a consuming fire." In harmony with what the writer of this epistle has taught in 1:8 concerning the fact of Christ's rule in this dispensation, we may conclude that this is the "unshakeable kingdom" he here refers to, of which believers are already a part, though he has looked beyond the present dispensation to view its culmination in the judgment of God. For God, as a consuming fire, will then not only purge away all the dross of his people, but will also consume his enemies in the fierceness of his wrath. That Christ is also the agent of this judgment is not here specified (cf. *Acts* 17:31). Nor need it be, for the writer's point has been made that only those who are members of the kingdom shall be immovable at the final judgment. Let us therefore serve God acceptably with reverence and godly fear!

It is true that the reference to the kingdom of God in James 2:5 can be given a present application: "Listen, my beloved brethren: has not God chosen the poor of this world to be rich in faith and heirs of the kingdom which he promised to those who love him?" For as Mayor puts it, "The son of God, as son, enjoys that which answers to his new birth (cf. *Matt.* 5:5, *Eph.* 1:14,18, *Col.* 3:24). This is described as 'eternal life'... or 'the kingdom of God'... or 'salvation'... an 'inheritance incorruptible', 'the eternal inheritance.'"[1] By equating the kingdom with the blessings of salvation, the text's application to the present may readily be made. But does this do full justice to its teaching? On the basis of the word "heirs" and the verb "has chosen", it is best to regard this text as referring to the future final glory of God's kingdom. For believers are members of Christ's kingdom now and participants in the blessings its salvation bestows, but as yet they are only heirs of that which they will enjoy in the final kingdom. God's promise of it to them, though certain of fulfilment, still awaits realization.

Concerning II Peter 1:11, it might be argued that a reference to the present kingdom of Christ is made because the kingdom is here specifically referred to as that of Christ: "For so an entrance will be supplied to you abundantly into the everlasting kingdom of our Lord and Saviour Jesus Christ." Two considerations, however, make the reference here to the future kingdom.

In the first place the accumulation of words in this verse suggests the splendour and fulness which will be realized only in the future kingdom of God. Then an entrance into the fulness of final glory shall be administered abundantly to the people of

---

[1] Joseph B. Mayor, *The Epistle of St. James* (London: Macmillan and Co. Ltd., 1897), p.83.

God. Already they have the blessings of salvation, to be sure, but rather as a pledge of that which they are yet one day to experience to the full.

In the second place, the word "everlasting" points to the final kingdom of God. Christ's mediatorial sovereignty, though presently exercised, is not everlasting. It will, one day, be handed back to the Father. That Peter here ascribes the everlasting kingdom to Christ must therefore mean that he views it in its final state where its dominion will be exercised by all three persons of the Godhead. But the Christians' part in that kingdom, Peter would remind us, is due to the salvation purchased for them by their Lord and Saviour, Jesus Christ, who, for this reason, is given exclusive prominence in this verse.

In the book of Revelation, there are a number of references to the kingdom. The first is found at 1:6, which in the AV and NKJV, following the *Textus Receptus,* reads "kings" rather than "kingdom", to agree with "priests". But *basileian* (kingdom) appears in other manuscripts which make the verse read: "And has made us a kingdom, priests unto God and his Father; to him be glory and dominion forever and ever. Amen." The reflection of this verse on the truth found in Exodus 19:6 is obvious. "As Israel when set free from Egypt acquired a national life under its divine king, so the church, redeemed by the blood of Christ, constituted a holy nation, a new theocracy."[1] Here, then, we have one of the clearest references to the kingdom of Christ as a present reality in this dispensation, a kingdom coming to focus in the rule he exercises over his people.

In the same way, the reference to the kingdom of Christ in 1:9 is to his dominion in this present age. "I John, both your brother and companion in tribulation, and in the kingdom and patience of Jesus Christ, was in the island that is called Patmos for the Word of God and for the testimony of Jesus Christ." Swete here makes this a reference to the future kingdom. "The obvious order is *thlipsis, hypomone, basileia,* i.e., tribulation, patience, kingdom: but that which is adopted here has the advantage of leaving

[1] Swete, *The Apocalypse*, p.8.

on the reader's mind the thought of the struggle which still remains before the kingdom is attained."[1] This observation may be true enough, but is it not a needless forcing of the text in the light of what John has just said about the kingdom three verses preceding? And if the reference to the present rule of Christ is preserved, there is no need for the transposition of "kingdom" and "patience". For the thought here is much the same as that expressed in Acts 14:22. Membership in the kingdom of Christ in this age is not without hardship and suffering. In fact, these are inevitable concomitants of such membership and serve to perfect the patience of the saints until the day when the final glory of the kingdom will spell their complete vindication. The reference to the present kingdom of Christ, therefore, should both be seen and maintained.

A reference to the kingdom in 5:10 is again obscured in the AV and NKJV where the change of "kingdom" to "kings" is repeated. But a translation of the original should be as follows, "And you have made them to our God a kingdom and priests, and they will reign upon the earth." The *Textus Receptus* also makes "them" "us" and "they will reign" "we shall reign".

At any rate, our interest lies in seeing yet another reference to the present dominion of Christ. For, according to the text, Christ has already made his people a kingdom. But that they will yet reign upon the earth reminds us of the glorious future goal which still awaits them. For Christ will one day make them participants with him in the exercise of his sovereignty.

The eschatological is clearly in evidence at Revelation 11:15, "Then the seventh angel sounded: and there were loud voices in heaven, saying, The kingdom (*he basileia* is singular and therefore not to be translated 'kingdoms', as in the AV and NKJV) of this world have become the kingdom of our Lord and of his Christ, and he shall reign forever and ever." Here we see the future merging of the kingdom of Christ with that of the Father, the result of which will be to usher in the eternal state. This will take place when Christ surrenders his mediatorial sovereignty

[1] *Ibid.*, p.12.

to the Father at the end of this age when his dominion of this world shall have reached its completion. "The words suggest the vision of a world-empire, once dominated by an usurping power, which has now at length passed into the hands of its true Owner and Imperator."[1] This does not mean that the Son will be excluded from sharing in the rule of the final state, as is further made clear in this book at 22:3 where the new Jerusalem, as the final order, has in it "the throne of God and of the Lamb".

A final reference to the kingdom of God is also found in the book of Revelation at 12:10: "Then I heard a loud voice saying in heaven, Now salvation, and strength, and the kingdom of our God, and the power of his Christ have come, for the accuser of our brethren, who accused them before our God day and night, has been cast down." Is this a significant reference to the present dispensation or is it eschatological? An examination of the broader context gives us the answer. In verse 6 we are told that the woman fled into the wilderness and at verses 13 and 14 we learn that she does so as a consequence of her persecution by the dragon who now vents his wrath upon her since he has been cast out of heaven. And when is he cast out of heaven? At verses 7 and 8 we learn that it comes about as the result of his defeat at the hands of Michael and his angels, which follows as a consequence of Christ's ascension (*v*. 5).

Therefore, the song of victory in verse 10 is the result of Satan's defeat at the ascension of Christ when he assumes his present rule, an authority (*exousia*) viewed as exercised within the larger realm of God's over-all sovereignty. The 1260 days of the woman's wilderness refuge must be then a symbolic designation of the length of this present dispensation based on the similar references to time made in Daniel 7:25; 9:27 and 12:7 but given the further development unfolded in New Testament revelation.

Having now briefly analyzed every New Testament verse from Acts to Revelation in which reference is made to the kingdom, we have seen how they substantiate our earlier conclusion on

[1] *Ibid.*, p.142.

the relationship between the kingdom of God and the kingdom of Christ; namely, that though the two are not synonymous, they may be spoken of in the closest of connections, because the latter is derived from, exists within and will ultimately be surrendered to the former. Once this truth is clearly seen, a basis for a better understanding of the New Testament references to the kingdom will have been established.

IV: THE CHURCH AS DISTINGUISHED FROM THE KINGDOM

We have been reminded by Bannerman (p.6) that the *Westminster Confession of Faith* identifies the church with the kingdom of Christ. The *Confession's* statement is as follows: "The visible church, which is also catholic or universal under the gospel (not confined to one nation, as before under the law) consists of all those throughout the world who profess the true religion; and of their children: and is the kingdom of the Lord Jesus Christ, the house and family of God, out of which there is no ordinary possibility of salvation" (*xxv*, 2). An up-to-date Roman Catholic catechism virtually identifies the church with the kingdom of God: "The church is to be grasped as both the People of God and as the kingdom of God... The kingdom will be present in its fulness only in eternity, when God will bring all things to completion. But the church is a realization of God's kingdom on earth."[1]

Neither of these positions is essentially different from that of Martin Luther: "Where he [Christ] speaks of the kingdom of heaven, he speaks of that in which we people are, which stands in the Word, in the faith, in the sacrament."[2] In other words,

---

[1] D.W. Wuerl, T.C. Lawler, R. Lawler, eds., *The Catholic Catechism* (Huntington, Indiana: Our Sunday Visitor Publishing Division, Our Sunday Visitor, Inc., 1986), pp.85,86.

[2] *Sämmtliche Schriften*, X, "Predigt auf das Fest der heiligen Engel" (St. Louis: Concordia Pub. House, 1885), p.1084.

Christ's kingdom for Luther was the *Glauben-Reich* (Faith-Kingdom), or church. The day will come when at the second advent of Christ the *Glauben-Reich* will give place to the *Schau-Reich* (Sight-Kingdom), for then Christ's supremacy over all shall be clearly manifested. But for the present, "Before the seeing comes, Christ has a kingdom of faith, here he is king."[1]

This view differs from Rome's position in that in it there is a recognition of Christ's kingdom as inclusive of the church invisible as well as visible, for the *Glauben-Reich* includes both. And though at first blush it might appear that the *Confession's* position is more in the direction of Rome than of Luther, an examination of the chapter proves otherwise, for in the first section the nature of the church as invisible is set forth. In other words, the *Confession*, in the interests of consistency and clarity, has divided into separate sections the treatment of the church as invisible and visible and has thereby set forth with little substantial change the position of Luther in identifying the church as the kingdom of Christ.

But this conception of the kingdom is too narrow to do justice to the scope of New Testament teaching. The sovereignty of Christ is all-embracing, including the principalities of heaven as well as the powers of earth. *So that, though the focal point of his rule comes to expression in his church, it is not correct to limit the extent of his kingdom or sovereignty to the church.* "Church and kingdom of God are not the same thing. They are not the same in the early church, which certainly regarded itself as the *ekklesia* while continuing the proclamation of the kingdom."[2]

We have seen how this is brought out in the book of Acts where the church's preaching of the gospel could be spoken of both as the kingdom of God and the things which concern the Lord Jesus Christ (*Acts* 28:31). Clearly the church existed as a vehicle in the proclamation of the kingdom of God but was not the same as that kingdom. The question to be settled therefore

[1] *Ibid.*, p.1085.

[2] K.L. Schmidt, "The Church", *Bible Key Words*, translated and edited by J.R. Coates (New York: Harper and Bros., 1951), pp.41-42.

is in what way the church and kingdom are allied and in what way they are different.

1. In what way allied?

Vos defines in the following way how the church and the kingdom of God are allied:

"The church actually has within herself the powers of the world to come. She is more than the immanent kingdom as it existed before Jesus' exaltation. She forms an intermediate line between the present life and the life of eternity. [Hence] the church is a form which the kingdom assumes in result of the new stage upon which the messiahship of Jesus enters with his death and resurrection... The kingdom, therefore, as truly as the invisible church is constituted by the regenerate; the regenerate alone experience in themselves its power, cultivate its righteousness, enjoy its blessings."[1]

In the effusion of the Holy Spirit at Pentecost, the church experienced the coming of the kingdom of God with power, as Jesus had promised his disciples (*Mark* 9:1). In the parallel passage of Luke (9:27), this event is referred to simply as seeing the kingdom of God, though Luke makes appropriate elaboration in Acts 1:8 where the kingdom's coming is associated with the power which the church would receive at the outpouring of the Spirit on her by the exalted Christ. Matthew's parallel (16:28) confirms the correctness of our judgment in that he speaks of the Son of Man's "coming in his kingdom".

When did this occur so that those standing with Jesus saw it before they had tasted death? — at Pentecost. Peter therefore properly spoke of this event as a fulfilment to be associated with the coming of the kingdom of God through the exercise of the exalted Messiah's rule, for the prophecy of Joel had envisaged it as a day when the Lord would manifest his power to the extent that the realms of nature and redemption would be clearly moved.

The church, therefore, as the recipient of the Spirit, received a pledge of the kingdom of God in its final form which was seen

---

[1] *The Kingdom and the Church*, pp.84-86.

in prophecy as a bestowal of "the last days" with the advent of the long-awaited Messiah. In the Spirit's presence the coming age has broken into the present age and by making the church the vehicle of his operation (*Acts* 2:38-39), the Holy Spirit has transformed it into an eschatological constituent, i.e., the firstfruits of that which is yet to be (*James* 1:18). It therefore both functions during this present age as a unit of the kingdom of God which has come in power and reflects the aura of the coming age of the kingdom of which it is already a part.

The apostle Paul also reflects on this, especially in the Ephesian epistle. We have seen in Paul's teaching Christ's present headship of the church so that her goal is to grow up into the fulness of his stature while already experiencing the transforming gifts and graces whose end is to accomplish this glorious destiny. But Paul also teaches that the church has been "sealed with the Holy Spirit of promise, who is the guarantee of our inheritance until the redemption of the purchased possession, to the praise of his glory" (*Eph.* 1:13-14). Here we are told that the Spirit, whose bestowal was in fulfilment of God's promise for the future (*Joel* 2:28-32, *Ezek.* 36:26, *Isa.* 32:15, *Zech.* 12:10), has been given to the church as a pledge of that which shall one day be her full inheritance.

In other words, the Spirit is the firstfruits (*Rom.* 8:23) of that final salvation which will be the church's blessing when the consummated kingdom of God will have become a reality. "The believer possesses already in reality, though but in part, the life of the future; the inheritance of the present and the inheritance of the future differing not in kind but only in degree, so that even now we have the life and blessedness of the future in the way of foretaste."[1] That is, the church, as the purchased possession of the Lord, is his people to whom he has given the pledge of the Spirit as a foretaste of their final blessedness, and in whom he has already made a replica, as it were, of what he will have done completely when the kingdom of God attains its full final reality.

When Christ said to Peter (*Matt.* 16:18), "Upon this rock I will build my church; and the gates of hades shall not overpower

---

[1] Salmond, *The Epistle to the Ephesians*, p.269.

(*katischuo*) it", he was promising his church that he would fill her with his own unconquerable life. The realm of the dead can no longer open its yawning maw to claim with indiscriminate finality the whole of humanity, for Christ by his resurrection made manifest his conquest of death and the truth of his assurance, "I am the resurrection and the life. He who believes in me, even though he dies, he shall live. And whoever lives and believes in me shall never die" (*John* 11:25-26).

To his people Christ gives eternal life, for having died with Christ, they have also been raised up together with him to newness of life (*Col.* 3:1-3, *Eph.* 2:5-6). If death yet remains, in a sense it does so only as an impotent foe (*I Cor.* 15:55). It claims none of Christ's own as victims, for "to be absent from the body is to be present with the Lord" (*II Cor.* 5:8). Yes, the church is an intermediate link between the present life and the life of eternity because the latter, bestowed by Christ on her through his Spirit, has become the church's portion already in this present life. She is possessor of the kingdom's eschatological life, if not in its fulness, then at least in the same kind. This eschatological life, therefore, as a present power of the world to come, is continuously active in unfolding itself in the progressive sanctification of the church individually and collectively (*Jn.* 3:3,16, *Eph.* 2:10, *Phil.* 2:12-13, *Rom.* 12:2, *Heb.* 12:14).

The church, in short, presently manifests the kingdom of God and in her the kingdom's transforming power operates and from her its life and blessedness flows to form an oasis in the desert of this world's sin and misery, darkness and death. To it the thirsty traveler may come and drink deeply at the well-springs of salvation. Braun, therefore, gives an appropriate summary of the way by which church and kingdom are allied: "From the standpoint of the 'new consensus' [concerning the biblical data], the church lies within the kingdom because she is wholly arranged upon it, and the kingdom lies within the church because the latter sets forth the former's normal sphere of operation."[1]

---

[1] *Neues Licht auf die Kirche*, pp.152-153.

2. In what way different?

But though church and kingdom are closely allied, they must nevertheless be clearly differentiated since they are not one and the same. This is equally true whether the church be viewed in the light of the final form of the kingdom of God or in relation to the present kingdom of Christ. Herman Ridderbos distinguishes church and kingdom in the following manner: *The basileia* [kingdom] *is the great divine work of salvation in its fulfilment and consummation in Christ; the ekklesia* [church] *is the people elected and called by God and sharing in the bliss of the basileia.*[1] This says in effect that the church is to be found within the kingdom but is not co-extensive with it. Ridderbos elaborates by saying, "It [the kingdom] represents the all-embracing perspective, it denotes the consummation of all history, brings both grace and judgment, has cosmic dimensions, fills time and eternity... The *ekklesia* is the fruit of the revelation of the *basileia;* and conversely, the *basileia* is inconceivable without the *ekklesia.* The one is inseparable from the other without, however, the one merging into the other."[2]

This statement sets forth the kingdom of God comprehensively. In it is made plain why the kingdom is necessarily of greater scope than the church, for it comprehends the present and that which is to come. This can be seen, for instance, in the aspects of grace and judgment. It is of course true that the kingdom in the present dominion of Christ has brought both grace and judgment. No verse presents these two aspects more clearly in their present relevance than John 3:36: "He who believes in the Son has everlasting life; and he who does not believe the Son shall not see life, but the wrath of God abides on him."

But in a more specific sense grace is the characteristic of the present age while judgment will not occur until his second advent at the end of this age. And though the church embodies grace before the world, and will furthermore have a part in the judgment of the world and angels (*I Cor.* 6:2-3), this latter will

[1] *The Coming of the Kingdom*, p.354.
[2] *Ibid.*, pp.354-355.

be a reflection of the glorious dominion her Lord will deign to
share with her and therefore cannot be an argument for her
co-extensiveness with the kingdom. For, as Ridderbos reminds
us, the kingdom has cosmic dimensions in which the church
shares but which she never encompasses. Her Lord, after all, is the
executor of the kingdom. And that kingdom includes dominion
over the forces of evil as well as the good, a dominion which the
Lord finally gains, not by means of the church alone or any
other instrumentality, but by himself in his sovereign, climactic
intrusion into history when he will bring every foe to submission
by the exercise of his omnipotence.

Dan G. McCartney[1] gives an additional insight into the Lord's
present rule and his people's place in the furtherance of that
rule toward the accomplishment of its ultimate purpose. He
points out that "the coming of the kingdom [i.e., the reign of
God]... is the *reinstatement of the originally intended divine order
for earth, with man properly situated as God's vicegerent*" [his ital-
ics]. He develops this thesis by first presenting "the connection
of the concept of divine rule (the reign of God) and the vicegerency of man in the Old Testament, and then how the person
and work of Jesus in the New Testament fulfilled that vicegerency." In developing this thesis, he gives significant attention to
Jesus' self-designation, "Son of Man" (*ho huios tou anthropou*),
which he considers to be a likely "literal rendition of the Ara-
maic *bar nasha*, which would be more idiomatically translated
as simply 'the man' (*ho anthropos*)... Hebrews 2 picks up on the
'son of man' of Psalm 8 and applies it to the representative
'Man' whose vicegerency is already restored on behalf of his
people." But he also does not lose sight of the fact that Jesus is
more than a mere human being, for he goes on to point out that
"the more idiomatic translation of 'the man' would obscure the
connection to Daniel 7, which is also in Jesus' mind, as we see
from Mark 14:62, etc. Still, if we think of 'The Man' as the
meaning of Jesus' self-referential term, it emphasizes his under-

[1] "Ecce Homo: The Coming of the Kingdom as the Restoration of Human
Vicegerency", *The Westminster Theological Journal*, vol. 56, No. 1 (Spring 1994),
pp.1-21.

standing of himself as representative of humanity, a 'second Adam' to use Paul's language (*Rom.* 5, *I Cor.* 15)." Then he makes the point, "The New Testament speaks not only of the restoration of *Jesus'* vicegerency; if Christ's inauguration of the kingdom is the restoration of human vicegerency, then the participation in the kingdom by believers is also a restoration of *their* vicegerency... When Jesus compares the kingdom of God to a mustard seed, or to leaven in a lump, he seems to suggest that the kingdom of God *grows*. Of course, the sovereignty of God does not grow. The restoration of man as proper vicegerent under God, however, does grow. It begins with Jesus as the one Man being enthroned, and continues as humankind in him is restored to vicegerency. In that sense the reign of God can 'increase'." That increase, moreover, in addition to the church, includes the Lord's ultimate openly-manifested dominion over all principality and power and authority "in this age and that which is to come" (*Eph.* 1:21).

The full conquest of now hostile powers is therefore a goal of the future awaiting the determinative action of Christ. While outside the realm of the church's scope, it nevertheless forms an integral part of the kingdom's realization, "for he must reign until he has put all enemies under his feet" (*I Cor.* 15:25). Then his enemies will be judged and forever excluded from the final glory of the eschatological kingdom (*Rev.* 20:15) in which the church will form so basic a part (*Rev.* 21-22).

The kingdom, therefore, encompasses the exercise of God's sovereignty in the broadest reaches of his dominion both for time and eternity, and consummates the full counsel of God decreed from all eternity and brought to pass by his providential outworking of history to the everlasting praise of his glory (*Rom.* 11:33-36).

The church remains as the cherished fruit of that kingdom, having been selected, nurtured and perfected by the grace her Lord has freely lavished upon her. The church is therefore an inseparable part of the kingdom but different from it in the same way that an organ of the body, though a part of it, is nevertheless to be distinguished from the whole. "[She is the community] of those who *await* the salvation of the *basileia*. Insofar as the *basileia* is already a present reality, the *ekklesia* is also the place where the gifts and powers of the *basileia* are granted and received. It is, further, the gathering of those who, as the instruments of the *basileia*, are called upon to make profession of Jesus as the Christ, to obey his commandments, to perform the missionary task of the preaching the gospel throughout the world."[1]

---

[1] Ridderbos, *The Coming of the Kingdom*, pp.355-356.

PART II

Church and Kingdom in
Eschatological Fulfilment

V: THE MERGING OF CHURCH
AND KINGDOM (the removal of the antithesis)

1. The realization of eschatological principles already present

In the earlier edition of this book, I wrote of church and kingdom "becoming synonymous." George E. Ladd took exception to this in his book, *A Theology of the New Testament*[1] by commenting, "The church is the people of the kingdom, never that kingdom itself. Therefore, it is not helpful even to say that the church is a 'part of the kingdom', or that in the eschatological consummation the church and kingdom become synonymous".

Ladd acknowledges that for the most part I adequately distinguish between the kingdom and the church, which means that I agree with his definition of the two, i.e., "The kingdom is primarily the dynamic reign or kingly rule of God… The church is the community of the kingdom but never the kingdom itself" (p.111). Ladd himself, however, recognizes the close relationship of church and kingdom by calling attention to such things as: (1) the fact that Christ will share his rule with the members of the church as his people in the final kingdom (*Matt.* 19:28, *Rev.* 2:27; 5:10); (2) "while the church in this age will never attain perfection, it must nevertheless display the life of the perfect order, the eschatological

[1] George E. Ladd, *A Theology of the New Testament* (Grand Rapids: Eerdmans, 1974), p.113; cf. also his footnote at the bottom of the page.

kingdom of God" (p.115); and (3) as the parable of the Wheat and Tares teaches, "the kingdom of God has invaded history without disrupting the present structure of society. Good and evil are to live mixed in the world until the eschatological consummation, even though the kingdom of God has come" (p.112).

The subject I wish to develop on the pages following is the ultimate eschatological vision in which the present antithesis that exists between the kingdom of God and the kingdom of the evil one begun by the fall is finally removed with the return of Christ, the consequent judgment of the world and the institution of the new heaven and earth. Therefore, while we may perhaps allow Ladd's point that church and kingdom do not become exactly synonymous, they will nevertheless have merged in the final kingdom.

Christians are members of a heavenly commonwealth because the church is an eschatological pledge of the state that shall prevail when the final order will have been brought to pass. In the preceding subdivision we saw how the church and kingdom are allied in that the Lord's dominion comes to focus in a community which already possesses the "powers of the age to come" (*Heb.* 6:5).

But we also saw that the two were to be differentiated in that the church is not as extensive as the kingdom. This, we noted, will continue to be true as long as good and evil, light and darkness, righteousness and iniquity, the kingdom of Christ and the kingdom of the evil one continue to co-exist throughout this present age. Now, since the Lord's kingdom includes ultimate dominion over both these spheres, his rule of the one means perfection in conformity to him, while his rule of the other consists in their complete reprobation, eternal destruction and final separation from him (*Matt.* 25:46, *Rev.* 20:15, etc.). During this present age, therefore, "the mystery of lawlessness is already at work" (*II Thess.* 2:7) and its "ripening process" will continue until the end when at the Lord's return it will have reached its ultimate development. Then it will be clearly differentiated and finally separated from that alone which shall endure (*II Thess.* 2:11, *Matt.* 13:41).

That which endures will be the church, for, following the

judgment and separation, the Lord Jesus declares, "Then the righteous will shine forth as the sun in the kingdom of their Father" (*Matt.* 13:43). The church is, then, to be distinguished from the kingdom in this present age while her antithesis, the world, remains. But her ultimate merger with the kingdom is inevitable; for, already possessing the finalities of the kingdom, she shall one day express them to the fullest in the day of her complete ascendancy. And then she will have become one with the kingdom.[1]

The Christian is therefore essentially a citizen of another world, the heavenly kingdom to come. "For our citizenship is in heaven: from which we also eagerly wait for the Saviour, the Lord Jesus Christ" (*Phil.* 3:20). The Christian may dwell in a hostile world among those "whose end is destruction, whose god is their belly, and whose glory is their shame — who set their mind on earthly things" (*Phil.* 3:19), but this description is not true of him because he has been rescued from the mire of destruction and has been placed on the firm ground of the world to come. And while he awaits the coming merger of church and kingdom, he labours to effect as much as possible the realization in the present of those finalities of which he is already a part. As Bannerman puts it, "It is the '*populus civitasque Christiana*' [i.e., the Christian populace and citizenry] ... in its full influence doing Christ's work in the world, seeking by his grace and Spirit to fulfil all righteousness as he did, in all the relations of human life, and to lead others to do so, to be actually consecrated to God and his service, that the will of God may be done on earth as it is in heaven."[2]

As they grow in grace and Christlikeness, his people render *obedience, service,* and reflect *patience* until their transformation to the fulness of Christ's image takes place at the consummation when he returns.

For if the will of the Lord should be done on earth as it is in heaven, then the goal of their obedience must be to perform it

---

[1] For the relation of this statement to the millennium, see the next chapter.

[2] *The Scripture Doctrine of the Church*, p.250.

to the same degree as it is done by the angels in heaven. Anything less is to be false to this final principle already present in the eschatological community and to betray the profession of their king's lordship over them. And considering their role as servants, they will vie with the angels to do service for their Master, remembering that he himself showed the way by his humiliation even to death in performing that service for them by which their salvation was purchased. And in all things they will exhibit patience, remembering that the full realization of kingdom finalities awaits the personal coming of their Lord.

Their success in the meantime can never be complete, but only relative to such actual victory as, by their Lord's grace, they are able to achieve over the world, the flesh, and the devil. This is because of what they are, saints in whom the remnants of depravity still linger (*Rom.* 7:18), and because of what the world yet is, the stronghold of the evil one (*I John* 5:19). While, therefore, the kingdom of God "has come and is even now in the world, it is also yet to come. In the tension between the two the church must live, and must always live, as the 'eschatological community'."[1] As the apostle John puts it in reflecting on what the church is but what she still awaits, "Beloved, now we are children of God, and it has not yet been revealed what we shall be, but we know that when he is revealed, we shall be like him, for we shall see him as he is. And everyone who has this hope in him purifies himself, just as he is pure" (*I John* 3:2-3).

2. The completion of the body of Christ

The depth of Christ's humiliation was reached when he "became obedient unto death, even the death of the cross" (*Phil.* 2:8) in order that he might make satisfaction for the sins of his people who had been given him by the Father from all eternity (*Eph.* 1:4). Christ "descended into the lower parts of the earth" (*Eph.* 4:9) on behalf of his people that they might be exalted with him to become heirs of the blessedness of eternity. He became a son of man that they might become the sons of God. And he, as the

---

[1] Bright, *The Kingdom of God*, p.237.

good shepherd, knows every one of his sheep by name (*John* 10:3), from the greatest to the least, and is furthermore known by them, for they recognize his voice alone (*John* 10:8) and follow him (*John* 10:27). And those who are his cannot be lost because of the omnipotence of sovereign grace (*John* 10:28-30).

The most glorious of Christ's triumphs will therefore come to its full realization when every member of the church he purchased with his own blood will have been added to his body, completely sanctified and finally glorified. The satisfaction of his victory in that day will be not only in his power to claim them as trophies from the "strong man" whom he bound in order to do so (*Matt.* 12:29, *Eph.* 2:1-3), nor yet in his sole ability to keep his own until that day when he presents them faultless before the presence of his glory with exceeding joy (*Jude* 24), but also contributing to the sweetness of his conquest will be the fact that he will be the reason for and object of his people's sweetest praises (*Rev.* 7:9-10; 14:3; 15:3). Sweet indeed will be his triumph in that day. For as Dijk says, it will be the apex of his mediatorial achievement: "And just as the mediator reached the goal of his humiliation when he had suffered and entered into death, thus the goal of his exaltation shall be reached in the great day of days when the bride of the Lamb is complete and the renewed world filled with the kingdom of God."[1]

As a result of his glorification of his church, there will be more than a mere exhibition of his mediatorial power. And there will be more than the mere grudging acknowledgment of his sovereignty by every present opposing power in heaven, on earth or under the earth (*Phil.* 2:10-11). Rather, in his glorified church will be imaged the resplendent perfection of his glory (*Eph.* 4:13, 5:27), and from her will sound forth the spontaneous anthems of praise. No wonder that this eschatological goal is painted in language of glowing colours: "Let us be glad and rejoice, and give him glory, for the marriage of the Lamb has come, and his wife has made herself ready... Blessed are those who are called to the marriage supper of the Lamb" (*Rev.* 19:7, 9)!

[1] K. Dijk, *De Toekomst van Christus* (Kampen: J.H. Kok, 1953), p.206.

3. Cosmic renovation

Eschatological realities also include cosmic renovation. The world as it was originally created by God was a reflection to man of God's glory (*Rom.* 1:20) and furnished the context in which God might delight to have fellowship with man as a creature made in his image (*Gen.* 3:8). In man's pristine state, the world in which he had been placed was a witness to him of God's loving provision for his every need, and it furnished the environment by which he might glorify God.

Man was to have dominion over the earth (*Gen.* 1:28), in order that he might discover the wonders of God exhibited in it, and interpret them according to God's relationship to them, declare his maker's praise and thus be fitted to dedicate the whole of his life to him who had made him. From then onwards, God would directly communicate with man in whatever situation he found himself (*Gen.* 2:16-17).

But with man's sin and fall came also a radical change in nature's constitution. Where man himself became subject to death and dissolution, nature for his sake was made subject to curse and corruption (*Gen.* 3:17-19). Man's experience of death in the wrenching of soul from body was merely indicative of a more basic death which he was to experience in the final separation of his being from his creator (*Rev.* 20:6, 13-15). And nature itself, while still witnessing to the wonders of God as his handiwork, would now do so only imperfectly because of its bondage to corruption. In short, the revelation of nature both within man and the world about him would be a continual witness to his need for redemption.

Now, though redemption has been wrought by Christ and is experienced by his church, its final goals have not yet been realized. The souls of Christ's people, in communion with God, have been redeemed and reconciled to him. But the bodies of men, which link them to the natural world, still suffer dissolution in death. And this is still true even for members of the eschatological community in order that they may ever be reminded by this witness that their hope is not to be set on the things of this world; for everything of which it consists is temporal and doomed to pass away (*I John* 2:17). The church's hope is to be set on the finalities of the new heaven and earth of the eschatological kingdom, and to this the cosmos in its present constitution bears stark testimony.

But since nature has been subjected to futility because of sin, its expectation too is one of redemption (*Rom.* 8:21). Paradise lost witnesses to the need of paradise regained. But paradise regained must itself consist of things eternal where every vestige of sin has forever been removed. And when the cosmos shall have been reconstituted, it will be both a witness of God's loving provision of his own's every need, and it will furnish the environment in which God's people may glorify him further in the activities of eternity which are beyond their comprehension on this side of the final state (*II Cor.* 12:4).

But in order to express this truth in some measure for our present understanding, the habitation of God's people in the final state is set forth in terms of a city in which they and their God dwell together (*Rev.* 22). In the city may be found a river in which flows the water of life (*v.*1). Also, the tree of life with its diversified fruits for nourishment is depicted (*v.* 2). The Lord God also provides light for his people but no longer in intermediary fashion with the sun and moon as lightbearers, but directly by the unending and unchanging glory of his person as he dwells with them (*v.* 5). Obviously with the full glory of God's personal presence in the city, it will in some way be seen by his people; for the Son, at any rate, is spoken of in redemptive connotation as the Lamb (*v.* 3).

The witness of nature to the glory of God in this dispensation (*Psa.* 19:1) will be merely secondary. Yet nature's environment will still serve a purpose, as the form of the city illustrates. We are told that the city has no temple because "the Lord God Almighty and the Lamb are the temple of it" (*Rev.* 21:22). But then, in order to direct us to the force of this truth, the description of the city discloses its form as a huge holy of holies (*Rev.* 21:16). In other words, its form directs attention not only to the place where God dwells in the midst of his people but also to the fact that he is to be worshipped by the redeemed host in eternity.

Furthermore, we learn that the new creation furnishes an environment in which the redeemed may fulfil their threefold office as prophets, priests, and kings, as at the very beginning.

For in Revelation 21:24 we read, "And the nations of those who are saved shall walk in its light, and the kings of the earth bring their glory and honour into it." This language must be understood symbolically, not literally, for the prophet has been shown visions and has seen realities which transcend the limitations of human language. Symbols are therefore used to portray the basic realities of his visions, though as we must realize, and as he, too, makes clear in the employment of simile (21:11, 18, 21, etc.), they have inherent limitations which express but do not embody the reality they portray.

As we look at the above verse, we detect in it the exercise of the threefold office by the redeemed. Kings are mentioned. Are we to understand by this the comparatively select number of monarchs who rule nations? That would be to follow the pattern of literalistic interpretation. Or does it mean that members of Christ's church are kings as he shares rule with them, and that therefore, in a sense, they are all kings? (cf. *Rev.* 22:5). This latter interpretation would be more in keeping with the eschatological prospect promised the believer elsewhere in the New Testament (*II Tim.* 2:12, *Rev.* 5:10). On either interpretation the kingly office is present and exercised by the redeemed. Therefore, wherever such kingly dominion is present, there is also present the conception of dominion, a dominion that was already manifested in the creation ordinance by which man was to rule the earth by subduing it (*Gen.* 1:28).

We also see the prophetic office revealed in the above verse in that glory and honour are brought into the city. This expresses the prophetic labours of discovery, selectivity and interpretation in order to distinguish and promote that which is glorious and honourable.

The priestly office is also to be seen in this verse in that things of glory and honour are brought into the city where God is. What is this but a dedication in worship of that by which the redeemed would promote the glory of God?

We can therefore see how cosmic renovation is an integral part of the eschatological picture to which we are directed as the merging of the church with the kingdom ultimately takes place. Only by its reconstitution with eternal forms will it be able to provide an adequate context in which to display the goodness and glory of God, and to form a proper environment for the fruition of the activities of the redeemed to the eternal glory of God.

VI: A MILLENNIAL RULE?

The considerations of the previous chapter have brought us to the threshold of contemplating the total victory of Christ. For when his people's citizenship in the new age has been fully realized at his coming, and the body of Christ has been brought to completion as the apex of his mediatorial reign, one might be prepared to conclude that little more remains than to set forth the aspects of Christ's total victory. This would be true were it not for the fact that there remains to be considered whether or not an intermediate reign of Christ takes place between the present and final age, a reign in an age commonly referred to as the millennium, and which, if true, would have bearing on church and kingdom.

1. Preliminary considerations

The arguments for a millennium have been of varied cogency. Besides the fact that its advocates find its support for it in various parts of Scripture, notably Revelation 20, a number of other considerations are offered to justify their position. For instance, it has been said by some premillennarians that there are at least four things out of place in the present dispensation which shall only be corrected by the millennium: (1) Christ is not now on the literal throne of David (*II Sam.* 7:12-13, *Matt.* 19:28, *Rev.* 3:21); (2) the church is not yet in the heavenlies (*Eph.* 2:6); (3) Israel, destined to be the head of the nations, is yet the tail; and 4) the devil is not yet in the abyss (*Rev.* 20:3).[1]

[1] These points come from lecture notes which were given by T. Leonard Lewis in a theology class at Gordon College in my student days, 1948-1952.

These considerations, however, are not necessarily the result of scriptural exegesis, but may be conclusions which merely reflect a presuppositional premillennarian bias. For example, Christ's rule already in the present dispensation cannot be denied. And his continuing rule in eternity is also acknowledged. Cannot all the scriptural references under the first point be explained in the light of either of these reigns without the necessity for positing a further intermediate reign? At any rate, the texts cited to prove this point are inconclusive, since they need no such reign to do adequate justice to their interpretation.

The second consideration, that the church is not now in the heavenlies, is a misunderstanding of New Testament teaching. She is in the heavenlies in the sense that she comprises heavenly Zion (*Heb.* 12:22) and has her citizenship there (*Phil.* 3:20). Granted that this eschatological principle will not become final until fully realized in the age to come. But this is not a concession which favours a premillennarian interpretation, for Christ according to that view is to rule on earth with his church. But would that place the church more in the heavenlies than it is now? Obviously the premillennarian mode of interpretation needs the full realization of the final kingdom for the church's complete ascendancy as much as does any other view. And the view that we suggest has the advantage of not being encumbered with the weight of something not shown to be necessary.

The third consideration, that Israel has not yet become the head of the nations, cannot be supported by a single verse from the New Testament. Such an interpretation rests on a form of exegesis of Old Testament passages that ignores the place the New Testament gives to Israel as a church in the unfolding redemptive plan of God, which place has been taken over by the messianic community, or church of Christ, in which the true Israel and not national Israel continues as the people of God.

Finally, the fourth consideration, that the devil is not in the abyss, rests on an interpretation of Revelation 20:3 which can be strongly disputed by such passages as Matthew 12:29, Luke 10:18, Revelation 9:2-11; 12:7 ff. This will be shown more clearly when we consider Revelation 20 in greater detail in the next chapter.

Three further reasons have been given to justify a millennium: 1) it will be a literal return of the nations to righteousness as all bow, outwardly at least, to Christ's rule; 2) the Lord must reign until he has put all his enemies under his feet; and 3) it will give the opportunity to put the full social effects of the gospel to a world-wide outworking.[1]

By way of answer to these: with respect to the first, we may ask, what particular point is gained by such a dominion by Christ? No dominion is truly worthy of the name that does not include complete mastery of the heart. That Christ does not gain this under this view is freely admitted in that this fact is supposedly demonstrated by the rebellion of Gog and Magog at the end of the millennium when Satan is once again released (*Rev.* 20:7-9). But, as a matter of fact, Christ's dominion includes the subjection of the heart as well as outward conformity to his will. And this is already occurring in the present dispensation and will continue until all who are his have been completely won unto total subjection to him (*II Cor.* 10:5). There is, therefore, no justification for a millennium in this claim, especially since it advocates a dominion that is decidedly inferior to that which is already taking place under Christ's rule.

The second claim states a scriptural truth which does not depend on a millennium for its realization. If Christ is already ruling, which rule includes subdual of his people to himself and subjugation of all his foes; then, what need is there for a further intermediate reign in which these aspects of his rule are only further carried out? If the Scriptures teach that such an intermediate reign shall indeed occur, then we bow to their authority and accept the teaching as true. But unless this is the teaching of Scripture, there is no reason why Christ cannot have accomplished both these aspects of his reign by the time he brings this present dispensation to a close; for both are presently in process of accomplishment.

The third claim is an argument that applies as much to the present dispensation as it does to the millennium. The

---

[1] This last reason particularly is advocated by D.H. Kromminga, *The Millennium* (Grand Rapids: Eerdmans, 1948), p.71.

responsibility to put into effect the social aspects of the gospel has already been committed to the church (*Matt.* 25:24-40), and that she can do so with any amount of success is due to her victorious Lord's enabling grace. She has, therefore, no excuse for any delay in the fulfilment of her Lord's mandate by the taking of a complacent attitude about a yet future golden age when this now present responsibility will be brought to its proper fruition. The church may already have been weighted down with this besetting sin too long! In the third major section of this book we will take up in greater detail the church's task in this present dispensation and show further how this third claim gives no justification for a millennium because it cites nothing different from what is already the church's present duty.

Cullmann advocates a chiliastic position because: "The one thousand year kingdom is neither to be identified with the whole reign of Christ nor with the present church."[1] He explains that the interpretation which equates the millennium with the present rule of Christ or with the church age began with the Donatist, Ticonius (circa 390 A.D.), and was subsequently made respectable by Augustine, after which it gained the ascendancy for a long while in the church. Yet Cullmann regards this view as a contradiction of the whole New Testament! He maintains that a millennium is needed, among other things, to fulfil such Scriptures as Matthew 19:28, Revelation 5:10; 20:4, II Timothy 2:12, and I Corinthians 6:2-3. "The one thousand year kingdom will be the church of this last phase."[2] That is to say, the millennium will be a time during which such Scriptures as the above which are not applicable to the church now will be fulfilled in the church of that age.

But is this view founded on the Scriptures? With the exception of Matthew 19:28 and Revelation 20:4, we have already considered all the above verses without finding a millennium necessary. Revelation 20:4 will be dealt with in detail in the next chapter. That leaves only Matthew 19:28. Does this verse need a millennium

---

[1] "Königsherrschaft Christi", p.15.
[2] *Ibid.*, p.23.

for its adequate interpretation? Jesus speaks here of the regeneration (*palingenesia*) and the throne of his glory, terms which carry the eschatological ring of the final kingdom with which the promise of Jesus to the apostles agrees when compared with such descriptions of the final kingdom as are found in Revelation 21-22 (especially 21:14; 22:3). As with the other verses, therefore, this one neither advocates nor needs a millennium for its interpretation. Rather, it demands the final kingdom. Cullmann, therefore, does not make any stronger case for a millennium than do others.

Then what do the Scriptures say concerning a millennium? Is it to be found in the Old Testament? Does it have support from the New Testament? A brief survey of relevant data is here appropriate before we draw our final conclusions.

2. The teaching of the Old Testament

Nowhere does the Old Testament refer to a millennium as such. That is to say, though in many places it speaks of a coming age of blessedness, it nowhere delimits such an age to a one thousand year period of time. This time span is found in Revelation 20 alone. But the question is, does Old Testament prophecy make necessary an intermediate era of blessedness between the present and final states, an era without which such prophecy cannot be adequately interpreted, and an era which may be designated as the millennium of Revelation 20? An examination of several representative Old Testament prophecies should give us the answer we seek.

Turning first to Isaiah 2:1-5, we read, "The word that Isaiah the son of Amoz saw concerning Judah and Jerusalem. Now it shall come to pass in the last days that the mountain of the Lord's house shall be established on the top of the mountains, and shall be exalted above the hills; and all nations shall flow to it. Many people shall come and say, Come and let us go up to the mountain of the Lord, to the house of the God of Jacob; he will teach us his ways, and we shall walk in his paths. For out of Zion shall go forth the law, and the word of the Lord from Jerusalem. He shall judge between the nations, and shall rebuke many people; they shall beat their swords into plowshares, and their spears into pruning-hooks; nation shall not lift up sword against nation, neither shall they learn war any more. O house of Jacob, come and let us walk in the light of the Lord."

We note the similarity of this prophecy with Micah 4:1-4. As it appears in Isaiah, the prophecy serves as a fitting introduction to eschatological concepts to which Isaiah consequently refers throughout his entire prophecy and upon which he makes further elaboration as his prophetic themes are unfolded and developed. For instance, the eschatological theme here introduced reappears at 11:1-6 with the elaboration that peace in nature and among peoples at the time of its realization will be the result of Messiah's rule. In 25:8 the redeemed sing of their expectancy of death's conquest by the Lord in the future, and in 65:20-23 further elaboration is made of this concept in language similar to that of 11:1-6. Moreover, the whole of chapter 35 gives further development to these eschatological strands of nature's regeneration (*vv.* 1, 2, 7, 9), of the removal of sin's curse (*vv.* 5-6), and of universal worship by the ransomed of the Lord (*vv.* 8, 10).

These instances are sufficient to show how Isaiah repeatedly returns to themes already expressed but in an ever rising spiral of elaboration and unfolding significance. So we are not surprised when at 65:17 ff. Isaiah, in reaching the climax of his unfolding of these eschatological themes, places their fulfilment in the setting of the new heaven and new earth; for this of course is their ultimate realization.

This is not to say that none of these strands have reference to the eschatology of messianic times inaugurated by Christ's first advent; for such a term as "the last days" in Isaiah 2:2 is shown by the New Testament to refer to this present dispensation (cf. *Heb.* 1:2, *James* 5:3, *Acts* 2:17, *I Pet.* 1:20, *I John* 2:18). But it is just for this reason that we must allow the New Testament to be the commentary on the Old, not only because it is a later revelation which fulfilled much of the Old, but also because it is only by its light that we may determine where the line has been drawn in the Old Testament prophetic revelation in relation to when its respective fulfilments occur.

The New Testament refers to these passages of Isaiah as applying to several different strands of history, i.e., to Christ's first ministry, compare 2:3 with Luke 24:47, John 4:22; 11:1 with Matthew 2:23; 11:2 with Matthew 12:18; 35:2 with John 1:14; 35:5 with Matthew 11:5; or to the dispensation now present, compare 35:3 with Hebrews 12:12; 35:6 with Acts 3:2, 7; 35:8 with John 14:6; or to the judgment at his second advent, compare 11:4 with II Thessalonians 2:8; or to the finalities of the new heavens and earth, compare 25:8 with Revelation 7:17, 21:4; 65:17 with Revelation 21:1, II Peter 3:13. Since the New Testament itself gives us this interpretation of how we are to understand these prophetic strands of Isaiah, we have no warrant to look further for an intermediate age just because we might yet hope for one to fulfil these prophecies.

We must let the Scripture be its own interpreter. And if Scripture interprets its prophecies as finding application, on the one hand, to "the last days" (i.e., this present age as it began with Christ's ministry) or, on the other hand, to the new heaven and earth, then our interpretation of prophecy for either designation as well as for what lies between them must be limited by scriptural specification, not personal preference. And in Isaiah nothing can be found that necessitates an intermediate era for the fulfilment of prophecy that would otherwise remain uncategorized. Isaiah saw eschatological goals as an undifferentiated whole, having their beginning with the "last days" of Christ's first advent and finally reaching their conclusion in the new heavens and new earth. Without exception his eschatology may be related to one or the other, as is borne out by his prophetic presentation when seen in the light of the New Testament. We must also remember that the prophets dealt with concepts, many of which in the struggle for their articulation, could be set forth only in figure, symbol or religious concept that was consonant with the Old Testament progress of revelation up to that historical period in which the prophets found themselves.

In Isaiah 2:1-5, therefore, the prophet does not envisage a geographical prominence which is one day to be given the house of the Lord any more than he envisages John the Baptist's ministry in his preparing of a way for the Lord as constituting a highway building programme (*Isa.* 40:1 ff., compare *Mark* 1:2-4). What he seeks, rather, to make clear here by figure is the ascendancy of the messianic salvation whose roots could be traced back to the Old Testament worship in which Isaiah participated, and whose significance it prefigured. Divorced from it as their worship was later to be by the Jews in the days of the apostles, it became worse than useless, a worthless husk soon to be destroyed by the Roman armies of Titus (*Matt.* 24:2, *Heb.* 8:13).

Therefore, when Isaiah speaks of swords being beaten into plough-shares and spears into pruning-hooks we are not to understand this literally, since it is a portrayal of peaceful times with concepts that applied to the prophet's current environment. Were he writing today, the parallel would be guns and bombs turned into tractors and threshing combines. But that which Isaiah symbolized by swords becoming ploughshares remains principially relevant for us, and is that for which God's people yearningly await; namely, the abolition of war by the Messiah and the institution of everlasting peace. And finally, when Isaiah speaks of the law as going forth from Zion, and the word of the Lord from Jerusalem (2:3), he sets forth in Old Testament terms the thought of union and communion with the Lord who would once again dwell with a people delighting in whole-hearted obedience to their king. The apostle John also uses practically the same language to describe the final kingdom in Revelation 21-22. Hence, for the present dispensation to which this prophecy applies, we may understand Isaiah's religious concepts not as a description of something yet to take place according to modern Zionistic notions, but as something that has already taken place, as indicated by Luke 24:47, John 4:22, Acts 1:8, etc.

Hosea 3:4-5 has also been cited as a passage which has millennial significance. "For the children of Israel shall abide many days without king or prince, without sacrifice or sacred pillar, without ephod or teraphim. Afterwards the children of Israel shall return, seek the Lord their God and David their king, and fear the Lord and his goodness in the last days." It is argued that the Jews have been without any of the above things since the dispersion of 70 A.D. Hence, the realization of this prophecy is bound up with Christ's return, who is referred to in the prophecy as David; and the setting up of the things in the ensuing millennium will be literally those things here set forth. Numerous objections, however, make this interpretation untenable.

In the first place, this interpretation seeks its strength in literalism. But it makes the David of the prophecy a symbolic reference to Christ. This is hardly consistent with its own literalistic canon of interpretation and reveals how difficult it is to be consistent using this method.

In the second place we may ask, Is a literalistic interpretation of this prophecy necessary, let alone possible? The New Testament tells us that the church is true Israel, not Jews after the flesh (*Rom.* 2:28-29, *Gal.* 6:16, *Eph.* 2:11-22, *I Pet.* 2:9-10); that the "last days" are to be equated with the New Testament dispensation, and that the Old Testament sacrifice and ritual are the weak and beggarly elements (*Gal.* 4:9) which, having fulfilled their purpose, are forever set aside (*Heb.* 8:13, and the entire epistle).

In the third place, one must remember that this prophecy was written before the exile during which, as a matter of fact, Israel was without a king, sacrifice, etc., as the prophecy indicates would come to pass.

How, then, is this prophecy to be understood? The various aspects of prophetic eschatology blend into a larger whole, being undifferentiated because they were all yet future. The New Testament, following Christ's first advent, separates for us those strands belonging to the fulfilment of his first coming and that which yet awaits the fulfilment of his second coming, together with what belonged to fulfilment in the Old Testament dispensation but which may yet have been future from the prophet's perspective.

As seen in the light of the New Testament, this prophecy becomes clear. Hosea tells his people in 1:4 of the coming exile, but then in verse 5 goes on to bring those of the remnant who are truly Israel the comfort of God by the promise of a restoration that looks beyond Old Testament boundaries to "the last days" of the messianic age when the one truly after God's own heart would rule God's people in a way that would make their obedience, service and worship what the Old Testament could never properly realize. The prophecy, therefore, neither envisions nor demands a millennium for its proper interpretation.

Other prophecies with supposed millennial reference such as Daniel 2:44; 7:14, Isaiah 9:6-7, etc., could be mentioned, but in them, far from a reference to a one thousand year period, we find mention of a messianic kingdom which is said to endure *forever*. A detailed examination of such passages is therefore unnecessary because if, on supposed literalistic exegesis, "forever" can be made to stand for the millennium, then it can also just as easily stand for the length of this dispensation under the present rule of Christ.

Joel 3:18-21 has been advocated as describing the millennium; "And it will come to pass in that day, that the mountains shall drip with new wine, the hills shall flow with milk, and all the brooks of Judah shall be flooded with water; a fountain shall flow from the house of the Lord and water the Valley of Acacias..." But no one may seriously press this language into a literal strait-jacket. When seen in its figurative significance, it opens the way to a true understanding of vistas on the prophet's horizon that defy description by the limited instrumentality of human language. Yet quite suggestively, the fountain flowing from the house of the Lord reminds us of the consummate state, for there also John saw a river, the river of life, flowing from the throne of God and of the Lamb (*Rev.* 22:1). In short, rather than being a reference to the millennium, Joel's language here describes final realities and their blessedness.

Amos 9:11-15 has been cited as a passage teaching "future kingdom [millennial] blessing of restored Israel."[1] "On that day I will raise up the tabernacle of David which has fallen down, and repair its damages; I will raise up its ruins, and rebuild it as in the days of old; that they may possess the remnant of Edom, and all the Gentiles who are called by my name, says the Lord who does this thing" (*vv.* 11-12). Following the promise to restore the Davidic dynasty, we are told in verse 13, "Behold, the days are coming, says the Lord, when the plough-man shall overtake the reaper, and the treader of grapes him who sows seed; the mountains shall drip with sweet wine, and all the hills shall flow with it." Then the prophecy concludes with the promise of Israel's restoration to their land (*vv.* 14-15).

Though by now we might be properly wary of a literalistic interpretation of all these details, the New Testament, with a direct

---

[1] The Scofield Reference Bible.

quotation of this passage, banishes literalistic exegesis for us, and opens the way for its proper interpretation. For in Acts 15:16-17, James, in explanation of the church's success in the conversion of the Gentiles through the recently conducted missionary labours of the apostles, cites Amos 9:11-12 as finding its fulfilment by this means.[1] Therefore, James makes the building of the tabernacle of David, not a future Jewish kingdom, but Christ's present rule on the throne of David as that rule began with his exaltation and his church's labours for him. Edom, too, no longer appears in James's quotation as it does in the original, since in consonance with the manner of James's interpretation, it had symbolic reference to the enemies of God's people, or the Gentiles in general, who were now by conversion becoming a part of new Israel.[2] With this principle of interpretation established, we may also understand the rest of the prophecy as a reference to the messianic age, which is not a future millennium but the present dispensation. Once more we have an example of symbolic language (v. 13) and concepts of religious significance current with the prophet (vv. 14-15) by which he clothes the spiritual of the messianic salvation with glorious apparel.

Perhaps one more prophecy should be mentioned, that of Zechariah 14.[3] We refer to this because it is different in one

[1] Scofield reflects his premillennarian position here by making, "After this I will return" (*Acts* 15:16) refer to Christ's coming after the present dispensation (1917 edition, p.1170). But if James did not mean his quotation of Amos 9:11-12 to refer to the fruit of the labours of the apostles, he was guilty of a remarkable *non sequitur.* In other words, Scofield, in order to preserve his artificial dispensational scheme, distorts what James truly does with Amos 9:11-12.

[2] We have deliberately refrained from discussing a variant of the unpointed Hebrew, *Adam,* which becomes *Edom* when pointed. This may have led the LXX translators to read it as *Adam* (man) and translate it as *anthropon* (man), and may also have influenced James if he made use of the LXX translation. But whether it is *Edom* or *men*, the sense is essentially the same; namely, that both Edom and men generally (Gentiles) were not the people of God originally. As a matter of fact, both were hostile enemies of the people of God. But an essential characteristic of the New Testament dispensation which Amos foresaw and James rightly discerned is that Messiah subdues his foes in redemption and makes them his friends and people.

[3] *The Dickson Reference Bible* says of this chapter, "The glorious messianic reign when the nations shall worship in Jerusalem" (Chicago: John A. Dickson Pub. Co., 1941), p.1073.

respect from the others in that it is post-exilic and may therefore stand as a representative example of the eschatology of post-exilic prophecy. Though it is true that, since this prophecy came after the exile, its eschatology looks forward more directly to the messianic salvation and its final goals than to any immediate post-exilic deliverance; nevertheless it is also true that much post-exilic prophecy merely reiterates that of earlier prophets but with further elaboration.

Two examples illustrating this should suffice. In the first, Malachi 3 and 4 reveals much concerning the way-preparer of the Lord of what is already given by Isaiah in chapter 40. In the second, when Matthew attributes to Jeremiah the buying of the potter's field with the betrayal money which the remorseful Judas returned (*Matt.* 27:9-10), he thereby reveals that, though his reference approximates to that of Zechariah 11:12-13, he considers that prophecy only an amplification of the earlier prophet's prediction (cf. *Jer.* 18:1-4; 19:1-3).[1]

As we read Zechariah 14, the basic eschatology associated with the Lord's advent and the final kingdom appears in harmony with what has already been set forth by the earlier prophets reviewed above.[2] For example, in verse 8 "living waters" are again mentioned as flowing from Jerusalem (the new Jerusalem in *Rev.* 22:1); and in verse 21, the description of Jerusalem's absolute purity, reminds us of Revelation 21:26-27.[3] It is not necessary, therefore, to develop the context further by examining all the

---

[1] Commentators are divided on this last example. For other interpretations, cf. John A. Broadus, *Commentary on the Gospel of Matthew* (Philadelphia: American Baptist Publication Society, 1886), pp.558-559. The view we have adopted is both consonant with the analogy and consistent with the integrity of Scripture. If our conclusion is correct, it is an example of amplification pointed out by Scripture itself.

[2] Keil says, "In chapter 14 (from *vv.* 6-21) there is predicted in Old Testament form the completion of the kingdom of God, which the apostle John saw and described in Revelation 20-22 in New Testament mode under the figure of the heavenly Jerusalem." Keil, *The Twelve Minor Prophets*, p.421.

[3] Keil says of this, "The reference cannot be to actual Canaanites because they were prohibited by the law from entering the temple, but only to Israelites who were Canaanites in heart." *Ibid.*, p.415.

details to be found there.[1] We simply note that nothing there either teaches or necessitates a millennium.

From this examination of Old Testament prophecy we may summarize our conclusions as follows: 1) the Old Testament has no teaching of a one thousand year, or millennial, period; 2) all Old Testament prophecy can be adequately explained either in the light of Christ's first advent and the resulting present dispensation or in the light of his second advent and the resulting consummation; 3) millennarianism is not demanded by the prophecies of the Old Testament.

3. The teaching of the New Testament

If the Old Testament neither teaches nor necessitates a millennial period, the New Testament is definitely against such a period. This might be suspected from the fact that no reference to a millennium is made by Christ in his Olivet Discourse (*Matt. 24-25*) where the history of this age with its eschatological conclusion is delineated. Having revealed that in this dispensation the gospel will be preached in all the world before the end comes (24:14), but having also revealed that this will by no means result in world-wide conversion (24:5; 24:6; 24:9-10; 24:12), and having further described the tribulation which precedes the end (24:15-28), Jesus then makes plain the manner of his coming which is a visible one of power and great glory (24:30). Then, having revealed that this will mean the gathering of his elect to himself (24:31), Jesus pauses to give several parables whose burden is warning and watchfulness (24:32-25:30) in order that his own may become neither unconcerned nor forgetful concerning his advent and the judgment connected with it.[2]

---

[1] For a satisfactory treatment of the whole chapter and its details, see Keil, *ibid.*, p.401-421.

[2] It is here that postmillennialists err, as well as at the point where they in effect deny the unexpectedness of the Lord's return. They must and do teach in fact that the world is getting better, and that until this takes place according to a variously defined millennium, Christ will not, and even cannot, return. They therefore deny: 1) the strength of evil's final and widespread development, and 2) the imminence of Christ's return. For an exposition of and apology for the postmillennialist position, cf. L. Boettner, *The Millennium* (Phillipsburg, N.J.: The Presbyterian and Reformed Publishing Company, 1958), pp.3-105;

Then Jesus climaxes and concludes the whole discourse with the judgment scene (25:31-46) in which separation of his people from the world takes place, the former going unto the kingdom prepared for them from the foundation of the world (*v.* 34), the latter into everlasting punishment (*v.* 46). Admittedly, it is possible to say that the millennium follows this scene, but to do so means: firstly, to de-emphasize the ring of finality that forms a natural climax to the whole of Jesus' eschatological teaching; secondly, to say in effect that Jesus does not take his disciples to the very end of eschatological triumph which would certainly be strange; and thirdly, it is to admit that Jesus himself here gives no disclosure of a millennium.

But where the Olivet Discourse disinclines us towards belief in a millennium, other passages in the New Testament actively militate against it. Romans 2:15-16, I Thessalonians 5:2-11, II Thessalonians 1:4-10, and Revelation 11:8 may be cited as passages which support the general character of the judgment depicted in the Olivet Discourse. In each of these passages the impression conveyed by the judgment described is that of contemporaneity of the reward for the righteous and punishment for the wicked, along with the finality which that judgment brings.

Romans 2:15-16 depicts Christ as the judge of the secrets of the hearts of all men gathered to him on the great day appointed by God the Father for this purpose. This can hardly be some form of preliminary judgment, or allow for other judgments to follow.

I Thessalonians 5:2-11 makes clear that the coming of Christ, besides being a day of salvation for his people, will be a day of wrath for his enemies (*vv.* 3, 9), as does also II Thessalonians 1:4-10 where again we are told, as in the Olivet Discourse, that the punishment of Christ's enemies will be one of everlasting destruction from the presence of the Lord (*v.* 9). Certainly, the tone of finality is again sounded here!

In Revelation 11:18, where, following the voices in heaven which announce that the kingdom of this world has become the

---

"Postmillennialism", *The Meaning of the Millennium: Four Views,* Robert G. Clouse, ed. (Downers Grove: InterVarsity Press, third printing 1979), pp.117-141.

kingdom of the Father and the Son, it is said that the time has come for judgment with its ensuing reward for the righteous and punishment for the unrighteous. In this passage we have a clear indication that not only is no room left for a millennium to follow, but it is definitely excluded by the finality of the kingdom which is announced.

It is also well to notice that in the above passages the coming of Christ is not something that occurs in differing ways or at different times. The exact time of his coming is known by no one, hence, the repeated admonition to the church to watchfulness (*Matt.* 24:44; 25:13, *I Thess.* 5:6). To the world his coming will be totally unexpected so that it will be as a thief in the night (*Matt.* 24:43, 50, *I Thess.* 5:2-3). But in both cases it will be one and the same advent as the ensuing general judgment proves. This is further seen in II Peter 3:3-14, where a parallel is drawn between the antediluvian judgment and the judgment at the end of the world (*v.* 7). As the one was unexpected, so also will be the other (*v.* 10). As the one issued in the destruction of the world, so will the other (*vv.* 10, 12).

It is at this point once again that a millennium is excluded, for the coming of the Lord, Peter tells us, is unexpected. It means judgment of the ungodly in the destruction of the world, and the institution of the final order with the creation of the new heavens and earth. Accordingly, it is to this that believers are to look (*v.* 13), not a millennium; for Peter, by the very order of events he outlines here, has made the latter impossible, since its locale (this present world) is to be destroyed as part of the judgment of the wicked in the day of the Lord's return (*v.* 7) so that what follows is the final kingdom described by John in Revelation 21-22. This is here referred to by Peter as the new heavens and earth (cf. *Rev.* 21-22).

There are at least two more passages in the New Testament which oppose a millennarian construction, though they are often used by premillennialists in support of their view. The one deals with the renovation of nature and the other points out when the destruction of the last enemy, death, occurs.

In Romans 8:17-25 we are told that creation is waiting for deliverance from the curse to which it was subjected as the result of man's sin. Then we are told that this will occur simultaneously with the resurrection (compare *v.* 21 with *v.* 23). But the resurrection takes place at the coming of Christ, at which time all the other eschatological events occur. The renovation of nature must therefore in this passage bespeak the glories of creation in the new heavens and earth rather than be identified with the millennium.

The premillennialist presupposition at this point, however, is that this resurrection is only that of the righteous and that judgment of the wicked follows the millennium. But we are prompted to ask whether the data of this passage have been sufficiently taken into account. For, if such renovation of which the apostle speaks takes place at the resurrection, how can the recurrence of such sin as issues in the apostasy at the end of the millennium be properly accounted for? Certainly, the renovation of nature includes man who is himself a part of that nature. His deliverance is described by the apostle in terms of the resurrection, a most glorious event. If sin can re-emerge after this, then no such deliverance as the apostle speaks of will take place.

Finally, in I Corinthians 15:22-28, the teaching of an alleged millennium has been found by some. For, do we not have here the order of the resurrection described, the millennial rule of Christ and the ultimate delivering up of the kingdom to the Father at the end? But a millennium is not the teaching of this passage because nowhere is mention made of it. Besides, no particular time lapse such as a thousand years is needed between the orders of the resurrection and the end (*vv.* 23-24). The language neither explicitly states nor demands one.[1]

Leaving aside the passage in Revelation 20 for the moment, does this passage whose climax is reached in verses 50-58 support a millennium? On the contrary. Paul tells us that Christ's rule will continue until all his enemies shall have been brought to

---

[1] George E. Ladd, a premillennialist, argues for a time lapse between the *epeita* and *eita* of verses 23-24 in which he would place the millennium (*Crucial Questions About the Kingdom of God,* Grand Rapids: Eerdmans, 1952, p.177 ff.); "Historic Premillennialism", *The Meaning of the Millennium,* Clouse, ed., pp.17-40. We cannot, however, accept his position, for Ladd's very example from verses 5-7 establishes only sequence, not a time lapse, let alone one of a thousand years' length. True, sequence may be admitted as being taught in verses 23-24, but to then aver that this creates a time lapse is to beg the question.

nothing, the last being death (*vv.* 25-26). After showing his readers that there will be continuity between the mortal and the resurrection bodies, though the latter will far transcend the former, the apostle returns to the subject of victory over death in verses 50-58; for having dealt with the reality of the resurrection body, he is now prepared to demonstrate how it is integrally bound up with that victory. Victory over death is achieved when the resurrection occurs (*v.* 54) which takes place at the return of Christ at the last trumpet (*v.* 52). Then his reign shall end, for then all his enemies will have been subdued. Then his victory will be complete, for even death will have been conquered! This passage, therefore, rather than supporting, clearly opposes the teaching that a millennium follows Christ's return.

To summarize the above New Testament data opposed to a millennium: 1) the coming of Christ issues in a final judgment which includes reward for the believer and punishment for the unbeliever; 2) the coming of Christ renovates nature into a new heaven and new earth, simultaneously with the resurrection and its consequent destruction of the last enemy, death; and 3) the coming of Christ ushers in the eternal state or the final kingdom.

4. The teaching of Revelation 20

It is to this passage that we now turn. It alone, in the final analysis, is the basis for millennarian views. And so allegedly clear is its teaching of a millennium, that exponents of it are willing to adjust the rest of scriptural data to it rather than vice versa, as might ordinarily be expected. As Sauer characteristically puts it, "But for ourselves this one reference of Holy Scripture suffices. We have no right to require from God that he must repeat a statement five or ten times before we can believe him."[1] Let us therefore give some attention to this passage.

---

[1] Erich Sauer, *From Eternity to Eternity* (Grand Rapids: Eerdmans, 1954), p.148. Sauer is a dispensationalist whose views, while allowing for the truth of symbolism, figure, and spiritual reality as present in Scripture, nevertheless further require a "literal" interpretation of a particular Scripture in question (cf. pp.137-194). His conclusion that Revelation 20 teaches a literal millennium, regardless of other scriptural data which militate against such an interpretation, is a typical example of his exegesis.

On careful examination, we are surprised at the rather meagre detail given if a millennium is indeed here described. It is true that a one thousand year interval is mentioned a half dozen times in differing connections. But in a book where symbolism is prominently used throughout, there is by no means unanimity even among millennarians in regarding this as a literal one thousand year period. For example, in a book where "ten days" means a specified period of tribulation but not that literal period of time (2:10); where "the seven spirits of God" stand for the fulness of the Holy Spirit and not a plurality of his being (4:5); where time references of "twelve hundred and sixty days" (12:6), "forty-two months" (13:5), and "time, times, and half a time" (12:14), refer to the entire present dispensation (cf. *Dan.* 7:25; 9:27; 12:7); where the number of the beast is given as "six hundred and sixty-six", which is very likely a designation for humanism carried to its ultimate development (13:18); etc., it is exceedingly hazardous, if not untenable, to maintain that this must refer to a literal one thousand year period, for it may quite properly stand for a significant symbolic designation.

Furthermore, though a reign with Christ is described (*v.* 4), those who reign with Christ are said to be souls, not persons. This, too, is highly significant because John does not use the word *psyche* (soul) in the loose sense as though it specified an embodied soul; for in 6:9 he has used the term to describe martyrs whom he sees in heaven in a disembodied state under the altar. In other words, as 20:4 reveals by a reference to "the souls of those who had been beheaded for their witness to Jesus", we have the same group as previously described in 6:9 but now shown to be reigning with Christ in heaven — not on earth as is sometimes uncritically concluded.

It may be here objected that a resurrection is referred to in verse 5 which, if language means anything, denotes the bodily reanimation associated with the resurrection in its fullest sense. Therefore, this must refer to a resurrection yet future because it is associated with the second death (*v.* 6, compare with *v.* 14).

We must, however, see this first resurrection mentioned in verse 5 as a spiritual rather than physical resurrection. For, since a second death is here spoken of, to which the first resurrection is linked, a first death is implied to have taken place, as we indeed see occurred in the case of the martyrs. Nevertheless, though the martyrs are dead physically, they are very much alive spiritually; in fact, they live and reign with Christ. The rest of the dead, however, do not live in this time (*v*. 5), being dead physically and spiritually. For them it is reserved to suffer the second death since they have not participated in the first resurrection.

Therefore, two kinds of death imply two kinds of resurrection here. Unbelievers are doomed to experience not only physical death, but eternal death (the second death) at the last resurrection (*vv*. 12-15) because they experienced no first resurrection. Believers such as the martyrs, on the other hand, because they have life, witnessed to by the first resurrection, may have suffered the first, or physical, death; but over them, when their second resurrection takes place, the second death will have no power.

To what alone then can the first resurrection be compared but to spiritual life (*John* 3:5; 11:25, *Eph*. 2:1-6, *Titus* 3:5), which, since it is the possession of believers ensures their victory over final death by the second resurrection?[1] The reference to *ezesan* (they lived), therefore, mentioned in verses 4 and 5 for both believer and unbeliever, should be translated simply as "they lived" and not "they lived again" as the AV and NKJV render verse 5; for the original gives no warrant for adding the word "again".

---

[1] An objection may still be made that it is rather far-fetched to equate spiritual life with a resurrection of any sort, though Titus 3:5 compares the impartation of spiritual life to a *palingenisia* (regeneration), the very term Christ uses in Matthew 19:28 to describe the new order of the final state which has integrally bound up with it the concept of resurrection. However, an application of John's meaning for *anastasis* (resurrection) may be found in Matthew 22:30-32. Here Jesus' reference to the resurrection cannot be limited to its final sense; for in speaking for God as the God of Abraham, Isaac, and Jacob, he says that God is the God of the living, though these patriarchs by that time had long since been physically dead. In other words, Jesus corrects the false notion of the Sadducees that the final resurrection alone will give life to the dead. Believers, such as the patriarchs, he asserts, are as a matter of fact living even now in the very presence of God. In Revelation, however, John is interested in bringing out the implications of the first resurrection as it specifically applies to the intermediate state between physical death and the final resurrection, rather than using it as applicable to spiritual life generally. This, we trust, will further become evident under point 4) below.

This is an important point because it is just the word "again" that conveys the false notion of a beginning to live or a not living during a then-alleged one thousand year period.[1] Actually, the word "lived" (aorist tense in the Greek), as it stands without the gratuitous "again", refers to life in its qualitative rather than animated form during this period. That is to say, unbelievers certainly have life of a sort after physical death, as well as believers (*Luke* 16:23). But in comparison with the life experienced by believers after death, it is no life at all. John therefore quite properly refers to them as "not living" (*ouk ezesan, v.* 5), during this period, while for believers, such as the martyrs, he says that "they lived" (*ezesan, v.* 4), because in this time they actually participate with Christ in his reign. They may have suffered the first death by a bloody and terrible martyrdom, but no matter, over them the second death has no power. In fact, they already live and reign with Christ in the enjoyment of a life properly described as "the first resurrection" (*v.* 6).

For unbelievers, however, physical death is but the portent of the second or final death. Not having spiritual life, they consequently have no part in the first resurrection but remain "dead" with reference to it. Their prospect can only be that of the second death which follows the "thousand years" of the first resurrection (*v.* 5) and which coincides with the bodily resurrection at the final judgment (*vv.* 12-15).

In short, believers experience one death but two resurrections. Unbelievers experience one resurrection but two deaths. There is therefore no need for a millennium on the basis of appeal to John's mention of a first resurrection and a second death, as though the former were the beginning and the latter the end of an alleged millennium.

There is, however, one further argument to which millenarians appeal, namely, that if the events of Revelation 20 are chronologically subsequent to those of chapter 19, then the doctrine of a millennium follows as a consequence, because the events of 19:11-21 are achieved by Christ at his second advent.[2]

---

[1] The NIV also conveys the same notion of "again" with its typically more free rendering, "they came to life" (*v.* 4) and "[the rest of the dead] did not come to life".

[2] Cf. Ladd, "Historic Premillennialism", p.35.

Millennarians, however, assume what needs to be proved. And that a strong case for discontinuity between chapters 19 and 20 can be made is seen from the following four considerations:

a. When does death's final defeat occur?

We have seen from I Corinthians 15:26 that the last enemy to be destroyed is death, whose destruction occurs at the coming of Christ and the resurrection of his people. But in Revelation 19 and 20, death is said to be destroyed not until 20:14, after the great white throne judgment. If a millennium were consequent to Christ's second coming in chapter 19, this would make the victory over death foretold here a flat contradiction to that given in I Corinthians 15, since a thousand-year period would intervene between the resurrection and it. Therefore, it is better to hold to the discontinuity of chapters 19 and 20, and make the great white throne judgment synonymous with or immediately after the events of chapter 19.

b. Do the battles of Revelation 19 and 20 signify the same event?

When the eschatology of Ezekiel is compared with that of the Apocalypse, striking similarities become evident. There is the mention of Gog and Magog coming to battle against the people of God, the active intervention and deliverance by the Lord of his people, and the description of the final state in terms of an ideal temple (Ezekiel) and of a city (John). The latter description freely borrows from the former, in that the city itself is a huge temple, the gates have on them the names of the twelve tribes (compare *Rev.* 21:12 with *Ezek.* 48:31-35), waters of life flow forth from the centre of both (compare *Rev.* 22:1 with *Ezek.* 47:1) and trees for the healing of the nations are to be found upon the bank of the river of each (compare *Rev.* 22:2 with *Ezek.* 47:12, etc.). Now, if Ezekiel 40-48 refers to the final state, as Revelation 21-22 by reference to it confirms, then a contradiction between Ezekiel 38-39 and Revelation 19-20 results on premillennarian presuppositions, because Ezekiel has no millennium whereas John allegedly posits one between two battles of similar imagery (*Rev.* 19:11-21 and 20:8-10).

May not these two battles be viewed as one and the same, but from differing aspects, so preserving a harmony between Ezekiel and John? Especially when it is seen that both Revelation 19:11-21 and 20:8-10 borrow from the same source (*Ezek.*

38-39), even to the concepts of the battle and the names Gog and Magog (cf. *Rev.* 19:17-21 with *Ezek.* 39:17-21, and *Rev.* 20:8-10 with *Ezek.* 39:1-7). Therefore, rather than saying that John has two battles which are so much alike that he uses imagery from the same source in Ezekiel to describe them though they occur a millennium apart, it would be better to posit discontinuity between the chapters of Revelation 19 and 20, with 20:8-10 reiterative of 19:11-21 but from a different standpoint. Whereas in the earlier depiction of the battle John shows that Antichrist's war is primarily against the Lord, in the latter battle he reveals that Antichrist's war is carried out against Christ's church.[1] Only the principle of discontinuity and reiteration in Revelation 19 and 20 create no conflict with the eschatology of Ezekiel because that prophecy, though very similar to the Apocalypse, makes no provision for a millennium. In chapters 38-39, after depicting the decisive battle between the world and the people of God which the Lord himself turns into decisive victory by his active intervention, it goes on immediately to set forth not the millennium but the final state (*chaps.* 40-48). Therefore, if the eschatology of Revelation 21-22 is in harmony with Ezekiel 40-48, the eschatology of Revelation 19-20 must be in harmony with that of Ezekiel 38-39. This becomes clear when we perceive that Revelation 19-20 does not set forth a continuous historical picture resulting in a millennium, but breaks off at the close of chapter 19, resuming historical sequence at 20:11-15 in the great white throne judgment. This in turn is depicted as the prelude to the final state which follows the battle of 20:8-10, this last being reiterative of 19:11-21. We are thus directed to historical sequence once more after the parenthetical break of 20:1-6.

---

[1] This interpretation is in harmony with the Apocalypse's own symbolism of the beloved city as being heavenly Zion, new Jerusalem, the city of God, the church; and which stands in antithesis to earthly Jerusalem (spiritually Sodom and Egypt – 11:8), imperial Rome, worldly Babylon, the people of Antichrist, the unregenerate world. In other words, the book presents to us a conflict between two forces, the people of God and the people of the devil. All the above-named symbols merely set forth and elaborate these two categories.

c. When is Satan bound?

There is a rather widespread misunderstanding that Satan is first bound at this point in history (*Rev.* 20) because Satan appears to be anything but bound at the present time, witness the widespread and increasing evil in the world today. Therefore this binding is thought to be something yet to take place, specifically at the return of Christ following the events of chapter 19. But is this a proper exegesis of the text? Satan's binding in Revelation 20:1-3 is not said to remove the curse or even necessarily put a check on sin flowing out of the depraved human heart. What is said is that he is bound *in order that* (*hina*) he should deceive the nations no more during the specified period of a thousand years. What we are being told is that Satan's power with respect to the nations is curtailed in the particular time during which he is bound. No longer is he able to control the nations as fell instruments of his kingdom so that the imperial might of a world power such as Babylon, or Persia, or Greece, or Rome, may be arrayed against the people of God. On the contrary, because he has been bound, he will be despoiled of such nations and peoples as formerly became the tools of his usurping grasp!

Now, when does such binding occur? Is it after the return of Christ and the events of Revelation 19? No! This would throw it into conflict with the eschatology of the New Testament. For, as we have already seen, Christ's victory at his second advent is total and leaves no room in the following eternal order for a consequent activity of Satan and a recrudescence of sin.[1] Can an explanation be given which better accounts for the whole of scriptural data?

There can be, if the discontinuity between Revelation 19 and 20 is recognized. Then the binding of Satan can be associated with the truth Christ taught in Matthew 12:29; namely, that because he had bound "the strong man", Christ was henceforth busily despoiling him of his possessions in the deliverance of his people from Satan's dominion. And that dominion, as Revelation 20:1-3 informs us, in agreement with Christ's teaching in the parable of the Mustard Seed (*Matt.* 12:31-32) and with Daniel's vision

---

[1] See above, pp.98-102.

of the stone cut without hands (2:34-35), will be a dominion that includes subdual of the nations so that they will never again rise in a mighty world federation to oppose the kingdom of God until allowed to do so by the unbinding of Satan and rise of Antichrist shortly before the return of Christ (*Rev.* 11:7; 20:7-8).

On this interpretation, Satan is presently in the abyss and will continue to be there until shortly before the end. On his release, his hostile activity will be embodied in the beast (the Antichrist) whose origin is also significantly spoken of as the abyss (11:7). This is where he indeed is when viewed in terms of the satanic power he is given by the devil to exercise. The abyss is a symbolic term, as is the chain by which Satan is bound, and represents a sphere of restricted activity, much as would be true for men if imprisoned. Again, we see how the language is couched in terms intelligible to human understanding.

Other places in the Apocalypse also bear out the thought that Satan's present activity is strictly limited. For example, in Revelation 9, with the sounding of the fifth trumpet, the abyss appears and is opened so that from it come evil spirits in the form of unearthly locusts whose king is Abaddon, or Apollyon (*v.* 11), terms which are at least descriptive of Satan's activity. In other words, we are again presented with a picture that reveals the imprisonment of the prince of demons with his unholy forces until such time as they are deliberately freed by divine action. This understanding also agrees with Revelation 20:7-8. In the twelfth chapter also, Satan's restricted sphere of activity is presented, but in the form of his having been cast out of heaven following the exaltation of Christ (compare *vv.* 13-14 with *v.* 6 for a fixing of the time of the war between Michael and his angels and the dragon and his angels). The events of verses 7-9 occur as a result of the exaltation of Christ (*v.* 5) so that Satan is no longer able to practise the role of accuser of the brethren (*v.* 10).

From this interpretation, which is consistent with scriptural data as well as the Apocalypse itself, we may conclude that the period of Satan's binding is this present dispensation, characterized as a one thousand year period of time to signify that it endures until all God's purposes have been fulfilled and will close only when God himself actively ends it. A thousand is ten, the basic decimal unit carried to the third multiple and therefore is most appropriate as a figure to denote this dispensation, a period which includes in its pericope every power as under the dominion of the Lord.

d. When do the martyred saints live and reign?

Having observed the decisive climactic victory of Christ at his coming over the hostile world forces arrayed against him by the Antichrist (*Rev.* 19:20-21), we might expect the apostle John now to unfold the details of the eternal state. This he proceeds to do in chapters 21 and 22. There is, however, one remaining factor which the seer, in his development of details by repeated recapitulation throughout the book, has not yet made completely clear; namely, the destiny of those saints who before Christ's final victory have died in him, particularly those who have suffered a gory death at the bloody hands of those powers who have ever opposed Christ and his church.

It is true that John has already depicted them in the form of souls under the altar in heaven (6:9), given white robes and told to await their vindication by the Lord himself after the rest of their company have been added to their number. In 14:13 another glimpse of the departed is afforded us, describing them as blessed, resting from their labours and enjoying the fruits of faithful labours performed in this life. But what specifically is the nature of their victory and the reward of their after-life during this intermediate state? Before this is answered, we should first notice that John has repeatedly shown that the church will not be overwhelmed, neither by the evil of hell's assaults nor by the justice of heaven's final judgment on the rest of the inhabited earth.

We see this already in chapter 7 where the elect company is presented both in its entirety on earth (7:1-8), and in its myriads in heaven (7:9-17). But in both places the elect are shown to emerge entire and triumphant from the judgment on the earth set forth at the end of chapter 6, for they are the purchased possession of the Lamb. Again, in chapter 11, though the two witnesses at length are overcome by the beast, they are at last vindicated in resurrection and ascension. Again, following the frightful picture of the beast's persecution (*chap.* 13), we are shown in 14:1-5 that the church once more emerges entire to stand in victory with the Lamb on heavenly Mount Zion prior to the execution of his avenging judgment on the ungodly (14:17-20). In these examples, John in his visions has focussed our attention on the eschatological victory of the church which is her glorious prospect and certain goal. Now, she may be persecuted, downtrodden, humiliated; but at last she will be vindicated, triumphant, glorious. In this patience she should possess her soul and endure to the end.

But can Satan and his instrument, the Antichrist, be said to gain a victory over the church in any way even at present? Jesus taught that the gates of hades would not *overpower* (*katischuo, Matt.* 16:18) his church, for he would fill her with his own unconquerable life. Consequently, merely killing the body is no triumph if there is nothing more that such an enemy can do. In Revelation 20:1-6, therefore, John now plainly shows that to which he has already alluded in chapter 12:10-12; namely, that the intermediate state is one of victory and reign for the souls with Christ. Satan, having been bound, no longer has any power or standing in heaven (see also *Luke* 10:18).[1] And, though upon earth he may manifest great wrath, this alone is the sphere of his limited domain until that, too, will be finally taken from him. In the meantime the full effects of his wrath in the persecution and martyrdom of God's people only hastens their release from this vale of suffering still lying under the curse of darkness, destruction and death. But on high, where even now their citizenship is already found, there is life, victory and rule with Christ.

The principle of discontinuity between Revelation 19 and 20 is here once more seen in that John's setting forth of the intermediate state, referred to in various places throughout the book but undeveloped until Revelation 20:1-6 is properly introduced by

---

[1] "Through Jesus' obedience Satan was cast out of his throne in heaven so that his demons could be cast out of men on earth. And this expulsion is the sign of Satan's coming banishment when God's kingdom comes in its fulness." Minear, *The Kingdom and the Power*, p.113.

reference to the binding of Satan. This is because firstly, the saints' victory and rule with Christ takes place just because of Satan's binding in defeat; and secondly, because their reign coincides with Satan's binding, or this present dispensation, referred to symbolically as a thousand year period (20:4, 6) as it was for Satan (20:2, 3, 7) because of that number's appropriateness to express the concept of completeness.

Our examination of all the scriptural data of the Old and New Testaments, including Revelation 20, has brought us to a negative conclusion about a millennial rule by Christ. In a comment upon the Gospels concerning this Vos has said, "There is no trace in the Gospels of the so-called chiliastic expectation of a provisional political kingdom, that strange compromise whereby Judaism endeavored to reconcile the two heterogeneous elements that struggled for the supremacy in its eschatological consciousness. What formally corresponds in our Lord's teaching to this notion is the idea of the invisible, spiritual kingdom, and how totally different it is."[1]

As we have seen, the basis of this statement can be broadened to include the whole of Scripture, not simply the Gospels. Should we then continue to recognize a view that originated with the exegetical compromises of Judaism whose efforts not only resulted in the violent wresting of Scripture along the erroneous byways of carnal notion and literalistic misunderstanding, but tragically led to the rejection of the Saviour himself at the time of his first advent? While the opening of error's floodgates is an all-too-prone operation of the human heart, the Lord, by divine grace and mercy, can close them. But he does so in connection with the truth of his Word. Let us therefore be more prayerfully dependent on the Spirit for the illumination he gives in connection with its study. Let us also strive for increasing consistency in its application to our faith and lives.

[1] *The Kingdom and the Church*, p.42.

VII: VICTORY OF CHRIST

1. The totality of Christ's mediatorial rule

Christ's victory will not be complete until the usurpers, sin,
Satan and death have been subdued under him (*Phil.* 3:21b).
The conflict with these usurpers which began at the incarnation
which was victoriously determined by the ministry whose
climax was his death on the cross in ransom for sin and which
is now since the resurrection and ascension carried on in the
heavenly realm, will be concluded only when his triumph is
universal. And that triumph awaits the cataclysm of the
consummation for its accomplishment. "The same omnipotent
power at work through the ages will also effect the consummation
at the end. But it will assume a new form when the end has
come, so as to work instantaneously, and will draw within the
sphere of its operation the entire physical universe."[1]

a. Over the world

Conquest over the world in the broadest sense means victory
over all creation. At the beginning, "All things were made
through him, and without him nothing was made that was
made" (*John* 1:3). But the world, having been finished by him
to reflect the light, beauty and glory of its creator, fell into
corruption and chaos due to the creature and his sin. What

[1] Vos, *The Kingdom and the Church*, p.45.

man therefore unmade by his sin, Christ set out to remake by his redemption. The destiny of the world, therefore, is once more to shimmer in the resplendent rays of celestial light as, garbed in heavenly glory, it reflects its author's divine aura. And Christ will achieve this "that in him all the fulness should dwell" (*Col.* 1:19). "Christ, mediator of the creation 'in the beginning'; Christ, mediator of the new creation at the end of the days!"[1]

But it is not enough to be general about the nature of Christ's victory over the world. It involves the subdual of every agency whose intelligence could be exercised in conscious opposition to him. And therein lies the reason for the lengthening of the process by which that subdual is achieved.

b. Over the devil

In this fallen creature, we have the fearful foe of God and man. His original sin was aspiration to supremacy over God himself (*Isa.* 14:14).[2] Though having suffered humiliating defeat in unceremonious eviction from heaven, he has by no means abandoned his attempts to achieve his original purposes as he exhibits the animosity of the reprobate and the rage of defeat's frustration. Seeking to overthrow God's dominion in the hearts of men whom God at the dawn of this world's history had made for himself, and seeking to enlist them on his side in his ceaseless conflict against God, he apparently achieved his purpose when, by means of a successful temptation, he turned the hearts of men to distrust of and rebellion against God. Thus it would seem that he had brought God's dominion to an end with the replacement of his own in the hearts of men who, in this state, are in bondage to the doing of his will (*I John* 5:19, *II Tim.* 2:26).

Therefore, in order for Christ as the promised redeemer of a renewed humanity and creator of a new world to accomplish

[1] Cullmann, "Königsherrschaft Christi", p.7.

[2] This Scripture verse, though basically a reference to the king of Babylon (*v.* 4), goes beyond him to the power "behind the throne" of whose sin his was but an impersonation within the sphere of humanity's limitations. The same will also be true with the Antichrist (*II Thess.* 2:3-4), though his power will be magnified by Satan to the climax of his evil power's concentration in this man more completely his instrument than any other.

this total victory, it was necessary for him to come to personal grips with this arch-antagonist and destroyer; for until he and all under his command have been brought to nothing, such power as might still remain would to that extent subtract from the total victory of Christ. It would furthermore constitute a challenge to his absolute sovereignty. The world has therefore become the battleground of these two opposing antagonists and history the tale of the battle's development. While this conflict rages, in which both invisible angelic powers and visible human forces are engaged, the world with its history continues until such time as Christ's sovereignty, assured since the victory of his resurrection, is demonstrated in the whole of that creation where challenge to it was originally made.

Satan's defeat with his hosts is consequently one of degrees. There is a threefold fall of Satan. First there is his fall out of the heaven of glory when sin was driven forth from the world of angels. Then there is the fall from the heaven of his power and glory of which Jesus speaks in Luke 10. And finally there is the fall of Satan at the day of judgment as he shall be thrown into the bottomless pit forever.

The first defeat, though humiliating, was not decisive, for it did not prevent the fall of humanity and the curse of creation by God after Satan's successful seduction which has put fallen mankind under his usurping power. Again, the second defeat, though crushing, is also not total because, though Satan's kingdom is now steadily being wrested from him, he is nevertheless allowed to exert his influence, either as a roaring lion, on the one hand (*I Pet.* 5:8), or a deceiving angel of light, on the other (*II Cor.* 11:14). That this enmity against God will never be repented of by him is to be seen in the damage he will seek to inflict on the church and kingdom when just before his final doom, he is unbound at the close of this age (*Rev.* 20:7-8). Only the third and final defeat, therefore, will be completely decisive because then his eternal destruction will terminate not only every part of his power and influence, but also every vestige and evidence of his opposition.

His doom, consequently, spells doom for all allied with him, whether angelic or human, because they, like him, are equally reprobate and share the same fate with him. Not only do they reap the full justice of God's punitive wrath, but they are also brought to nothing in terms of opposition to the Lord. That Christ is able to enforce the decrees of just condemnation on all his implacable foes, from the greatest to the least, is but another exhibition of that power by which he shall bring his total victory to its proper consummation. For in this also, Christ's complete sovereignty in the proper punishment of his enemies will be openly demonstrated.

Then shall the way have been prepared for the final display of his total victory. "For, *every part* of the kingdom of God that Satan has disturbed shall be restored through Christ. Has Satan made the soul sinful, Christ shall make it holy. Has Satan darkened the understanding, Christ once more gives enlightened eyes of understanding. Has Satan brought our body under ailment, Christ shall glorify it in awakening it from the dead. Has Satan poisoned human social relationships, Christ shall establish the community of the saints. Has Satan brought the earthly sphere under the curse, Christ shall re-fashion a blessed creation. In all this he brings to realization the kingdom of God through his power, and sees to it that his throne is established in heaven, and that the kingdom of the LORD rules over *all*."[1]

c. *Over the flesh*

We might suppose that, with such an eloquent statement by Kuyper concerning the total victory of Christ over Satan and those elements of perversity, depravity and curse for which he may be accounted originally responsible, nothing more could be added to the subject of Christ's total victory. However, the aspects of depravity and curse should receive a somewhat further explication: the first finding development under the subject of the flesh, and the second under the subject of death.

The biblical view of the flesh is not that of Greek philosophy; namely, that the flesh is inherently evil. This concept found its way into the church at an early date: the attempted flight of the

---

[1] Kuyper, Jr., *Van het Koninkrijk*, pp.288-289.

anchorites or hermits was as much from the flesh as it was from the world. Viewing the flesh as inherently evil still remains today in Romanist doctrine, which holds that in the fall man lost the divine gift of superabundant grace by which he could originally resist and overcome every inherently evil tendency. Now, no longer possessing that grace, he needs those resources which only the church of Rome with its multiplied means of grace can give him in order to combat and overcome the evil tendencies of the flesh.

But the teaching of Scripture is not that the flesh is inherently evil, but that it is the instrument of man's inherent depravity. Man's evil is much more basic than the weakness of his flesh. It is his whole being, soul and body, with his faculties of mind, reason and will which expresses itself in the perversity of his nature (cf. *Gen.* 6:5, *Matt.* 12:33-34, *Rom.* 8:7-8, *Eph.* 2:3, etc.).[1] In his natural state, sin reigns in man's bodily members which are instruments of unrighteousness as his evil nature expresses itself through them (*Rom.* 6:12-13). It is to this total complex the Scriptures refer when they term it "the flesh".

However, Christ's redemption effects a radical change. In Christ his people become new creatures (*II Cor.* 5:17) because they are now indwelt by his Spirit, the firstfruits (*Rom.* 8:23) and guarantee (*Eph.* 1:14) of their salvation's final inheritance. But it is just because their salvation is not yet complete that they await the total victory of Christ which will involve the transformation of the flesh.

It is true that even now they experience victory over the old nature so that their flesh becomes the instrument of righteousness, but this is only because of the power which is theirs by the gracious operations of the Holy Spirit dwelling within them. The old nature is ever at war with the new, seeking to regain that mastery which it formerly had (*Gal.* 5:16-17). The Christian, therefore, is to put on the Lord Jesus Christ, for he is a citizen

---

[1] We do not feel it necessary to prove the doctrine of total depravity here. This has been adequately done by Reformed theologians. We wish at this point merely to recognize that man's basic ill is much more deep-seated than the failings of the flesh.

of his kingdom and must consequently exhibit its righteousness, and no longer cater for the flesh and its lusts (*Rom.* 13:14).

In its primary sense, the Christian's victory is one of principle moving by degree to complete realization. As long, however, as he is linked to the old world by something that has not yet experienced Christ's full redemption, i.e., the flesh, neither his victory nor his salvation are complete. His victory is not total because he is not yet clothed with that habitation (*II Cor.* 5:2) of the final age in which he will have a completely adequate vehicle by which to glorify the God of his salvation. Hence, his full salvation awaits the day when the body of his humiliation will be transformed to be fashioned anew in the likeness of that glorious body which Christ himself now possesses (*Phil.* 3:21) following his resurrection.[1] That Christ rose from the dead in such a body as the firstfruits (*I Cor.* 15:23) guarantees that the corruptible tabernacles of his people shall be further clothed (*ependusasthai, II Cor.* 5:4)[2] with incorruption (*I Cor.* 15:53), and then shall mortality with all of its fleshly limitations be swallowed up in life (*II Cor.* 5:4). Then shall every lingering effect of sin in Christ's people be forever removed. Then shall the means by which they shall be able to glorify their king to the full and for all eternity have become their portion. Then Christ's victory over the flesh shall be complete!

d. Over death

Death is the consequence of sin. In its most basic sense it means more than the violent rending of the soul from the body.

---

[1] As we have seen earlier, the transformation of the natural world will take place at the same time this takes place (*Rom.* 8:21-23). Wendland therefore says, "This end of history is *redemption from history in the sarx* (flesh)." *The Kingdom of God and History,* p.165.

[2] The significance of this verb, used by Paul both in *vv.* 2 and 4, should be carefully noted. H.A.W. Meyer is correct when he calls attention to it by saying, "Paul is presently 'put on' with an earthly body, and sighs full of longing 'to put on over it' the heavenly body" (*Critical and Exegetical Hand-book to Epistles to the Corinthians,* Winona Lake, USA: Alpha Publications, 1979, p.511). Vos confirms this view: "*ependusasthai* signifies 'to put on one garment over another garment'; it is the preposition *epi,* that effects this plus in the meaning" (*Pauline Eschatology,* p.189).

It means that man, as a sinner, being ethically alienated from God, is to suffer the separation of his very being from God in a spiritual death of which the physical is but an image. Christ's people can therefore still suffer physical death because the old nature is flesh and blood which will not inherit the final kingdom (*I Cor.* 15:50). Until the final kingdom is a reality, all that is not part of it continues to suffer from sin's curse whose climax is death. Death is therefore the last enemy to be destroyed, for two reasons: In the first place it continues to exist as the ultimate fruit of the old order. As long as any part of that order stands, so long will death continue as its product. But after the old has given way to the new, then will the death of the old be swallowed up in the life of the new. For Christ's people, therefore, death's final destruction will be a witness to the total victory of Christ, because it will exhibit the absolute completion of his redemption whose end is unconquerable life, the condition and atmosphere of the new order.

In the second place, since death is the ultimate fruit of the old order (*Rom.* 6:23), it will continue until it, as the final reward of sin, is the full portion of all the unredeemed who suffer it. Death, as final and complete separation from God, will be the experience of the ungodly, the execution of the judicial sentence of Christ in eternal destruction (*II Thess.* 1:9) as the climax of his total victory over his enemies (*Matt.* 25:41, *Rev.* 20:12 ff.). After this has been accomplished, death will have fulfilled its purpose and will then itself be forever banished along with its recipients (*Rev.* 20:15), for in the new creation of the final order, all the former things to which death was the final witness will have passed away (*Rev.* 21:4).

We can therefore see how church and kingdom in the final order merge completely. Christ is presently sovereign over all, but only the church enjoys the eternal state. When Christ will have completely subjugated all his foes and sent them to their doom, when he shall have removed every vestige of the old order in making all things new, and when the church will have entered into the fulness of its inheritance to enjoy the final kingdom with its sovereign Lord, the new order will be the context in which the church experiences consummate blessedness and glorification.

Every former encumbering restriction, as part of the old order, will have passed away. Therefore, "blessed are those who do his commandments that they may have the right to the tree of life, and may enter through the gates into the city. For outside are dogs and sorcerers and sexually-immoral and murderers and idolaters, and whoever loves and practises a lie" (*Rev.* 22:14-15).

2. The termination of Christ's mediatorial rule

As Vos points out: "After the last enemy, death, has been conquered, there is no further need for the kingdom of Christ: hence it is delivered up to God the Father. Christ's kingdom as a process of conquest precedes the final kingdom of God as a settled permanent state."[1]

In this statement, Vos gives the reason for the termination of Christ's kingdom in that it is primarily a kingdom of conquest. Christ has been seated as king upon the holy hill of Zion (*Psa.* 2:6). Sending the rod of his strength out of Zion, he rules in the midst of his enemies (*Psa.* 110:2). That rule consists in making a people his willing subjects (*Psa.* 110:3). It also consists in the exercise of his power until all his foes have been completely subdued (*Psa.* 110:1). Until these objects have been completely attained, Christ's rule continues. But the day will come when these goals will have been reached. Then his mediatorial reign, delegated to him by the Father after his ascension, will come to an end. When will this occur and what will follow?

a. The second advent of Christ

The second coming of Christ marks the close of Christ's present mediatorial rule. As it began with his ascension, it will end with his coming again. That is to say, when Christ ascended up on high, the Father declared him to be the Son of God with power (*Rom.* 1:4), by which he was set forth as Lord and Christ (*Acts* 2:36), these latter two terms implying the whole of his present rule which began at that point. That he is Lord guarantees

---

[1] *The Kingdom and the Church*, p.53.

his ultimate dominion over all. And that he is Christ ensures the full salvation of every one of his own.

As his reign began at his ascension, so it will end at his return. For when the angels would assure the disciples from whose sight the bodily presence of Christ had disappeared in the clouds of the ascension, they stated that Jesus would come again in like manner as they had seen him go into heaven (*Acts* 1:11). Therefore, just as Jesus returned to heaven only once, there to begin and conduct his reign to its successful conclusion, so he will return only once.

Yet we must not lose sight of the complex of events which will occur in connection with Christ's return. With his coming is to be associated: the resurrection, the general judgment, cosmic renovation and his total victory. Of course, since these things occur on the threshold of eternity which his advent will usher in, their exact chronology is not a consideration of primary importance. But that they must all occur before Christ's mediatorial reign ends should be kept in mind when it is said that his rule ends with his second advent.

In a sense, the mediatorship of Christ will never end, for there will be an everlasting recognition of it by the church. She will have a consciousness for eternity of him as the Lamb slain in sacrifice for her sins (*Rev.* 22:3). This concept bespeaks his redemption which in turn bespeaks his mediatorship. Yet his mediatorial sovereignty will nevertheless end by its surrender to the Father. In the words of Kuyper, Sr.: "The mediatorship of Christ is and ever will be the burden of the grand hymn of the tongues of men and the voices of angels, but even this mediatorship has for its final end the glory of the Father; and however grand the splendor of Christ's kingdom may be, he will at last surrender it to God and the Father."[1]

In a sense, therefore, the mediatorial rule of Christ will end with his second advent. Kuyper has suggested why it thus ends; namely, that the final glory may be the Father's. This is our next point.

---

[1] A. Kuyper, Sr., *Calvinism* (Grand Rapids: Eerdmans, 1943), p.119.

b. The handing over of the kingdom to the Father

By handing over the kingdom to the Father, Christ bears witness to the complete fulfilment of his mediatorial office made necessary because of sin. With all the hostile forces defeated and banished, with the salvation of his people fully won and their lasting happiness secured, no further reason for the exercise of his mediatorial office remains. But this, as we realize, is not the only reason for Christ's giving up the kingdom to the Father. For, "when all things are made subject to him, then the Son himself will also be subject to him who put all things under him, that God may be all in all" (*I Cor.* 15:28). In other words, "for of him, and through him, and to him, are all things: to whom be the glory forever" (*Rom.* 11:36). The goal of creation, as was its beginning, is the ultimate glory of God. And this will have been achieved only when at last God is all in all.

In this connection it is well for us to distinguish that which Christ, as the Father's appointed mediator, surrenders from that which remains inherently his by virtue of his place in the Godhead. To see exactly what rule it is that Christ surrenders, we must first distinguish the various spheres of the kingship he exercises.

There is, first of all, the kingship of his deity. This is everlasting, and one which he enjoys to all eternity as a person of the Trinity (*Rev.* 11:15, *II Pet.* 1:11). When his mediatorial sovereignty shall have been given over that God may be all in all, he will, in his deity, enjoy this final and supreme act of God's glorification along with the other persons of the Godhead.

In the second place, there is his kingship as head of the church. The Lamb shines forth as the glory of the sun in the eternal state (*Rev.* 21:23). The throne of God and of the Lamb are in the eternal city, new Jerusalem (*Rev.* 22:3). And it is the Lamb who is the husband of the church who sits down with her to enjoy the marriage feast of eternity's final blessedness (compare *Rev.* 21:2 with 19:7). It is also as the Lamb that Christ cares for his church for all eternity, ensuring his people's well-being and felicity in a manner comparable to the tender ministrations of a good shepherd for the sheep of his flock (compare *Rev.* 21:3-4,6, etc., with *Rev.* 7:15-17). In a word, the concept of Christ as a Lamb has redemptive significance which continues to all eternity for his church; for only by their redemption (*Rev.* 7:14) and union with him as head and husband do they have access to fellowship with God and right to final felicity.

When this is seen, it can be understood why Christ glorified the body of his humiliation by rising again from the dead in it, ascending to heaven in it, ruling in it, and dwelling with his church in it for all eternity (*Phil.* 3:21). As we have already seen, he became a son of man that his people might become sons of God. And he continues forever as the Son of Man because this, too, is a redemptive title, not only because bearing it he wrought his people's salvation, but also because in it he became the first-fruits of a harvest that would not be complete until his people, as his body, were wholly transformed into his image. And that image, though one of humanity transformed, is nevertheless human, receiving its perfection by its divine exemplar who brings all his own to share the full dimensions of its glory for endless ages.

How such concepts as Son of Man and Lamb in Christ's kingship as head of the church are to be reconciled need not concern us. The fact remains that the concept of the Son of Man expresses an actual reality in that our resurrection bodies assume the form of Christ's as the Son of Man who is the firstfruits, while the concept of the Lamb serves to express the thought of redemption. Suffice it to say that Christ's office as head and king over his people continues for all eternity.

Only the third sphere of his kingship, therefore, is remitted to the Father, i.e., the present sphere of his mediatorial dominion by which he subdues all things to himself, for it is this which the Father has given him (*Heb.* 1:13; 2:8-9; 8:1), it is this alone of the three aspects of his kingship which is temporal since it was given for Christ's mediatorial mastery of this world, and it is this, when returned to the Father, which makes the glory of God complete.

3. God is all in all

a. The eschatological goal (to make the revealed and secret will of God coincide with each other)

God's being all in all is the furthest goal of eschatology. We must cast ourselves completely on the revelation of Scripture for our understanding of this great point. Human experience can be of no help whatsoever. It is consequently hardly to be wondered at that not a few of the many modern writers are agnostic with respect to eschatology generally and the aspects of the final state specifically, having an eviscerated eschatology that is hardly adequate for this world's history, let alone illuminative of eternity. For example, Bright says, "But of that final victory which faith announces, the kingdom coming in power, we have said little. Indeed, in one sense, there is little that can be said; for it is a victory that cannot yet be seen; nor do we know when it will come, or how."[1]

Such a statement can be made only if the eschatological teaching of Scripture is ignored; for the Scripture is not silent about the when and how of the kingdom's coming, nor does it fail to reveal some of its major aspects. The kingdom will come in power when Christ returns. It will be an irruption into history that will bring this present age to a close, to be succeeded by the final state. It will bring to culmination and consequent fruition God's being all in all. But we fear that, too often, where Scripture's eschatology is unalterably supernaturalistic, it is found to be uncongenial to the rationalistic bent of the modern mind accustomed to the continuance of all things "as they were from the beginning of the creation" (II Pet. 3:4).

Neither is God's being all in all a concept compatible with that too narrowly-conceived view, also current in modern fundamentalist theology, that the ultimate goal of history is God's salvation of souls. The grand truth of Christ's redemption of his people is a cardinal doctrine whose clarity should never be obscured and whose importance should never be de-emphasized. But it is not the sole aspect of redemption, whose final end includes the cosmos, nor is it its principal goal, which is the consummate glory of God. This view is anthropocentric rather than theocentric. As Kuyper has said: "In keeping with this [the creation of heaven and earth at the beginning], the final outcome of the future, foreshadowed in the Holy Scriptures, is not the merely spiritual

[1] *The Kingdom of God*, p.272.

existence of saved souls, but the *restoration of the entire cosmos*, when God will be all in all under the renewed heaven on the renewed earth."[1]

The eschatological goal, therefore, in God's being all in all is the complete fulfilment of his will by all created things. This means that though God has already determined for his own glory whatever comes to pass, and brings it to fulfilment by the providential development of history, he himself is not the author of evil. His decrees include evil as he works all things together according to the counsels of his will. But evil acts are not the doing of his will, for evil seeks to oppose, thwart, bring to nothing that will. Evil is the sin of Satan and his invisible angelic and visible allies. It is the sin of the world under his influence and the secular history it produces until the termination of this age.

When, however, the eschatological goal shall have been completely attained, then the dualism of secular and sacred history will have been brought to an end. Presently the two exist side by side and are often interwoven, if not even at times indistinguishable. For the world may take the values of the church and simply call them its own; or the church may profane her mission by incorporating the ways of the world into her life and even giving to them a measure of legitimacy, or a combination of the sacred and secular may be interwoven together.[2] But it would be sheer hypocrisy to say that the will of God was being done when in fact it would be more accurate to regard the church as having blurred the antithesis between good and evil by losing the savour of being the salt of the society in which her Lord has placed her for that very purpose.

When, however, despite the failure of his people to bring the will of their Lord for them and society to effective expression, God in his sovereignty will bring this world's history to its destined culmination, so that when God is all in all, his will shall be done as perfectly on earth as it is in heaven. For everywhere and in everything he will have the pre-eminence. Even so, Lord,

---

[1] *Calvinism,* p.119.

[2] For a fuller development of this subject, see below under, "Transforming Society".

"Thy kingdom come, Thy will be done on earth as it is in heaven"; for then Thou shalt truly be all in all.

b. The settled, permanent state of the eternal order

"That God shall be 'all in all' does not mean that the all will be dissolved in God and lost in him, but that everything will be filled and permeated with God's sovereignty, will and salvation."[1] This is an important consideration to remember concerning the final kingdom. God's creation has always been distinct from him and will ever continue to be. To say anything else would be to open those sluice gates which would release an inevitable flood that would inexorably engulf one's *Weltanschauung* (world-and-life-view) in pantheism. The new world will be as distinct from God in eternity as the old world was in the history of time. With this concept we find the picture of the final state as presented in Revelation 21-22 in hearty agreement. The picture of its conditions is simply the portrayal of that ideal state which might already have permeated this present world had not sin brought disruption, disharmony, disunity and death. In other words, the present world sets forth the sad state of paradise lost. The final kingdom of Revelation 21-22 is an eloquent portrayal of paradise regained. "Rebellious creation [as it now is] has been inveigled into accepting the sovereignty of Satan. Consequently it forms a single body of sin, of law, and of death. The unity of the holy city may best be grasped by its contrast to the fellowship pervading the old age."[2]

As much was already taught by Christ in his setting forth of the kingdom ideal; namely, its character of absolute perfection in doing God's will (*Matt.* 6:10), and reproducing his character (*Matt.* 5:48), which bespeaks the mirroring of his fulness in a new creation that is nevertheless not to be identified with him. For his people, in doing his will perfectly, perform those self-determined acts of worship (*Rev.* 21:22), rule (*Rev.* 5:10), and

---

[1] Wendland, *The Kingdom of God and History*, p.166.

[2] Minear, *The Kingdom and the Power*, p.151.

research (*Rev.* 21:24) by which God, then dwelling among them, is further glorified (*Rev.* 22:3).

If this conception be grasped, we shall understand that the final state will not be different in kind from the church's present experience (entangling alliances with the world, the flesh, and the devil excepted), but rather that it will differ only in degree. Things now true in principle will then be realized in fact. But finitude, though the continued experience of the creature even in the final kingdom, will not be static, for the goal of Christ's people will still be the model of their Lord's infinite perfection. Hence, unity, harmony and life will not only be a blessed realization, but their fruits will exercise the maturity of increasing influence in a sinless society continuing to grow in the infinite perfection of Christlikeness. And as sun and moon will then no longer wax and wane (*Rev.* 21:23), so neither shall personal powers of experience, wisdom, comprehension, love and service by the servants of the living God rise to a meridian in the maturity of life only inevitably to decline to a nadir of nothingness at death.

Vos describes the kingdom's present perfection in principle which will attain its full realization when the supremacy of God is such that he will be all in all: "The supremacy of God in the kingdom [already] reveals itself in various ways. It comes to light in the acts by which the kingdom is established, in the moral order under which it exists, in the spiritual blessings, privileges and delights that are enjoyed in it."[1]

These aspects of the kingdom are presently true for members of the final kingdom because its power and blessing have broken into this age. But their full portion and possession are yet awaited by the people of God, for they will be theirs only when the final form of the kingdom has been established. The supreme blessedness of the eternal order will be that, since God is all in all, he will be able to give himself to his people to the full in a way which because of sin in them now, together with the curse on their present environment, he is unable to do so. Hence, "As the point of departure for Jesus' kingdom-conception lay in God, in

---

[1] *The Kingdom and the Church*, p.52.

the active exercise of God's royal sway, so its point of arrival [and consummation] lies in God, in God's gift of himself to man for everlasting possession. It is the teaching of Jesus, as well as of Paul, that from God and through God and unto God are all things."[1] As God's people have been taught to give themselves and their service wholly to him already in this life (*Matt. 6:33, Rom.* 12:1) which self-giving service remains incompletely realized because of the debility inherent in this age, so also God's giving of himself to his people for full experience and everlasting enjoyment cannot be fully realized in this age. But when the new order is established, God will be all in all, filling all things with the fulness of all his perfections, and loving and being loved with the grand ardour that this greatest of graces involves. "Behold, the tabernacle of God is with men, and he will dwell with them, and they shall be his people, and God himself will be with them and be their God" (*Rev.* 21:3).

In this connection, the observation of Kuyper, Jr. needs to be modified. He says, "The kingdom of God in its perfection shall gleam and glisten as though there had never been sin. The goal of its full sheen and lustre will have been attained, and in nothing any more will it be perceived that Satan once brought a breach into the kingdom of God. Therefore the organization [e.g., offices] of the church life, which is tied together with the fact of sin, also will be terminated, and this is true for all positions of service as well. 'No more shall every man teach his neighbour, and every man his brother saying, Know the Lord: *for they shall all know me,* from the least of them to the greatest of them' (*Jer.* 31:34)."[2] We agree that all God's people shall know fully, for then the obscurities of this age's imperfect mirror will have been taken away (*I Cor.* 13:12). But for two reasons it may be doubted whether Kuyper is correct in saying that all present offices in the church shall cease.

In the first place it may be questioned whether these offices came about, according to Kuyper, as the necessary result of sin.

[1] *Ibid.,* p.76.
[2] *Van het Koninkrijk,* pp.303-304.

After all, the cultural mandate (*Gen.* 1:28) was already a prelapsarian duty giving room for diversity of callings among men. And we have seen how Revelation 21-22 portrays the threefold office of the cultural mandate as continuing to find expression in the final kingdom, so that diversity of function will make up a part of the continuing activity of the church, just as each member now plays its part in the function of the body as a whole. This would be consonant with the infinite variety which the activities of heaven suggest when God will be all in all.

In the second place it may be wondered whether Kuyper has not perhaps unintentionally oversimplified the task of the church. It is evangelistic, to be sure. And this teaching of one by the other to know the Lord (*Jer.* 31:34) will certainly cease in the coming age, for all God's people will have been brought into a proper and saving knowledge of him. But as the work of the church for the present is also one of edification of the saints, we would suggest that such work may well continue in the final kingdom. For, as we have already seen, since the perfections of Christ are infinite, does this not suggest the possibility of continuing growth on the part of his people rather than a static condition of fixed maturity? This would also suggest that gifts of service will still have their place and function in the eternal order of paradise regained, the new heaven and earth (*Rev.* 21:24).

We have gone as far as we possibly can in searching out the reaches of the rarefied atmosphere of the eternal order when church and kingdom blend in eschatological fulfilment. Further we cannot go, for we must stop where the revelation of Scripture ends. We have doubtless merely glimpsed over the threshold into eternity and must turn away with the conviction borne home to us afresh that, "Eye has not seen, nor ear heard, nor have entered into the heart of man the things which God has prepared for those who love him" (*I Cor.* 2:9). But our interest has been aroused and our pulse quickened as we contemplate the church's glorious destiny yet enfolded within the finalities of eternity. Subjects of the king should therefore even now promote his cause! Citizens of the kingdom should be diligently engaged in the prosecution of its present task! To this we now turn our attention.

PART III

The Task of the Church in the Kingdom of God

VIII: THE CHURCH VERSUS
THE KINGDOM OF DARKNESS

Introduction

In the earlier chapters we have seen that Christ is already Lord, having been given a name which is above every name to which one day every knee in creation will bow, that the goal of history is that God's will shall be done perfectly as it is now done in heaven and that the church shall enjoy the final blessings of the eternal order.

Consequently, it behooves the church to be diligently engaged in the prosecution of her king's business during this present dispensation, for she is an instrument in the outworking of his sovereignty that will leave no sphere untouched. Granted that the ultimate goal of this world's final form depends on the sole exercise of Christ's power when he brings his mediatorial sovereignty to a close in judgment at his return; it must nevertheless be ever remembered by the church that she is, during Christ's present mediatorial rule, the locus in which the powers of his regenerative life are manifested and from which they are to radiate forth in ever-widening influence on the world. Anything less is to fall short of that influence which the symbols of salt and light (*Matt.* 5:13-16) as applied to her[1] by Christ himself are intended to illustrate.

---

[1] It is conceded that Christ's references may well have been to the kingdom of God which therefore includes in the broadest sense more than the church. But the church is, nevertheless, the locus from which the power of the kingdom of God goes forth and in this sense we make use of these references.

In this final division of the book we shall seek to trace out the task of the church in the kingdom of God in this present dispensation. For the church must affect with her influence both those people whom God has chosen to be his in Christ from the foundation of the world, and the world in general. In this way she manifests and applies her triumphant Lord's victory which will not be complete until he has subdued all things to himself (*Phil.* 3:21). Hence, to the extent that the world is christianized by the church's efforts, it exhibits to that degree at least the all-inclusive power of Christ by which his victory since Calvary is actualized, as well as forming a context for the conversion and edification of God's people by means of gospel truth. And to the extent that the world and its forces resist the church's transforming power and light, its inhabitants lay themselves open to Christ's just condemnation with its consequent final punishment. For in despising God's longsuffering goodness on which their very existence depends, and impenitently opposing his grace and its influences, they show themselves worthy recipients of that divine wrath, which, when finally poured out on them, makes Christ's sovereign rule complete.

So the church must labour to make the influence of the powers of the age to come world-wide. Not that its effects will be one hundred percent successful in conversion, but those transforming influences shall become world-wide in order that the church may be an aroma either of life to life for the elect or death to death for the reprobate (*II Cor.* 2:14-16).

The church's task in the kingdom, therefore, is never complete as long as this present dispensation endures because, on the one hand, the imperfections within and the opposition without will prevent her from attaining her goal. On the other hand, she is without the criteria to judge either the intensity of that final opposition her Lord will allow to be raised up against her or the degree of the relative goals she reaches before her task is judged by her Lord to have been completed when he comes.

With these qualifications before us, we can now proceed to trace out the development of our subject in its application to all the spheres of influence which the church must exercise in the discharge of her task in the kingdom of God.

1. The battle against invisible foes

We consider this first because the kingdom of darkness is the church's most basic enemy. "For this purpose the Son of God was manifested, that he might destroy the works of the devil" (*I John* 3:8). Since the church is Christ's primary instrument for this purpose in our present age, all the forces of hell are arrayed against her, since her defeat would mean in effect the defeat of Christ. The church must, therefore, realize what her chief opposition is in order that battle against it be properly waged.

"For we do no wrestle against flesh and blood, but against principalities, against powers, against the rulers of the darkness of this age, against spiritual hosts of wickedness in the heavenly places" (*Eph.* 6:12). In this reminder to the members of the church, the apostle Paul merely reiterates what Christ has already taught his own concerning the opposition arrayed against them under the evil machinations of the prince of this world (*Matt.* 16:18, *John* 14:30). This is not to say that the church must be unmindful of flesh and blood. She indeed knows all too well of their resistance to and opposition against the things of the Spirit (*Gal.* 5:17).[1] But the church must recognize that flesh and blood are all too often merely instruments of demonic powers in their battle against the Lord's dominion. Conquered they are because of Christ's victory over them on the cross (*John* 12:31-32). Conquered they must be by the church as long as there remains anything of the old order which can be used by them as bases of operation.

They will oppose the church by means of the world (*John* 16:33) whose shrinking dominions (*I John* 2:8) are yet under Satan's control, and the flesh which even as the Christian's cannot inherit the kingdom of God (*I Cor.* 15:50). And the devil employs every stratagem in the execution of his cunning devices. Where he cannot overthrow by frontal assault, he will seek to paralyze by deception. Where he cannot decimate by the martyrdoms of persecution, or control by active embodiment, he will attempt to neutralize by arousal within the church herself those

[1] This is more particularly dealt with under the next heading.

works of the flesh which, if not kept under faith's control by the power of the Spirit, erupt to her shame and his glee.

The church should not, therefore, be ignorant of the devil's devices, for all the above means have been used successfully by Satan in times past, are employed with varying success at present, and will become an alarming means of success in the future under the Antichrist (*II Thess.* 2:9-10, *Rev.* 13, etc.).

What is then the church's armament against this implacable foe and his forces? Viewed from the human standpoint, the situation might seem well-nigh hopeless, for how can an unseen enemy be coped with, let alone defeated? The church can, however, be of good cheer, for her Lord has already engaged the enemy and having brought him down to defeat has given his church the means by which to share in his victory. As in the day of his humiliation he overcame the devil by means of his Word's truth and the power of the Spirit (*Matt.* 4:1-11), so today he gives the same means to those he has delivered from Satan's grasp and the power of death in order for them to sustain victory. It is to this that the apostle refers when he tells the members of the church to put on the whole armour of God, which is the truth of the Word with its sanctifying effects applied through faith by the Spirit. Relying on the latter for power in prayer, intercession and the truth's dominion in personal application to self and persuasive proclamation to others, they are enabled to share in their Lord's victory.

The result of this victory is that Satan's power is broken by the release truth brings (*John* 8:32) as applied by the Spirit to its recipients, and the dispelling of error's blindness and darkness by which Satan keeps his own in subjection to himself (*II Cor.* 4:3-4). Spiritual foes can therefore be overcome by this spiritual equipage alone. And its sufficiency is such as to put the devil and his evil hosts to a total rout. "Therefore submit to God. Resist the devil and he will flee from you" (*James* 4:7). However, the adversary's power can never be underrated for two reasons: (1) The church's battle against the foe, being spiritual, must be waged in the Spirit — and what member of the church is free from lamenting the fact that he is not as spiritual as he should be, and even could be? (2) Satan and the powers of darkness have two natural allies, world and the flesh, which are effective saboteurs of the church in her battle against her invisible foes. To these two elements we must give further consideration.

2. The battle against visible embodiments of enmity against the kingdom of God

The world and the flesh as arrayed against the church may be viewed from two aspects.

a. In connection with the church

In a sense, at least, the world and the flesh should never be completely isolated from the church, even if this were possible. For, in the first place, the church is in the world, though not of the world (*John* 17:14), and its mission, if it is to be properly fulfilled, must ever be directed to the world because from it the Lord saves his people and to it the power of his grace is directed for transforming influence. In the second place, the flesh, operating in a tabernacle of clay, is the abode of believer and unbeliever alike while alive in the world. These factors, though self-evident, should nevertheless be recognized by the church, so that she may exercise proper vigilance at all times, for in dealing with these two entities she deals not with allies but with foes.

Insofar as both can be profitably employed by the Christian as he lives to the glory of God, he is to use them for, "Whether Paul or Apollos or Cephas, or the world or life or death, or things present or things to come — all are yours. And you are Christ's, and Christ is God's" (*I Cor.* 3:22-23). The Christian, as a wise steward of the manifold grace of God, makes friends for himself by means of unrighteous mammon, that when it fails, as all in this life inevitably must, they may receive him into everlasting habitations (*Luke* 16:9). And his earthly tabernacle, the flesh, is to be employed as an instrument of righteousness (*Rom.* 6:13). However, he remembers to set his affection on things above and not on the world soon to pass away; and he suffers no illusions concerning the flesh as an effective instrument to deceive him, for he remembers that, all too often, though the spirit is willing, the flesh at best is woefully weak.

b. As opposed to the church

In this respect, the world and flesh may be thought of primarily in connection with unbelievers who use both as instruments of unrighteousness against God and his church. How then is the church to face and do battle with such opposition? The church again is to remember that the weapons of her warfare are spiritual not carnal (*II Cor.* 10:4). As much as is possible for the church to do so, she should act from the highest principle of love regarding her neighbour's welfare (*Luke* 6:27-36), subordinating her own interests to those of others, even her enemies, for only in this way is she an imitator of her God who is thus disposed to act towards the sons of men in this age of grace before the coming of final judgment. The church therefore does good to her enemies and overcomes evil with good, leaving the final judgment to God to whom it alone properly belongs (*Rom.* 12:19-21), and recognizing, too, that by so doing, firstly, her erstwhile foes may yet be won to become her friends and fellow-citizens in Christ by means of the saving activity of God's grace and, secondly, by despising the goodness of God as reflected in the Christian, her foes treasure up further wrath and condemnation on themselves for the day of judgment.

However, overcoming evil with good is not to advocate pacifism, so that members of her communion as individuals cannot bear the sword or actively resist evil; because, in the first place, they are citizens of the state as well as of the church and must live in obedience to the laws and demands of the former, as long as they operate within their realm and do not encroach upon the latter (*Matt.* 22:21, *I Pet.* 2:13-20).[1] In the second place, the highest interests of love toward the foe may demand resistance to and correction of his evil insofar as possible, much as a parent would be acting only in the highest interests of love by punishing a disobedient child. Anything less would not be love at all, but sanction of, or complicity with, his evil. Even Christ rebuked the soldier who unjustly struck him (*John* 18:23). But this must be carried out by the individual members of the church in personal relationships or in spheres under the state's jurisdiction; for the church, as a spiritual organism and eschatological entity, can only exercise ministerial and declarative power. Christ's kingdom,

[1] The subject of the relation of church and state is dealt with more particularly in chapter 11.

after all, is not of this world, though it is in the world. Hence, its members do not fight the world with worldly weapons (*John* 18:36).

The church, therefore, does battle against visible embodiments of opposition against her by means of the spiritual weapons of love and truth. She does not bear the sword. That is the prerogative of the state (*Rom.* 13:4). She defends herself and conquers by spiritual power. By so doing, she recognizes that she cannot raise the spiritually dead to life by physical force or legislative injunction. Any such attempts not only prove futile, but also provoke retaliatory efforts in kind against her by the hosts of evil. Regeneration is the work of her Lord alone, which he performs in grace by means of his Spirit through the truth committed to her as she proclaims it in love.

We must remember that the devil's lie is the fundamental foe which must be overcome. For without it he would be powerless to blind the subjects of his kingdom and keep them in bondage to his will in opposition to the Lord and his church. Truth, therefore, needs the width of freedom's full room. And truth needs the undergirding drive of love's selfless zeal (*I Cor.* 13)! By these forces alone the church really conquers. So she will labour to give truth greater freedom and ever more effectual expression, knowing that by so doing she is not condoning tolerance or encouragement of error; but recogizing rather that in this manner alone are error and wickedness conquered. This will be the tolerance for which the church pleads; for this is not the tolerance of indifference to or denial of truth, but a tolerance that gives truth the full elbow-room of freedom for its effective working.

If error appears stronger today than ever before, and the world and flesh's evil are so little conquered, may it not be because the church has either forsaken her spiritual weapons or makes too little use of them? The church has the truth. But is she hiding her light under a bushel? Then let her beware, lest her Lord come and remove her lampstand from its place (*Rev.* 2:5). The church is to minister in love, working while it is day before the night comes when no man can work. But is she as cold and lifeless as a corpse (*Rev.* 3:1)? Then, may God have mercy on her, for his coming will overtake her as a thief, and can her appointed portion be otherwise than with the hypocrites (*Matt.* 24:51)?

In the final analysis, the world, the flesh and the devil are not such foes that the church's concern must be to exercise such compromise with them as will preserve her earthly life. Such preservation is properly her Lord's business, for he has promised to preserve her. May her primary concern rather be to lose her life in complete dedication to his cause. For only in so doing will she find both that the gates of hades will not overpower her and that she has gained her life eternally (*Matt.* 16:18, *Mark* 8:35).

IX: THE CHURCH AND THE INDIVIDUAL

Turning now from the foes against which the church does battle, we centre our attention upon her efforts in behalf of the society in which she finds herself in the performance of her labours. Moving in the direction from the most basic unit toward society as a whole, we begin with the church's ministry to the individual.

1. Reconciliation with God

Bright defines the church's ministry to the individual in the following way (my italics): "She is the church militant; she campaigns for the spirits of men; she captures men for the redemptive fellowship of the kingdom of Christ... There is no hope for man until he can find some citizenship higher than that which national loyalty, class interest, and political ideology can impart... *Man must find a saving community...the kingdom of God and his Christ*."[1]

Linton adds: "The church belongs to the *soteriological realm*... One may say that the church is God's institution of salvation, and one may regard the sentence of Cyprian: 'There is no salvation outside of the church' (*extra ecclesiam nulla salus*), as of primitive Christian origin — though, of course, with reservation... *Out of the association with the world and the evil powers, the Christian*

[1] *The Kingdom of God*, p.257.

is rescued into a new association, out of isolation into the community of the people of God."[1]

Linton also gives us this added thought of Charles Gore: "From the beginning of Christianity it [the church] came to men and took them up, one by one, out of their isolation and alienation from God into its holy and blessed fellowship. *It was never a creation of their own by free association.*"[2]

Finally, Kuyper, Jr., observes: "In the Jerusalem that is above and free, the spiritual temple is being built out of living stones: so you yourselves also *as living stones* are being built into a *spiritual house, a holy priesthood, in order to offer up spiritual sacrifices that are well-pleasing to God through Jesus Christ (I Pet. 2:5).*"[3]

Several observations emerge from these statements. In the first place we notice that the church is primarily a redemptive institution. As the church militant, she campaigns for the souls of men. She may, to be sure, be interested in their physical and material welfare, for she shows to others the saving mercy of her Lord which includes the well-being of the whole person. But she is not simply another of the numerous philanthropic organizations in our society whose aims, though commendable, do not approximate those of the church. The church's business is one of salvation — the reconciliation of alienated man to God and the placing of him in that redemptive community in which, under God, he may find wholeness of being and fulfil the purposes of his existence in glorifying God and enjoying him forever. To that end the church has been founded by God, not man, and for that purpose her reason for existence is justified. If this aim is obscured or lost by the church, to that degree it is no longer a church but only another human institution, though it may continue to exist and even still call itself a church.

In the second place, the church is not only a divinely-founded organization, it is also an organism — the body of Christ. This means, therefore, that the solitary are removed from isolation

---

[1] *Das Problem der Urkirche*, pp.151-152.

[2] *Ibid.*

[3] *Van het Koninkrijk*, p.242.

and alienation, and are placed in the household of God as members of a family whose ties bind its members into the closest of relationships at the head of which is God himself. As members of this family, they work together for the attainment of their common goals, complement one another in the gifts they may pool for the attainment of their ends and please one another and their Lord in the exercise of mutual love. As an organism, this family cannot be delimited into visible or invisible categories. Its great head is himself invisible, and the church of "firstborn ones" (plural, *prototokon*) has in its company the spirits of just men made perfect (*Heb.* 12:23). But this only describes the unity that exists between the visible and invisible; for it is the members of the visible community who have been brought to Mount Zion, the heavenly Jerusalem, in which their names have been recorded as citizens. It is they, though one with the invisible, who are nevertheless the visible manifestation of that organism. They are living stones built into a spiritual habitation, and the emphasis to be noted here is that of their physical "aliveness" (*I Pet.* 2:5).

The saved sinner, therefore, by his adoption into the community of God, becomes a member of the church of Christ catholic, and his labours, talents, gifts and love should be, as much as possible, for the practical good of the whole. For it is sin that alienates, separates and isolates. But where sin has been put away by the provisions of the divine head, so also should every lingering effect of it be put away by us. We must resist all that would presently mar the expression of that unity whose final goal is to be expressed by the whole body's attainment to the stature and fulness of its head. Visible disunity by the church catholic is, therefore, not only a lingering manifestation of sin and its effects, but a factor which presently nullifies much of the church's power both without and within. It entails failure and inability on the part of the members of that body to perform properly those tasks for which they were engrafted into it by the divine head himself.[1]

---

[1] For a further discussion of this subject, see further chapter 12, "Cultivating special gifts of grace."

In the third place, we can see how there is no salvation for anyone outside the church. The body severed from the head is a corpse, and any member cut off from the body is equally lifeless and useless. The church alone is the living organism of eternal life because it is joined to the head who is the fount and source of life. Life comes to individuals who are grafted into this living organism as they too partake of its derived life from the head. So the church comes to individuals with a gospel that is really good news because it brings to them the means of the conquest of sin along with its effects, and a reconciliation with God that is life-bestowing, life-transforming, life-fulfilling and life-abounding.

The church, therefore, brings to the individual the blessings of the kingdom of God which are mentioned by the apostle Paul in Romans 14:17. Received into the redemptive community's membership, he has imputed to him Christ's own righteousness (*Rom.* 5:18) which accompanies the new birth and is thereafter the pattern of his sanctification by the Spirit's operation within him. He has the inward peace of God which is the fruit of the indwelling presence of Christ's Spirit who bears witness to the spiritual primacy of the kingdom of which the world has neither experience nor knowledge. He abounds in joy which comes as a fruit of his reconciliation to God, peace with God and the certain expectation of ultimate glorification by God. There is no salvation outside the church, for it alone is the means of redemption and replacement of every loss. And not only is there no salvation in the world, but there is every conceivable loss to suffer in it and from it at the end.

Where so much benefit, therefore, is offered to and received by the believing individual, a newness of expression in his life-walk must follow. This expression cannot be restricted solely to the terrain of the redemptive community's activity. Rather, it is one which must suffuse the whole realm of the believer's life and labours. And herein is fulfilled indirectly by the church those aspects of philanthropy by which much good is wrought, but which should never be her primary concern. "The kingdom of God, after all, encompasses the whole life and covers every terrain of life in order to claim it for the honour of God. The demand of the kingdom asserts: *everything* must listen to his laws. The whole world is his dominion. Ultimately all things shall be subjected to Christ, and then the Son shall give the kingdom over to the Father. *But the task and the calling of the church does not go this far* [italics mine]. She has the Word to preach, the sacraments to administer and Christian discipline to exercise. To her are entrusted the means of grace, and she has very particularly to labour upon the terrain of grace. But then this must also first occur before the battle for the kingdom of God is begun upon the other terrains of life."[1]

In a word, the church's energies must be husbanded for those labours whose fruit is primarily redemptive. Benefits which ought to follow in other areas of society as the result of the church's saving ministry should be achieved indirectly by the activity of her members in those realms to which God has called them to labour for his glory.[2] Anything other than this for the church would make secondary things primary and dissipate her energies on minors to the detriment of her major mission — to win adherents to the realm of grace, and to strengthen, perpetuate and make fruitful this terrain in which her life and activity is chiefly to be found (*Matt.* 28:19-20).

This is not to be misconstrued so as to make the church an end in itself, as though her functions were for the sake of men alone. For the church is solely the Lord's and exists for his glory. In this sense Kuyper, Sr., is correct when he cautions, "That purpose [of the church] cannot be human or egoistic, *to prepare the believer for heaven*... Nay, upon the earth also, the church exists merely *for the sake of God*... For the glory of our God it is necessary to have regeneration followed by conversion, and to this conversion the church must contribute, by means of

[1] Kuyper, Jr., *Van het Koninkrijk*, p.271.

[2] As the church brings saving grace to the individual, so the whole realm of his life can be fruitful only as he abides in and derives benefit from that institution, for it is in this manner that he, as a branch, abides in Christ, the vine (*John* 15:5). To the point therefore, is Filson's comment: "The New Testament, like the Old, knows no purely individualistic way of life with God. It does indeed demand a personal decision and responsible living, but all that God gives and all that man should do are set in the framework of that covenant relation. Christ, the risen and exalted Christ, is the rallying centre and head of the people of God" (*Jesus Christ the Risen Lord*, p.186).

the preaching of the Word... In the second place, the church must fan this blaze, and make it brighten, by the communion of the saints and by the sacraments. Thus the purpose of the church does not lie in us, but in God, and in the glory of his name."[1]

2. Continuance in the apostolic doctrine

Since the individual's being numbered with the people of God is contingent on his acceptance of their gospel and his trust in their Lord, it is also incumbent upon him to continue in their doctrine if he is to abide in that relationship.[2] Salvation is of the Lord, and he saves by means of his church. Of that church he is the chief cornerstone, and on that cornerstone are successively built the apostles, prophets and believers as living stones (*Eph.* 2:20-22, *I Pet.* 2:5). Christ's people hear his Word, for no other foundation can any man lay. And that Word has been given by his Spirit through the medium of his apostles. Therefore, to hear them is to hear him. Their testimony, acordingly, has become the faith once for all delivered to the saints (*Jude* 3). Therefore, "Whoever goes ahead (*proagon*), and does not abide in the doctrine of Christ does not have God. He who abides in the doctrine of Christ has both the Father and the Son" (*II John* 9). Here then is the touchstone by which membership in the body of Christ may be discerned — abiding in the apostolic doctrine — for no one can learn of, let alone keep the things Christ has commanded except as his voice is heard through the apostolic Word.[3]

[1] *Calvinism*, pp.66-67.

[2] Herman Ridderbos says, "Christ will build his church. This is the unconditional promise. But he will do so through those whom he 'knows' as his (*Matt.* 7:23) in their readiness to listen to his Word, to accomplish his will and to build upon the foundation laid by the apostles" (*The Coming of the Kingdom*, pp.366-367).

[3] We here presuppose that by the apostolic Word is meant the entire corpus of Scripture, since the New Testament is the fulfilment of and commentary on the Old. It is also recognized that a proper foundation for the extent of Scripture is based on the doctrine of inspiration; but this is not here discussed because it would take us too far afield from our immediate subject. We have, however, presupposed the inspiration of the entire canon of Scripture as presently constituted. For able apologies on the inspiration of the complete canon, see E.J. Young, *Thy Word Is Truth* (London: Banner of Truth, 1963); *The Infallible Word, A Symposium by the Faculty of Westminster Seminary* (Philadelphia: Presbyterian Guardian Publishing Corporation, 1946); John Warwick

It is consequently imperative that the church proclaim no other gospel than that entrusted to her by the Lord's apostles lest she preach a different gospel, which is no gospel at all and, consequently, subject herself to the divine anathema: "But even if we, or an angel from heaven, should preach any gospel to you other than what we have preached to you, let him be accursed" (*Gal.* 1:8). In this realm, therefore, the church can brook no false tolerance as though there were latitude of gospel definition, or that truth itself is more or less relative to the existential situation which is modified in one way or another with the passage of time. The church has but one gospel and its truth is absolute. Anything else, whether more, or less, or other, is no longer either building on the cornerstone, Christ, or the foundation, his apostles; and great will be the destined ruin of such a house, for it is no longer the true and abiding temple of God through the Spirit!

And likewise it is imperative that the individual respond to and remain in the apostolic doctrine. Not every church, so called, is of the body of Christ. Not every Christian, so called, is of the number of God's people. And he who is not for Christ is against him, and he who gathers not with him scatters (*Luke* 11:23). Therefore: "Beloved, do not believe every spirit, but test the spirits, whether they are of God; because many false prophets have gone out into the world" (*I John* 4:1). Yes, Christ will build his church, and to every individual the invitation is to be given to be a part of it (*Matt.* 28:19-20); but the genuineness of his church may be discerned only in that company which abides in the apostolic truth, as is also true only of those individuals who embrace it. The church of Christ is truly catholic, but her ecumenicity can only be as broad as its acceptance of apostolic doctrine, and her visible witness and practical fruit-bearing. Where anything less is present, the true church must remain aloof and the individual beware, lest in the end the Lord's

---

Montgomery, ed., *God's Inerrant Word* (Minneapolis: Bethany Fellowship, Inc., 1973); D.A. Carson and John D. Woodbridge, eds., *Scripture and Truth* (Grand Rapids: Zondervan, 1983).

judgment be, "I never knew you; depart from me, you who practise lawlessness" (*Matt.* 7:23).

3. Discipline in the community of God's people

One point yet needs further detail, namely, the means by which the church's integrity is ensured. The church is to make disciples of the nations, but, as we have seen, she cannot assume that all within her ranks will be true disciples. Already in his day the apostle John speaks of false disciples when he says, "They went out from us, but they were not of us; for if they had been of us, they would have continued with us; but they went out that they might be made manifest, that none of them were of us" (*I John* 2:19). But what about false disciples who do not voluntarily go out? Or true disciples who may be guilty of sin concerning which the church must take action? What recourse may the church here employ?

Christ, in founding his church, gave her the keys of the kingdom (*Matt.* 16:19; 18:15-20). These keys involved the ministry of the gospel in that through its acceptance or rejection the kingdom of God is accordingly opened or closed to its hearers. This is undeniable, for we see it demonstrated by the apostolic ministry recorded in the book of Acts (cf. 2:14-42; 10:34-48; 13:46, etc.). But more than mere gospel declaration is to be associated with the concept of the keys as is made clear from Matthew 18:18. Here, the keys are connected with the ministry of discipline, as the context reveals, along with the fact that it is not something exclusive·to the apostles, as might be concluded if Matthew 16:19 were considered in isolation. Discipline is to be a continuing ministry for the church as a whole in her subsequent history (cf. 18:20).

As Ridderbos says: "To the general viewpoint of Matthew 16:18-19 is to be coupled the special [18:17-18]. They are not contradictory but complementary. For the *ecclesia* is the community of those who have been given the promise of entry into the kingdom. Expulsion from the kingdom, therefore, also implies expulsion from the church, and vice versa. In both cases, the point is that of the disciplinary, judicial authority exercised on earth and confirmed in heaven. This authority certainly cannot be detached from doctrinal authority; for in a certain sense it depends upon the latter."[1]

From this it becomes clear that the church has been entrusted with the responsibility for maintaining her integrity by the due exercise of discipline in the community of God's people. If an individual from her company acts contrary to his profession by a breach of faith with his Lord caused by one manner of sin or another, so that in effect a breach has been created in his fellowship with God's people (or vice versa, his breach in fellowship with God's people creating also a breach of faith with his Lord); he is to be dealt with in progressing degrees of severity so long as that breach remains by his failure to repent (*Matt.* 18:15-18). For the honour of Christ, the purity of his body and the warning of others is at stake, as well as, if possible, his due reclamation by repentance (*II Thess.* 3:14-15, *II Cor.* 2:5-8).

Obviously, such discipline is limited, for it can deal only with public or manifested sin. The heart cannot be judged by the officers of the church. That must be left to the Lord who, in the end, alone knows those who are truly his. But discipline cannot be minimized or disregarded by the church because of her inability to ferret out hypocrites in her ranks. Her purity may only be relative to this extent, it is true. But as we have seen, purity itself in this present age is only relative with the true people of God according to the degree of their sanctification. Yet discipline, though relative, nevertheless restrains evil, ensures integrity and promotes purity. On the one hand, it separates from the wheat those who are obviously tares, and, on the other hand, prunes the excrescence of evil from the wheat where necessary in order that greater fruitfulness may result. Discipline is therefore a tool that the Lord has given his church for her protection and well-being and it cannot be neglected by her without putting her very existence in jeopardy.

Fellowship in the community of God's people is not something, therefore, to be taken for granted either by the church or by the individual. The church must ever be aware of the melancholy

---

[1] *Coming of the Kingdom*, pp.361-362.

truth that former companies of God's people have degenerated into synagogues of Satan (*Rev.* 2:9; 3:9) and the breakdown invariably has had its beginning either at failure to abide in apostolic doctrine or laxity in the exercise of discipline. And the individual believer has the continual responsibility of self-scrutiny. "Examine yourselves as to whether you are in the faith. Prove yourselves. Do you not know yourselves, that Jesus Christ is in you? — unless indeed you are counterfeits (*adokimoi*)" (*II Cor.* 13:5)?

It is at this point — her ministry to the individual — that the crux of the church's success or failure in its ministry as a whole lies. For, although the Lord in his grace works along the lines of his covenant which embraces the families of God's people, the church nevertheless consists of self-determining *individuals* to whom the ministry of the church must come with effective impact, and from whom it must go forth in ever broadening and deepening outreaches of transforming power. But how often the church's programme is limited by the failure of her weak links! Oh for more divine grace to revitalize, empower and transform the ever-present and all-too-numerous weak links of Christ's church! The church's ministry to the individual must therefore become increasingly more effective, for herein, from the human standpoint, lies the secret of her success for the impact of her total programme in the world.

X: THE CHURCH AND THE FAMILY

1. The distinction of the family from the church

While the individual is the most basic unit of society, the family is the most basic unit of fellowship in society. When Eve was formed from Adam by God and brought to him, the initial and primary social unit was constituted. All other social groups are subsequent and derivative. Even the church traces her beginning back to the first family of the human race, and it is in the family unit that God still delights to perpetuate his covenant. He is a God to his people and their seed after them for, while he visits the iniquity of the fathers on the children unto the third and fourth generation of those who hate him, he nevertheless shows mercy to the thousandth generation[1] of those who love him and keep his commandments (*Exod.* 20:5-6). It can almost be said that the church is minimally constituted in the covenant-keeping family unit as was once true at the very beginning. This statement, of course, needs to be qualified, for the church is more than the individual family or the aggregate of individual families who may gather together for worship. For her to be properly constituted, she needs both members and office-bearers.

[1] The word "generation" does not appear in the original (*Exod.* 20:5-6), but is a valid rendering of "third and fourth" which are in the plural in Hebrew. Likewise, "generation" may be added to the plural "thousands" in verse 6 (cf. Keil and Delitzsch, *Commentary on the Pentateuch*, Grand Rapids: Eerdmans, 1951, vol. 2, pp.116-118).

From the beginning, the head of the household directed his family at the altar of worship, was responsible for the religious instruction his children received and exemplified the godliness after which the family's piety was to be modelled. Later, in Old Testament Israel, we see clearly manifested the father's representation of and accountability for his entire family by virtue of the covenant sign made by God in his flesh from the time of forefather Abraham (*Gen.* 17:10-14). A father, therefore, might be commended and rewarded for his religious zeal with respect to his family, as Abraham was (*Gen.* 18:17-19); or he might be condemned and suffer loss affecting him, his immediate family and subsequent generations, as was true in the case of Eli (*I Sam.* 2:30-36). In this we have the truth borne out that from the beginning God dealt with his people not only as a church but also according to their separate family constituencies. Israel might be a church but the family unit and its responsibilities remained inviolate.

This same relationship and distinction between church and family remains true for the present New Testament dispensation. Salvation is promised to believing heads and their families (*Acts* 16:33-34),[1] and the head of the family is consequently responsible for rearing his family in the nurture and admonition of the Lord (*Eph.* 6:4). Fathers generally, and those particularly who would aspire to the offices of the church, must rule well over their own houses, having their children in subjection (*I Tim.* 3:4, 12, *Titus* 1:6). That is to say, church officers, as fathers of the church, must first exhibit their reliability as fathers of their own families before being entrusted with similar responsibilities in the church. Where disciplinary measures or corporal punishment are necessary, it is by fatherly administration or authorization that these are to be carried out. Failure here means that the father does not love his

---

[1] It should not be overlooked that, in keeping with the household principle of salvation, it is the jailer's faith, not his family's, that is referred to in verse 34, for *pepisteukos* ("he believed") is in the singular, not plural. This truth, however, does not negate the personal responsibility of individual members of the family, when they come to years of discretion, actively to accept Christ as personal Saviour and publicly to confess this fact in the church and to the world.

children as he should, and that he does not rear them properly as he must (*Heb.* 12:6-10).

The family, while in closest association with the church, nevertheless exists distinct from the church and has responsibilities to exercise that belong solely to it as a divinely constituted unit. But though this be true, there is a necessary dependence of the family on the church; for no area of its collective life from the cradle to the grave is left unaffected by the transforming power of the church's ministry.

2. The dependence of the family on the church

The apostle Paul was conscious of the varying needs of the families in the churches to whom his epistles were directed.[1] His word to them was the Word of Christ given through his servant and it shows the church ministering to the needs of the family unit. The husband must exemplify the love of Christ for his church in his love for his wife (*Eph.* 5:25). The wife needs the exhortation to place herself under her husband's authority in the same way that the church submits herself to Christ (*Eph.* 5:24). Fathers are warned against impatience and harshness in the discharge of parental discipline. The nurture and admonition of the Lord must ever be kept in mind as a guide and goal. Children are to be shown the same manner of love and tenderness as that which the heavenly Father shows toward his own, and thus they are to be directed toward such full-orbed personal faith as would become the means of their mature and independent sanctification (*Eph.* 6:4).

There are also children who need the injunction to give obedience in the Lord to their parents, for this is his will for them (*Eph.* 6:1). In this way they will be preserved from the foolishness of youth, being taught the good and right way of loving the Lord from their tenderest years of life. And in learning submission to visible and immediate authority over them, they are moulded

[1] "In general, the family was for him, as for the entire New Testament, the most important social unit outside of the church, and it deserved honour and support from all Christians" (Filson, *Jesus Christ the Risen Lord*, p.252).

along such pathways of obedience as will later make them good citizens of larger earthly power and effective servants of higher, all-embracing heavenly sovereignty. Such was the ministry of the apostle as he took into account the entire family unit, speaking to each's need and advising according to the welfare of the individuals in relation to their function in the family unit as a whole.

In addition, the New Testament warrants the performance by the church of such service to the family as she alone may properly perform as the institution of Christ. "Marriage is honourable among all, and the bed undefiled" (*Heb.* 13:4). What more fitting way, therefore, can be found for two young people in 'pledging their troth' of lifelong love, oneness and mutual enrichment in the holy estate of matrimony than by doing so before the church who has enfolded, cherished and ministered to them from the earliest years of their infancy? It is surely fitting and appropriate that a Christian couple, before the church, anticipate together a future service in the kingdom of God which will be more fruitful than they could attain to singly. And if in due time the Lord should give them the blessing of children, with the responsibility of their physical and spiritual development, how necessary it is that they should grow up in the larger environment of the church as the wider family of God. To that wider family they belong by God's covenant of grace, and spiritual gifts are given to the church for a ministry which must include the smallest lambs as well as the maturest sheep.

This ministry of the church will begin with the covenant infant's baptism whereby the witness is given before the Lord's people that this one is his own by the grace of covenant faithfulness, and a pledge is made that the parents will fulfil their covenant obligations to God, with prayer that their child(ren) will one day be active and fruitful in the work of God's kingdom. To this end the parents will be the primary instruments, though the church will also give invaluable supplementary assistance through her service of worship and her diversified programme of religious education.

However, it should be made clear that the church is no more the *primary* agent for the religious instruction of children than is the state for their general education. This duty belongs to parents both with regard to religious and general education. For there is no disjunction in the realm of education as though it were made up of religious and secular realms. The God of heaven and earth is Lord of all, and everything he has made should be in some way revelatory of him as the people of God learn ever more effectively to discharge their threefold office as prophet, priest and king in the service of their Lord. The sphere of education is therefore a unity and the fear of the Lord is the beginning of wisdom (*Psa.* 111:10).

Parents are thus responsible for the whole of their children's educational knowledge. This is not, of course, to say that they must personally teach their children everything it is necessary for them to know. They will no doubt need help and this need becomes ever greater with the increasing complexity of modern society. But they must remember that all that their children learn should have as its unifying basis love for God and desire to become his effective servants. Anything less is to create a contradiction of values, aims and allegiances in the child's mind, the result of which may spell disaster to his faith and shipwreck of his life.

It should therefore be seriously questioned by Christian parents whether they may safely entrust their children's education into the hands of a secular state whose constitutional policy at best ignores God and at worst actively opposes him.[1] It is a marvel of ignorance, blindness, complacency, apathy, or a combination of all these, that has allowed the situation to progress so far that even so-called Christian parents have relinquished their divinely-given obligation to the state and abandoned their personal responsibility for their children's education. Efforts by Christian organizations, awakened to this perilous condition, to provide a God-centred education for children are too often given cool reception or warm opposition!

In this dire situation, the prophetic voice of the church must again sound forth. It cannot be denied that church-sponsored,

---

[1] Kuyper, Sr., even goes so far as to say, "A people therefore who abandons to state supremacy the rights of the family...is just as guilty before God as a nation which lays its hands upon the rights of the magistrates" (*Calvinism*, p.98).

or parochial, schools have in many instances been successful in providing Christian education for children. But the implementation of such schools by the church in an effort to provide at least some remedy for this need is not really the biblical way to go. For it means a transfer by the parents of the responsibility for their children's education from the state to the church. This relinquishment of responsibility by the parents does more than simply encourage the very situation which now needs remedy. For, too often, the church, by acting as a parental substitute, diverts her energies which should rather be directed toward the accomplishment of her primary goal of fulfilling the great commission (*Matt.* 28:18-20). However, the church, at the same time, should do all that she can to encourage the establishment and promotion of Christian parent-controlled schools.

The church must arouse herself to her task as watchman on the walls of Zion. The enemy has made a breach in her defences at that place where untold damage may yet further result; for where God has been shunted to one side in a realm of life (in this case, children's Christian education), then secularism, like a malignant growth, will not stop until the whole of life has been affected. The walls must be repaired, but those who alone can properly perform these repairs, the parents, must be awakened to the peril which is ready to engulf them and unborn generations of the holy seed! Is the cry of the watchman a clear clarion call, or is it at best only an uncertain sound?

The church's responsibilities to the family, however, are not yet exhausted by her children's education. There are the aged and poor who may have physical needs that only the church can supply. True, here again the church must not invade the realm which should first be discharged by the family concerned; in fact, the church's first duty is to stir up such responsibility as may be directly connected with the situation. For the injunction of Scripture is clear: "If anyone does not provide for his own, and especially for those of his household, he has denied the faith and is worse than an unbeliever" (*I Tim.* 5:8). There are, however, two factors which make the needy the church's relevant concern.

In the first place, God is a Father of the fatherless, and a defender of the widows (*Psa.* 68:5). He takes up, as we have seen, individuals here and there from the isolation of their sin and consequent miseries, and places them in the household of God. This is true of families or individuals alike, so that there can no longer be strict isolation or lonely solitude for a member of God's family. For when the Lord makes a family for his people (*Psa.* 68:6), then even abandonment by father and mother will not make such an individual bereft (*Psa.* 27:10). Obviously, since such a family relationship exists among her members, the church has a continuing responsibility for ministering to the needs of her own who may require it. Quite rightly, therefore, the church, from the earliest days of her New Testament existence, set apart those from her number who were qualified by divine endowment for this ministry of mercy (*Acts* 6:2-3, *I Tim.* 3:8-10). And if caring for the widows and fatherless is still a mark of pure and undefiled religion (*James* 1:27), then it is incumbent upon the church to continue the prosecution of this labour of love with vigour and diligence lest the apostolic warning given with particular regard to individuals (*I Tim.* 5:8) becomes applicable in the corporate sense to the church!

In the second place, the church has been given by her risen and ascended Lord a gospel of mercy. As he came preaching the gospel to the poor, healing the broken-hearted, liberating the bruised, and delivering the captives (*Luke* 4:18), so his church also is to go and do likewise. It cannot be otherwise, for how can she come to the needy sons and daughters of men mired in the miseries of sin and claim to have relief for their spiritual infirmities if she does not also show true sympathy for their physical afflictions? For what does it profit if the destitute are told to depart as though warmed and filled if nothing has been done for their bodily needs? This is nothing less than indifference and hypocrisy (*James* 2:15-17).

The church must therefore ever remember that her ministry of mercy is of primary obligation. It is striking to observe that the Lord's condemnation of the "goats" in the final judgment is on the basis of a failure to execute a ministry of mercy which he regards as indifference and disloyalty to him (*Matt.* 25:45). There-fore, rather than move in the direction of ever greater relinquishment to the state of this ministry of mercy, the modern church must bestir herself to this responsibility and return to it as one of her tasks; for it is not only a practical demonstration of the gospel to the world, but it is also, in more cases than may be immediately apparent, simply a caring for her own (*James* 2:5).

Finally, the church's ministry to the family does not end until the grave, and even here she performs a twofold ministry. This, let it be remembered, is limited to the bereaved, for the dead have passed beyond the help of the visible church. The doctrines of Rome in praying for the dead and seeking to aid in shortening the soul's stay in a non-existent purgatory are wholly erroneous (*Heb.* 9:27, *II Cor.* 5:10).

The church has, in the first place, a ministry of comfort and hope to administer to the surviving members of the family (*I Thess.* 4:18, *II Cor.* 5:8-9). Death, after all, holds no terror for the life hidden with Christ in God. For it has become for the saint a doorway separating the temporal from the eternal, and to pass through it is to enter upon the blessed realities of salvation which now are only dimly seen and partially experienced in this vale of heaviness and heartache. In this ministry the good news of the evangel should sound forth in its sweetest tones of solace to the believer, and in the clearest notes of tender appeal to the burdened and distressed soul yet wandering in the arid wastes of sin's desert. The church should be conscious of the truth that the Lord often wounds most deeply so that the healing balm of his grace, being necessary, may take full effect.

In the second place, the church should dignify the discarded garment of the flesh by tenderly committing it to the elements, designating thereby that in doing so this is not its final destiny. For he who raised up Christ from the dead will also give life once again to the mortal bodies of his people by his Spirit who indwelt them and who once made them his temple (*Rom.* 8:11). The mortal body may therefore be sown as a seed destined to experience the corruption and dishonour of its being planted in the earth but it will yet exhibit its ultimate life in the form of a glorious, incorruptible spiritual body (*I Cor.* 15:42-44). Death is not therefore the body's defeat. Its humiliation is only as temporary as a seed planted. Its glorification in due time is as certain as was Christ's, the firstfruits of the dead, by the fact of his bodily resurrection.

A funeral is not therefore the dread and dismay of the church. It is an opportunity once again to bear witness to a living faith, a continuing life and a certain hope. May the church then discourage the modern practice of disguising death as though perhaps there may yet be lingering mortal life in the "seed" after all. May she rather turn the eyes of the sorrowing from the immediate realities of the temporal to the permanent joys of the eternal. Although the final salvation is now only seen through the curtain of death by the eyes of faith, that faith enables believers to anticipate the time when the full height of eternity's goals will be achieved by every single one of God's own. Then the church's ministry to the family unit will be finished, for then the family of God as a whole will be inseparably complete and fully perfected!

XI: THE CHURCH AND THE STATE

"Without sin there would have been neither magistrate nor state order; but political life, in its entirety, would have evolved itself, after a patriarchal fashion, from the life of the family... Every state-formation, every assertion of the power of the magistrate, every mechanical means of compelling order and of guaranteeing a safe course of life is therefore always something unnatural; something against which the deeper aspirations of our nature rebel."[1]

Kuyper gives us in simplest form the reason for the state, i.e., to ensure order and to guarantee a safe course of life. In recent years our society has grown so accustomed to the increasingly paternalistic role which the state is assuming that there has arisen a tendency to ignore the warnings of divine revelation.

We should note that even the pagan political philosophy of the pre-Christian world discerned the tendency which a state always has to assume a totalitarian form. Aristotle pessimistically taught that the state inevitably degenerates from its better to its worst forms, "owing to the badness in the rulers, who do not distribute what the state has to offer according to desert, but give all or most of its benefits to themselves, and always assign the offices to the same persons, because they set supreme value upon riches".[2] Quite surprisingly, to our thinking at least, Aristotle

[1] A. Kuyper, Sr., *Calvinism*, p.80.

[2] Aristotle, *The Nicomachean Ethics* (Cambridge: Harvard University Press, 1947, The Loeb Classical Library), p.491.

did not regard democracy to be the best form of government which to him was a perversion of a republican or constitutional form of government (timocracy), itself the least desirable of the three types of government he distinguished.[1] To Aristotle, the best type of government was the monarchy because a king is able to study and effect that which is of most advantage to his subjects. But if the monarchy was the best, its perversion, the tyranny, was the worst form of government because a tyrant studies his own advantage and pursues his own good at the expense of his subjects. And interestingly enough, the Apocalypse in Scripture leaves us in no doubt as to what form the final government of society will take. It will be a world-wide tyranny under the iron-fisted rule of the Beast, or Antichrist (*Rev.* 13, 17, *II Thess.* 2).

1. The separation of the church from the state

Government is, as Kuyper correctly defines it, a later divine innovation in the social life of man because of the consequence of sin. Its formal beginning came in the postdiluvian period immediately following the flood.[2] In its most primitive form it was essentially negative in function (*Gen.* 9:5-6), ensuring the peace and order of society and guaranteeing justice by capital punishment when necessary. And, at first, it need not have been distinct from its predecessor, the patriarchal form of government,

[1] The three types were: monarchy, aristocracy, timocracy (*ibid*, p.489). Their perversions: for monarchy, tyranny; for aristocracy, oligarchy; for timocracy, democracy. Aristotle here does not tell us why he held democracy in least estimation. But it seems rather obvious from the standpoint of his political philosophy; namely, 1) a democracy cannot and does not always secure the best interests of its citizens as can be true of a monarch. We would agree only if the monarch is a theocratic king, namely, Christ himself. 2) Democracy has latent within it those forms of despotism which he expressed as the perversions of the other two forms of government. In other words, it is also possible for a democracy to degenerate into an oligarchy and ultimate tyranny — even without necessity of its first passing through the other forms of government from which these perversions usually come.

[2] Since Scripture is silent concerning any specified form which prediluvian government may have taken, we can only conclude that its form must have been simply an extension of patriarchal family rule which we have previously seen is Kuyper's presupposition also.

but may well have been enforced by the patriarchal constituency with the duties of justice devolving about the nearest of kin as the avenger of blood. However, we detect in this investiture of power, with the nearest of kin to be the avenger of blood, an unnatural social necessity inherent in government's enforcement that has been brought about as the result of sin.

But here, too, are already seen the limitations in any government formed from sinful men. In primitive times, the absence of formal civil government left sin to run its wild course, thereby making greater centralization and complexity of government necessary. For, on the one hand, would it be certain that the avenger of blood would always act according to strict justice? Apparently not, for ancient Israel had six cities to provide refuge for the man guilty of blood until his case was properly judged by the congregation which acted up to this time in the interests of family and national solidarity in accordance with the dictates and propriety of divine law (*Num.* 35).

On the other hand, would it be certain that proper justice could be executed by the avenger of blood even if he would? Supposing the murderer were too strong for him, were unapprehendable in another unit of an ever-expanding society? Obviously this primitive and limited role of government, though desirable from the standpoint of individual freedom within the family, could not continue indefinitely. Sin's power, after all, was too pervasive and increasingly extensive. Society's growth would bring with it too much complexity in enforcement of law and the safeguarding of the peace by such a decentralized government.

Without the presence of sin, the patriarchal system would have been quite adequate. With the presence of sin, however, not even the addition of capital punishment would be sufficient to guarantee its continuing proper operation. The enforcement of the divine sanction would not always be possible.

The growth of a more centralized government as an instrument of authority and power was inevitable, though its justification and structure devolved about this basically negative divine sanction, together with its necessary and proper enforcement (*Rom.* 13:1-4). The existence of such a centralized government would ensure the safety and protection of its citizens, but its price would be the curtailment of their freedom and the ever-present threat of their servitude to it. The very lives of the innocent might be endangered if this entrusted tremendous power, always liable to abuse, was put to wrong use by the ascendancy of an unscrupulous state.

Furthermore, because the state is necessarily more comprehensive than the church, since it embraces the whole of society with its social interests and its religious bias, it can hardly be expected to act for the uniform good of the church. And it must also be remembered that covenant-breakers almost always outnumber covenant-keepers in a given society and, hence, may be able to exert an influence that proves disastrous to a state-linked church.

One may therefore readily understand how the principle of jurisdictional separation between church and state takes form on the basis of these considerations: namely, 1) the primary power of the state being based on force, even to the taking of life where it is considered necessary; 2) its comprehensive jurisdiction over all society of which the church herself is but a part; and 3) the primacy of unbelievers over believers in society.

A question may be raised, however, as to the validity of this third point because it simply states rather than proves the primacy of covenant-breakers in society and the dominance of their interests in the realm of government.

Such dominance was certainly true historically when Christianity first existed in its incipient form in the New Testament era. What however might be the case with a government arising from a society where believers were predominant, or if not predominant, at least in governmental control? Could not the church then labour in closest association and union with the state, as was true for example in the ancient theocracy of Israel? To this point we will now give attention. For the reasons given below, our answer to the question will be negative, not only since the example of Israel as a theocracy no longer can be applied to the present relationship between church and state in the New Testament era but, more pointedly, because the teaching of the New Testament directs us to the separation of church and state.

In the first place, it must be remembered that regeneration and heavenly citizenship cannot be legislated. The church cannot make members or perpetuate herself by mere external compulsion or coercion. In colonial New England, when the townspeople were also members of the church, it was safe to give the townspeople the vote in matters of government and to have the church and state in closest liaison under a virtual theocratic system. But the consequence was more speedily disastrous than it was for the ancient Israelite theocracy because, though the same inherent weakness was present in the latter, i.e., numerical ascendancy and predominance of unbeliever over believer, there was still the safeguard of the theocratic king who could ensure the best interests of the theocracy by the maintenance of standards in harmony with divine law. Only after the law was later disregarded by him did it lead to the undoing of the theocracy.

But in democratic New England, there was no such mechanism as a theocratic king to maintain the decisive control of the godly minority. It was therefore only a relatively short time before unbelievers, outnumbering believers but having the same voting privilege, could take out of the hands of the godly minority not only the government of the locality but also the government of the churches as well. This was eloquently attested to in the Unitarian defection whose outcome led to the exclusion of believers from the churches erected by their fathers but wrested from their control by a legitimate majority in a "society" or "parish" no longer in sympathy with the historic orthodox Christian faith.[1]

---

[1] This history makes most instructive reading. Actually, the way for eventual control of the local government and church by unbelievers was prepared for by the church's employment of the Half-Way Covenant (*circa* 1670) whereby, "Children whose grandparents were members of the church, but whose parents were not, could be baptized, although such persons were not received into full membership. They did not have the right to communion, but males so received, when they came of age, had the right to vote in town elections" (G.G. Atkins and F.L. Fagley, *History of American Congregationalism*, Boston and Chicago: The Pilgrim Press, 1942, p.93). When the Unitarian defection occurred approximately 150 years later, "The poor communicants, the actual church members, did not own anything, in the contemplation of the law. The titles to their 'meeting houses' were vested either in the 'town' or in an ecclesiastical corporation specifically organized to maintain public worship. Such a corporation must have trustees, directors, and voting members. But the voting members need not be communicants and a church member might not be a voting member of the ecclesiastical body which, again, was the only body existing in the contemplation of the law" (*Ibid.*, pp.132-133).

The framers of the USA's constitution, in advocating the separation of church and state, may have done so with other reasons in mind than the truth that the church cannot hope to keep a democratic society in control by means of its numerical majority. For it to do so, the church would need a godly theocratic king who would ensure that the standards of government were maintained in harmony with divine law, even when the majority of the unregenerate populace might not necessarily be in favour of that law. But since a democracy is ruled by popular vote rather than a godly theocratic king, an unchristian society, either by sheer numerical force or in periods of spiritual decline, will inevitably gain the upper hand in government to the ultimate hurt of the church if thus linked to it. Hence, the church must exist in separation from the state.

In the second place, the church, in the interests of justice, should respect the rights of the unbeliever in the same way that she expects the unbeliever to show respect to her rights (*Matt.* 7:12). In so doing, the church does not sanction or give approval to the position of the unbeliever, but remembers that she cannot force conversion on anyone. That must come as the result of the Holy Spirit's enlightenment in connection with the heralded truth he sovereignly chooses to apply. The church's only proper spiritual results, therefore, are achieved, not by earthly might, nor by the human power of the flesh, but by God's Holy Spirit. Consequently, she should ever strive to create and maintain that environment which is most favourable to the gospel's reception, but she will recognize that coercion is not one of its ingredients, and so will avoid it at every turn.

The church exists within the framework of the state of which she is a part but from which, since it has ever present within it a greater or lesser unbelieving proportion, she must be separate for the sake of her continuing identity and witness. The church is, after all, a heavenly commonwealth with divine laws and a heavenly king. She cannot therefore be joined to Belial (*II Cor.* 6:15).

But though the church exists in separation from the state, the latter must nevertheless continue to exist, both for the sake of the church and society generally, over which the state presides. New Testament teaching, following that of Christ, recognizes the place of the state as a preserver of law and order in society as a whole. From this the church benefits directly and indirectly as her individual members render the state their support. Christ himself taught as much both specifically when he said, "Render unto Caesar the things which are Caesar's and unto God the things that are God's" (*Matt.* 22:21), and generally, as Cullmann has pointed out, by his attitude to the state during the time of his ministry: "On the one hand we see that he consistently did not view the state as an *eschatological* [i.e., permanent] divinely-instituted entity. On the other hand he nevertheless accepted it and radically declined every temptation to overthrow it."[1]

In other words, Jesus came to found a kingdom that was not of this world. He therefore rejected every overture to advance himself as a mere political messiah. But until such time as the dominion of this world shall become wholly his (*Rev.* 11:15), this world's government, though not necessarily Christian, has its task to perform with respect to its citizenry, a part of which consists of the church.

Christ's people are therefore to be in subjection to governmental authority, as Paul was to reiterate, recognizing that in the proper discharge of its tasks, it is a minister of God for good (*Rom.* 13:1, 4). Furthermore, they are to pray for kings and for all in authority, that they may lead a quiet and peaceable life in all godliness and honesty (*I Tim.* 2:2). But the Christian should never forget that he is primarily a citizen of the kingdom of heaven and to it he owes his first allegiance. This will mean not only his resistance to the state if it invades the spiritual realm (*Acts* 5:29), but his dispensing with dependence upon the state where its existence is not threatened by his doing so.

A good example of this principle is furnished us in I Corinthians 6 where members of the church there were admonished by the apostle not to bring lawsuits against one another to the courts of the state because, firstly, it would be a shame to the saints to seek justice from a power whose judges, since they do not keep the law of God, cannot judge righteously (*v.* 1), i.e., Christians should

---

[1] Oscar Cullmann, *Der Staat im Neuen Testament* (Tubingen: J.C.B. Mohr, 1956), p.12.

recognize that moral issues belong to the church and therefore if she cannot judge them she is denying her character as God's representative. In the second place, even though magistrates may judge some issues "righteously" on the basis of God's law which has been written on the hearts of all men (*Rom.* 2:14-15), an attitude of mind that would bring a lawsuit before pagan judges would be indicative of a culpable lack of love (*v.* 7). This does not necessarily mean that a believer should suffer loss without redress. But he should be willing in the first instance to take advantage of the means which the church offers him (*v.* 5); and above all else, exhibit an attitude of love that is not overcome by the loss of mere material gain.

From all this, we may conclude that the best government is the least government, and that the state's powers should be basically negative as it presides over society in jurisdictional separation from the church. We will return to this consideration of the extent of state power in chapter 12, "The Church and Society".

2. The rule of the state by Christ

Christ rules his church. But he also exercises universal power which comes to active expression in this world. How then does he exercise rule over the state, especially if his body, the church, is to remain separate from it? To the answer of this question we now give our attention.

a. *The state as a world-power*

The state is a world-power in that through its various forms it exercises universal control over humanity. It could be argued, as Kuyper does, that, logically, there should be only one state. He says: "The *shady side* for this multitude of states [is that] they ought not to exist; there should be only one world-empire... [for mankind is one family]. But the *light side* also, for a sinful humanity, without division of states...would be a veritable hell on earth; or...a repetition of that which...God drowned...in the deluge."[1]

[1] Kuyper, Sr., *Calvinism*, p.81.

Sinful man's bent for building his own kingdom rather than God's was already demonstrated by the antediluvians in their attempt to build the tower of Babel. In so doing they sought a sinful unity which would consolidate their collective power in opposition to God (*Gen.* 11). What once took place in antediluvian times and which called down God's judgment upon it, will yet again come about in the future under Antichrist before he and his forces are brought to nothing and the rightful sovereign of this world assumes his perfected rule.

The state, therefore, whether in its destined future unified form, or in its present collective totality, is a world-power, but not acting for the Lord. It is in the power and under the control of the hostile demonic forces who seek to enlist it — as they ever attempt to do with all else — as an instrument in their total warfare against the sovereignty of God.[1] When they succeed, as they finally will, in unifying all the separate states which now exist into one world power in opposition to the Lord, his programme and his church, the end will be near. In the meantime, however, as Kuyper has pointed out, the oppositions existing among the states cancel out in appreciable degree a unified opposition that would otherwise be against God and his cause. In this way we have at least one manifestation of the Lord's present rule over states, in restraining form at least. The nations, though not actively seeking to do the Lord's will, will not be permitted to succumb to that deception by the devil which culminates in Antichrist until so permitted by the Lord when he unbinds Satan just prior to the end of this age and his second advent (*Rev.* 20:3, 7-10).

b. *The state as subservient to Christ*

To pursue the subject from a more positive standpoint, Christ's sovereignty over the state as a world-power comes to

---

[1] "They [demonic powers] already at that time stood behind the state authorities [Herod, Pilate, etc.], who consigned Christ to the cross. They are the 'princes of this world' who in their ignorance of the 'hidden wisdom of God' crucified the 'Lord of glory' (*I Cor.* 2:7-8)." O. Cullmann, "Königsherrschaft Christi", p.25.

expression in that all forces, whether visible or invisible, have been brought under his sovereign control, though not as yet to the termination of their evil practices.

Cullmann's comment is to the point: "We are not to think that the place of Christ's present kingly rule is heaven alone or the invisible world. Christ also rules upon earth, and not simply over the church, but also over the state. To be sure, he does not rule over the states directly, but rather, through the instrumentality of 'powers and forces' that he has vanquished and that are provisionally bound."[1]

Kuyper adds: *"All authority of governments on earth originates from the sovereignty of God alone*... God only — and never any creature — is possessed of sovereign rights in the destiny of the nations, because God alone created them, maintains them by his almighty power, and rules them by his ordinances. Sin has in the realm of politics broken down the direct government of God, and therefore the exercise of authority for the purpose of government, has subsequently been invested in men, as a mechanical remedy. In whatever form this authority may reveal itself, man never possesses power over his fellow-man in any other way than by an authority which descends upon him from the majesty of God."[2]

A further comment by Cullmann is in order: "In the formulae mentioned and in other New Testament texts it is said that these powers have already been vanquished (*Col.* 1:16, 2:15, *Phil.* 2:10, *I Pet.* 3:22): in other texts, on the contrary, the conquest by Christ is still an expectation (*I Cor.* 15:25, *Heb.* 10:13)... As long as they remain in bondage to Christ, however, they stand in God's order [but when Satan is unbound at the end of the age, he will unite them to his cause in a totalitarian opposition against God]. Therefore they must finally be conquered yet again, at the end of the days although the issue has already been decided."[3]

[1] "Königsherrschaft Christi", pp.24-25.

[2] *Calvinism*, pp.82, 85.

[3] *The State in the New Testament* (New York: Charles Scribner's Sons, 1956), pp.68-69.

In these statements the nature of Christ's sovereignty over the state as a world-power becomes clear. Since all power in heaven and on earth has been committed to him, the exercise of all sovereignty by the state, whether in recognition of the fact or not, descends from him. While his control of the visible powers is not exercised directly, nevertheless it is present. Similarly, Christ continues to maintain control over the invisible powers which animate the ungodly.

In the end, the state as a world-power will be actively brought under submission to Christ, as it is included in his final conquest of the world at his triumphal return. Prior to this, it will have manifested its complete subjection to demonic power when unbound by Christ and will have become the totalitarian instrument of the lawless one, himself practically an incarnation of Satan. Human government is therefore of this world alone, continuing to exist as it fulfils the Lord's purposes for it, but destined to pass away at the time of his final triumph.

3. The relationship of church and state

We have seen that, though Christ rules over both church and state, he does so over the former directly in that his people render him willing though imperfect obedience; while he does so over the latter indirectly in that those not his people accomplish his sovereign will in spite of their rebellion. The former has been referred to as Christ's *regnum gratiae* [kingdom of grace], while the latter is his *regnum potentiae* [kingdom of power]; or as Luther put it, the former is Christ's kingdom in his right hand while the latter is the kingdom of his left hand.[1]

---

[1] Igor Kiss gives two quotations from Luther's *Hauspostille* (family sermons): "The worldly realm...is indeed also our Lord God's kingdom...and is the kingdom of the left hand, but his proper kingdom is where he rules" (in 1532). "Such preaching of the law is God's Word and such a realm of Moses is also our God's realm in the same way that the worldly realm may also be considered God's realm... But it is only the kingdom of the left hand. His proper kingdom is rather this, that the gospel is preached to the poor" (in 1544). *Lutherische Monatshefte* (Hannover: Lutherisches Verlagshaus, 1979), p.666.

The church, as a redemptive institution and the body of her Lord, is the present *eschaton*[1] of the eternal order, while the state, being part and parcel of this world, partakes also of its character and will share in that end which is reserved for all temporality, namely, to pass away. But since the church's duty is to subdue as much of the earth as possible to the active obedience of her Lord, the state is by all means included in the reaches of her mandate. What then are those duties which the church is to fulfil with respect to the state?

a. The duties of the church to the state

We have already seen in some measure what duties the individual members of the church's communion should perform in relation to the state. Citizens of the church, being members of society, are also citizens of the state. They should therefore see that the leaven of their influence comes to active expression in the determination of government by vote where it is theirs to exercise, and by holding governmental office where attainable by them, since this would be quite consonent with both Christian principle and practice. As Filson points out: "Whether Christians could take part in imperial administration was rarely a question at first for these politically unimportant people, but Erastus was the city treasurer at Corinth (*Rom.* 16:23), and it appears that soldiers could be Christians (*Acts* 10). All could and should pray for the rulers (*I Tim.* 2:1-2), and payment of taxes was a duty that Christians did not seek to evade."[2] With such responsibility already exercised by the infant church right from the start, her influence inevitably increased as her general impact on society became greater. In a word, her members were to subdue the whole of the created realm to God's glory. In so doing, they would pervade government as a sphere of the temporal order, and seek to control, direct and guide political activity, insofar as possible, to the glory of God alone.

[1] A technical term which refers to a final reality already present in this age.
[2] *Jesus Christ the Risen Lord*, p.256.

So much, then, for the duties of the church's individual members. Cullmann suggests three things that make up the church's corporate task with respect to the state: "The abiding task which is given to the church regarding the state is:

1. She must loyally give to the state whatever is necessary for its existence. She must combat every form of anarchy and all zealotism in her ranks.

2. She must fulfil the role of a watchman with respect to the state, i.e., she must remain principally critical with respect to every state and be prepared to warn it about transgression of its bounds.

3. She must deny to the state the right to transgress its bounds where such may be the case in the religious-ideological realm which delimits its legitimate sphere of operation. In her declaration of denial, the church must courageously point out that this transgression of the state is antitheistic."[1]

A few comments on these points are appropriate. In the first place, we are reminded that the church must be in subjection to the state where that subjection falls in the sphere of citizenship as marked off in the authority which God has given the state. If the state has the divine injunction to preserve the peace by the enforcement of law and order (*Rom.* 13:3), then the church, as a part of society under the state, should lead the way in exemplary obedience to its ordinances as of God (*Rom.* 13:2). "Therefore submit yourselves to every ordinance of man for the Lord's sake, whether to the king as supreme, or to governors, as to those who are sent by him for the punishment of evildoers and for the praise of those who do good. For this is the will of God, that by doing good you may put to silence the ignorance of foolish men" (*I Pet.* 2:13-15).

If the church continues to do this, she will never fall prey to the temptation to take governmental matters into her own hands (e.g., as has been historically true of the church of Rome), and so, become as guilty in taking from Caesar the things which belong to him as he would be if he invaded the church's realm to take from her the things which belong to God. For the church to

[1] *Der Staat*, p.65.

follow such a course would be as disastrous for her as it would if the state were to invade her realm; for the end result would lead only to the secularization of the church. Then the state, rather than becoming more spiritual, would only become deified in the process as it illegitimately employs the church's spiritual sanctions in the prosecution of its evil purposes.

In the second place, the church has the duty of a watchman to fulfil with respect to the state. This applies in the same way as for any other sphere of life concerning which she raises her prophetic voice. She, as the proclaimer and interpreter of God's Word, must make clear its application to the state, setting forth the scope of the state's duty to its citizens and defining the bounds of the realm in which it exercises its authority. Again, at this point the church must resist the temptations: 1) to remain silent concerning the duties of the state where God's Word clearly speaks; 2) to misinterpret the Word in its application to the state particularly and its citizens generally; 3) simplistically to affiliate the Word with the current situation in the false assumption that the status quo may automatically be that taught by the Word.

The duties of the church in being a watchman are an ever-renewed challenge to her in whatever generation she may find herself, lest the mystery of iniquity, in its ceaseless develop-ment, exceed its bounds and win by the church's default what should have been defended by her at all costs. Scripture warns that as the end of the present era approaches, apostasy with its doleful consequences will come, but woe to that generation who is guilty of it, for such sin, like all other sin, will be inexcusable.

In the third place, the church must be prepared to resist all attempts by the state to deify itself by arrogating to itself such authority and prerogatives as belong to God alone. This defection comes about usually in two stages. There is at first indifference to, if not resistance of, the prophetic voice of the church. The initial manifestation of rebellion ever takes the form of disobedience to God's revealed will as expressed in his Word. Then the next step follows in which that rebellion breaks out into the open conflict of assertion of personal independence from God and self-deification by promoting autonomy. Anything (including the church) resisting this process, when it has once been set in motion, must be opposed and overthrown since it is the conquest of God himself which is being sought.

The continuing temptation of the state is to invade the church's realm, though it does not necessarily take the form of physical persecution. The state may just as likely seek to achieve its usurping ends by other, more cunning stratagems. If, for example, the state can capture the church and make her its mouthpiece (which would be a greater coup than present efforts in democratic states to make her irrelevant), its diabolical ends may have been achieved with more devastating effect than by making a martyr of the church by means of persecution (cf. *Rev*. 6).

That both persecution and manipulation of the church will be practised by the state in its ultimate process of self-deification is made clear in the Apocalypse. True, the church will be persecuted (*Rev*. 11:7; 13:7; 17:6; etc.). But the Antichrist will also have an ideological spokesman who is referred to as the false prophet (*Rev*. 13:11-17; 19:20). He will give religious-ideological foundation to Antichrist's actions. It is tragically possible that this figure will represent some form of apostate Christianity (*II Thess*. 2:10-12).

With this fair warning in Scripture, therefore, the church must be vitally concerned. Sad will be the day when the state refuses to hear and purposely rejects her prophetic voice. But what can be said if the state takes this first step because the church herself has muffled her prophetic voice in apostasy? Will she not then be ripe for the judgment which ultimately ensues as a consequence of the state's self-deification? The false prophet and the beast will be thrown into the lake of fire (*Rev*. 19:20). If an apostate church either actively causes or passively allows herself to become so identified, her final doom will be just.

b. The duties of the state to its subjects (including the church)

We have already seen that the state exists to preserve law and order and ensure justice for the benefit of its citizens. For the fulfilment of these ends, its citizens are responsible for the active support of the state. But there is yet one point which still needs further attention, namely, to what extent the state exists for the welfare of its citizens. We have already noted that the best government is the least government, but this statement itself is relative and one which can be interpreted differently by successive generations in ever-changing times. Kuyper, Sr., has suggested the duties of the state which we set forth here and then evaluate.

1. [The magistrate's duty to God]: "God's supremacy is to be recognized by confessing his name in the constitution as the source of all political power, by maintaining the sabbath, by proclaiming days of prayer and thanksgiving, and by invoking his divine blessing. God's *Word* must rule, but in the sphere of the state only through the conscience of the persons invested with authority...statecraft flows from Christ.

2. [The magistrate's duty to the church]: It is the duty of the government to suspend its own judgment and to consider the multiform complex of all these denominations as the totality of the manifestation of the church of Christ on earth... *because the government lacks the data of judgment,* and because every magisterial judgment here *infringes upon the sovereignty of the church.*

3. [The magistrate's duty to the individual]: In the first place, it must cause this liberty of conscience [before God] to be respected by the church; and in the second place, it must give way itself to the sovereign conscience."[1]

It may be questioned if Kuyper, in presupposing the conditions of the governmental situation of his own time, has not perhaps unconsciously involved himself in inconsistencies between the first and the other two points. The church would delight to have the state acknowledge all that is specified under the first point, and in a democracy where the large percentage of the populace is at least nominally Christian, the state may be able to operate in this manner. But in a pluralistic society aspects of Kuyper's second point become questionable. If the state is "to suspend its own judgment and to consider the multiform complex of all these denominations as the totality of the manifestation of the church of Christ on earth" what is it to do about the different religions which are present when the society is pluralistic? The

[1] *Calvinism*, pp.103,104,105,108.

state obviously cannot consider different religions as "the manifestation of the church of Christ on earth." But in the interests of justice
for all, it should give these groups the right to practise their own
religion. Kuyper in effect recognizes this in his third point.

Moreover, since the state must act justly toward all its citizenry,
it cannot enforce the principles of one religion at the expense of
another. If it seeks to do so, we ask, which god's supremacy must
be recognized by the state from among those which are worshipped
by the multi-faith groups of its varied constituency? Again,
which sabbath is to be maintained? Friday (Islam's), Saturday
(Judaism's and certain sects'), Sunday? So also with prayer.
Which god should be invoked for blessing? If the state's duty is
to provide protection, security and justice for *all* its citizenry, it
must of necessity assume an official attitude of impartiality
toward the pluralistic society it governs.

At the same time, while doing so, it must, as a matter of justice
and liberty of conscience (which is the same right it gives to other
faith groups as well), permit the church to proclaim the truth of
the gospel and practise its implications for behaviour so that,
with the Holy Spirit's blessing, this brings about the conversion
of unbelievers and needed changes in the social climate of which
the church is a part.

When Kuyper avers that "God's Word must rule, but... only
through the conscience of the persons invested with authority",
we must include in this the work of God's law which is written
on the hearts of mankind (*Rom.* 2:14-15). The church's task is
to inform this "work of the law" with the revelation of God's
Word, in order that the increasing conversion and christianizing
of society may result. Moreover, the state can be unofficially
Christian (through Christian magistrates in authority) and it
should seek to govern as Christianly as it can within the framework of democracy. To be more in an official capacity would be
not only to violate the separation existing between church and
state,[1] but also to transgress the liberty of conscience which the
state should foster among its citizens.

---

[1] It is paradoxical to observe that in the United States, repeal of Puritan "blue
laws" is judged as justified since they are a remnant of the colonial theocratic

Cullmann's statement is in harmony with the position we have presented: "From the standpoint of the state, however, the prerequisite is — not that it must be unqualifiedly Christian — but, to be sure, that it know its *bounds;* and that it is able to do this we may see in the epistle to the Romans [13:1-4]. But, in the second place, it should make the effort to *understand* as much of the position of its Christian subjects as it is *able* to understand. The cross of Jesus in this connection [where state powers unknowingly crucified the Lord of glory, *I Cor.* 2:8] should be a warning-indicator to it."[1]

The above presents a rather bleak view of state paternalism, and rightly so! It is only because of a Christian veneer which centuries of the church's labour have put on the state, plus the fact that society has increasingly entrusted into the hands of the state a paternalism not authorized by God's Word, that a false picture of the state has been created. This is but a mask that it may one day tear aside, revealing underneath a naked desire to execute evil purposes which it may then be too late either to resist or overcome. Citizens who progressively relinquish liberty and personal responsibility to the government as the price of promised security are paying too dearly with divinely entrusted capital which is not theirs to barter. And if they persist

---

principle of oneness of church and state. Yet there is alarm at "this increasingly secularistic trend" when opposition is leveled on the same grounds to the teaching of religion in state-controlled schools. Opposition to the latter, however, as with the former is made by the consistent application of the constitutional principle of the separation of church and state, and its ultimate success will probably be inevitable in much the same fashion as has already been true for the abolition of most of the "blue laws". While in one sense this may be alarming (for this secularistic trend obviously goes well beyond the intention of the founding fathers who embodied the principle in the constitution), in another sense it can be welcomed. For the state at best in an increasingly pluralistic society can only hold to unitarian principles of religion acceptable to all (atheists excepted) members of its constituency which is then no better than a false religion it might otherwise impose. The moral for Christians is therefore obvious. They must not relinquish to the state such areas of their life and responsibility (for example, their children's education) that are vitally connected with their Christian faith and practice and which have originally been entrusted to them by divine grant.

[1] *Der Staat,* p.66.

in doing so, may they realize before it is too late that they are moving in the direction of Antichrist's ultimate unveiling (*Rev.* 13:16-17). We are, consequently, prompted to ask if our society which entrusts to the state responsibilities for welfare programmes, education, etc., and which, in turn, is already in bondage to multiplied forms of taxation, bureaucracy, inflationary losses, etc., has not become the seed bed from which the man of lawlessness may soon arise?

This is not to deny that the state has certain powers of regulation in the lives of its citizens. The enforcement of law and order itself will necessitate some curtailment of liberty. The cost of the state's existence will necessitate taxation. And the complexities of our modern society necessitate the imposing of certain regulations by the state with respect to morals or the standards of education; for the state's very existence may ultimately depend on the quality of its citizens' education and morals. Also, there may be no legitimate objection to the erection and support of educational institutions by the state where such education has for its subjects mature citizens who are no longer under the private jurisdiction of the home; just as in the same way the church may also be justified in the erection and support of seminaries and higher institutions of learning to ensure that an educated ministry in her realm be perpetuated.

In both these instances there is no invasion of the home as a separate institution because its educational jurisdiction is directed in Scripture to be given to minors. After maturity has been reached, the young citizen, especially if he is Christian, must take responsibility for his own decisions as he moves in the realm of the state as well as in the home and church. In any case, the principle of the purpose of his liberty must be kept uppermost because he has been freed by God so that he may completely be the Lord's servant (*John* 8:36). Therefore, to the degree that this is curtailed by the state, to that degree the discharge of his divinely-given responsibilities is hindered, and he in turn has become the slave of another. The ramifications of sin's actual or ever-threatening bondage is an always-present peril against whose encroachment constant vigilance must be exercised.

Evaluation of the state's duties to its citizens is thus exceedingly complex, and ever more so as time progresses. We have maintained 'that the less government the better' is the teaching of Scripture. But were a Reformed interpreter from the past living today, he might well view with alarm what we presently regard as the necessary functions of government which are yet in harmony with Scripture. For some of this alarm there might be little proper cause. But for much there might well be more than adequate justification.

The church is therefore faced with a prophetic task with respect to the state the sheer weight of which is well-nigh overwhelming; but if she does not arrest the darkness of mischief afoot by rekindling the light of truth, then the cause is lost and the knell of defeat is already ringing in her ears. The answer does not lie in her invasion of the political realm. That must be the duty of her individual members. Neither is the answer to be found by usurpation of prerogatives that belong to the home. The answer lies solely in the proper use of the means already at her disposal, namely, the Word and Spirit. May she pray for more of the Spirit's power! May she labour for more diligent and consistent application of the Word's truth!

Excursus: Another Look at Theonomy[1]

In 1982 I wrote an extended review of Dr Greg Bahnsen's *Theonomy in Christian Ethics* which was subsequently published in the May issue of *Vox Reformata,* the theological journal of the Reformed Theological College in Geelong, Australia. In this review I took note of Bahnsen's threefold definition of theonomy, namely, that "God's Word is authoritative over all areas of life (the premise of a Christian world-and-life-view), that within the Scripture we should presume continuity between Old and New Testament principles and regulations until God's revelation tells us otherwise (the premise of covenant theology), and that therefore the Old Testament law offers us a model for socio-political reconstruction in our day".

From the above definition there would appear to be little to fault about theonomy; in fact, shouldn't it be wholeheartedly welcomed by Reformed Christians? This is especially the case when in developing the thesis of his book Bahnsen devotes worthwhile chapters on such things as: the unjustifiable legalism of the Pharisees, the integrity of the law even though it is unable to justify and empower, messianic obedience and atonement, sanctification by the Holy Spirit, covenant unity between the Old and New Testament dispensations, etc. A closer examination of Bahnsen's position, however, especially in the area where he proposes that Old Testament law should serve as a model for

---

[1] This excursus is largely a response to and evaluation of Greg L. Bahnsen's book, *No Other Standard: Theonomy and Its Critics* (Tyler: Institute for Christian Economics, 1991). My earlier article, "Theonomy in Christian Ethics", *Vox Reformata,* May 1982, pp.11-24, was a review of Bahnsen's book, *Theonomy in Christian Ethics* (Nutley: The Craig Press, 1977). Other worthwhile evaluations of theonomy are the following: William S. Barker and W. Robert Godfrey, eds., *Theonomy: A Reformed Critique* (Grand Rapids: Academie Books, 1990); Walter J. Chantry, *God's Righteous Kingdom* (Edinburgh: The Banner of Truth Trust, 1980); T. David Gordon, "Critique of Theonomy: A Taxonomy", *The Westminster Theological Journal,* vol. 56, No.1 (Spring, 1994), pp.23-43; H. Wayne House and Thomas Ice, *Dominion Theology: Blessing or Curse* (Portland: Multnomah Press, 1988); Meredith G. Kline, "Comments on an Old-New Error", *The Westminster Theological Journal,* vol. XLI, No.1 (Fall, 1978), pp.172-189.

present socio-political reconstruction, reveals questionable factors that invite various criticisms.

Since theonomists "presume continuity between Old and New Testament principles and regulations", they maintain that the Old Testament penal sanctions are still in force. Bahnsen says that "Scripture lists the following capital offenses against God [which therefore warrant the death penalty]: murder, adultery, unchastity, sodomy, bestiality, homosexuality, rape, incest, incorrigibility in children, sabbath breaking, kidnapping, apostasy, witchcraft, sorcery, false pretension to prophecy, and blasphemy" (*Theonomy in Christian Ethics*, p.445).

In my review I sought to point out (in agreement with Meredith Kline's article, "Comments on An Old-New Error", Philadelphia: *Westminster Theological Journal*, Fall 1978, pp.172-189), that Israel as a theocracy had unique features in connection with regulations of the law, some of which as moral aspects still apply to people generally, but some of which as ceremonial laws were fulfilled in Christ's redemption and no longer apply. While Bahnsen agrees that ceremonial laws no longer apply, he rejects my next point that, since some laws were geo-political, they no longer apply, for they were bound up with Israel's dwelling in the land of Canaan. As the *Westminster Confession* puts it, "To them [Israel] also, as a body politic, He gave sundry judicial laws, which expired together with the state of that people, not obliging any other now, further than the general equity thereof may require" (XIX, 4). In other words, the *Confession*, contrary to Bahnsen, teaches that judicial as well as ceremonial laws are no longer applicable today except where they may embody moral aspects which remain abidingly valid.

1. Are Old Testament case laws to be enforced today?

The most controversial aspect of theonomy is the insistence by its exponents that the Old Testament case laws[1] with their penal

---

[1] Case laws refer to law principles which were applied in terms of very specific Old Testament cultural details (e.g., goring ox, flying axehead, rooftop railing, etc., as given for example in *Exod.* 21-22). See further, Bahnsen, *No Other Standard*, p.46.

sanctions still apply today and are to be enforced by the civil magistrate. In maintaining their continuing validity Bahnsen says that if this were not so, "One would have to conclude that the penal sanction of capital punishment for murder has also been abrogated since it is not reaffirmed [in the New Testament]" (p.461).

As a consequence, Bahnsen has maintained that there is New Testament evidence that case laws together with their penal sanctions are to be regarded as continuingly valid. In my review I sought to show that the verses Bahnsen cites as evidence (i.e., *I Cor.* 9:9, *Mark* 10:19, *Matt.* 15:4 and *Heb.* 2:2) do not support his conclusions. A brief reworked presentation of my previous comments on this so-called evidence follows, since it takes into account Bahnsen's reply in his *No Other Standard.*

In I Corinthians 9:9 Paul quotes Deuteronomy 25:4 which says, "You shall not muzzle the ox while he is threshing." But is Paul referring to this ordinance of the Mosaic economy to establish a law for oxen that applies equally in this present era? Is he not, rather, simply referring to this ordinance by way of an example that has an *a fortiori* application, i.e., if God in the old economy made provision in his law for oxen, how much more will he provide for his servants in the service of the gospel now? As a matter of fact, Paul himself tells us that this is exactly what he means, for in this same verse he goes on to say, "God is not concerned about oxen, is he?" And then he adds, "Or does he say it altogether for our sakes? For our sakes, no doubt, this is written, that he who ploughs should plough in hope, and he who threshes in hope should be partaker of his hope [i.e., a sharer of the crops]." Then his application follows in verse 11, "If we have sown spiritual things for you, is it a great thing if we reap your material things?" Paul then goes on to use another example from the Old Testament to reinforce his point. In verse 13 he points out that, since the priests of the old economy in the performance of their temple duties were entitled to eat of the food of the temple and had a share in the sacrifices of the altar, support from God's people for his ministers should still be true today. If Bahnsen agrees that the priesthood, belonging as it did to the ceremonial aspect of the old economy which has been fulfilled and superseded by Christ, therefore no longer applies today, though Paul could still use it for illustrative purposes in making his point; why should not the same be true of his reference to Deuteronomy 25:4? I Corinthians 9:9 therefore in no way supports Bahnsen's advocacy for the continuance of case law in the present era.

Bahnsen holds that in Mark 10:19 the Lord Jesus, in adding "Do not defraud" to the commandments of the Decalogue he cites to the Rich Young Ruler, was casually inserting a case law from Deuteronomy 24:14, and thereby showing that he viewed the case laws to be on a par with, if not undifferentiated from, the Decalogue. Therefore, according to Bahnsen, if the latter is still valid, why should not the former? But is Bahnsen's contention valid? Isn't the command, "Do not defraud" so closely related to the commandments of the Decalogue that it could be considered as an explication of the moral law? And if this is so, then isn't our Lord simply teaching "the general equity" of a case law where it agrees with the moral law? This aspect of the case law would indeed have abiding validity for our day. But this does not mean that its Old Testament accoutrements also apply, any more than do even the accoutrements of the ten commandments (e.g., that of the fourth commandment's seventh day observance) apply today.

In addition to the above alleged examples of case laws in the New Testament which we have seen do not support Bahnsen's contention, he gives a further two examples of penal sanctions from the Mosaic economy which he alleges prove that penal sanctions are still valid for today.

In Matthew 15:4, the Lord Jesus reproves the Pharisees for setting aside the law of God in favour of their own interpretations. In citing the fifth commandment Christ also adds the penal sanction originally found in Exodus 21:17, "He who curses father or mother, let him be put to death." Of this Bahnsen says, "It was not simply the fifth commandment that Christ cites as binding, but even the penal sanction specifying capital punishment for incorrigible children is held forth by our Lord as an obligation" (p. 256). We concede that the Lord may have regarded the penal sanction as of valid application for Israel in the old economy of which he and the Pharisees were still a part, though evidently he did not insist on it for the woman taken in adultery who was brought to him (*John* 8:11), nor as a matter of fact did Joseph when he learned that Mary was pregnant, though he was "a just man" (*Matt.* 1:19). Such examples of the possibility of relaxing case law penalties already in the old economy support our contention that these penal sanctions are not to be regarded as applicable today.

Bahnsen feels that even to suggest that a change of economies might bring with it a change in the application of penal laws would be "a trivialization of Jesus' teaching here (after all, the Pharisees were ignoring a law which within months God would have them ignore anyway) if such laws could thus be set aside after Christ's resurrection."[1]

An immediate response to this assertion would be to point out that such an assertion is hardly valid when it is remembered that, regardless of what the various aspects of the old economy

---

[1] This quotation is taken from Bahnsen's book, *No Other Standard*, p.222. In this book Bahnsen answers his literally dozens of critics in number (Kline, Chantry, the Westminster Seminary faculty, House, Ice, Harris, Lightner, Dager, Geisler, Bibza, Carl Henry, Neilands, Lewis, Schrotenboer, O. Palmer Robertson, Sider, Skillen, Spykman, Dunkerley, Robert Strong, Zorn, etc., etc.). This book is an effort both to answer and refute the positions of theonomy's critics. For Bahnsen, dialogue appears to be a virtual impossibility. He considers Kline's critical article "scandalously bad", p.8, with "defects in … logic, lack of Biblical citation to support it, and the conspicuous misrepresentations of the theonomic position [which has] thoroughly discredited his attempt at criticism" (p.116). Moreover, he professes to be hurt by Chantry's "vitriolic name-calling under the guise of Christian scholarship" (p.41). However, he gives as good as he gets. Waltke's article contains "hit-and-miss criticisms" (p.93); Muether "tries simplistically to dismiss the theonomic outlook for its alleged 'unwillingness to make important redemptive-historical distinctions'" (p.48); Gaffin, Lightner, House and Ice, Kline, make the "error" of identifying theonomy with postmillennialism; in fact, Neilson goes so far as to devote "one-fifth of his booklet…[to being] against postmillennialism" (p.52); "the muddled character of Zorn's reasoning should be apparent" (p.224), etc. On the back cover of the book Bahnsen's critics are accused of "hit-and-run attacks when they think their readers and listeners will never read Bahnsen's response. But, we are told, Bahnsen "corners them all, and one by one, [like a prize-fighter?] floors them." One has only to read this book, therefore, to understand why Bahnsen's critics are reluctant to reply to his attacks. For in his book Bahnsen makes it obvious that his critics are not the only ones who may be be guilty of acid criticism and perhaps even misrepresentation of "opponents'" positions.

were, they would have been in force right up to its end, including the Levitical priesthood, temple worship, sacrifices, the Mosaic regulations, etc. Therefore, not to expect Jesus to teach in a way in keeping with the current demands of the old economy because some aspects were to pass away after the new economy had come, would be anachronistic to say the least. In fact, in the Olivet Discourse (*Matt.* 24-25), Jesus gave a prophetical warning about persecution and his people's flight from it, and in a specific instance related to their time warned that they should pray that their flight be not on the Old Testament sabbath (*Matt.* 24:20), which, since it had been abrogated with the inauguration of the new economy (*Col.* 2:16-17), would no longer have applied to them when the destruction of the temple occurred in 70 A.D.

The fourth example which Bahnsen gives as an alleged evidence for the continuance of the Mosaic law-code for today is Hebrews 2:2-3. Bahnsen puts great reliance upon this passage as an evidence for his position. In *No Other Standard* he lists some nine references to it (p.330). He takes notice of the fact that the writer in Hebrews 2:2 uses an *a fortiori* argument in pointing out that if in the old economy "every transgression and disobedience received a just reward, how shall we [in the new economy] escape if we neglect so great a salvation" provided by Christ. Bahnsen's point in maintaining the present validity of old economy penal sanctions is, "It is *precisely because* those (lesser) civil sanctions *are* valid and just that one must see that the (greater) eternal sanction will be valid and just. The eternal is not put in place of the civil; it is argued on the basis of the civil! If the civil sanctions could be mitigated or set aside in any way, one might perhaps hope that the eternal penalty might also be avoided; if the civil sanctions were somewhat arbitrarily harsh, then perhaps the threat of eternal damnation might turn out to be likewise overstated" (p.179).

But is Bahnsen here making a proper assessment of the writer's point? Is it not simply this: if a temporal Mosaic law because God-given was certainly enforced, how much more will eschatological punishment be enforced on those who presently despise the gospel? Bahnsen maintains that in order for the latter to be true, the former must also presently apply (hence, the continuing validity for case laws). But why must this be so? Cannot what was valid in the old economy be used for illustrative purposes in the same way as the apostle Paul does in I Corinthians 9:9? Why then must this mean that, unless case law is still valid, that of which it was illustrative (the eschatological) would be bereft of force? Bahnsen makes an application here which neither logically follows nor is ethically necessary and therefore, once again, does not with this New Testament reference establish the continuing validity of case laws and their penal sanctions.

2. What does "fulfil" in Matthew 5:17-20 mean?

Even more to the point is a correct interpretation of Matthew 5:17-20. What did Jesus mean by fulfilling the law (v.17)? Bahnsen maintains that, basically, Jesus meant that he came to confirm or establish the law, hence, the continuing validity of the Mosaic law-code for this present era. Moreover, he claims that he learned this interpretation of "fulfil" (*pleroo*) from John Murray (p.318). Bahnsen devotes a number of pages in defence of his view and goes to some length in his attempts to oppose those who disagree with him about the meaning of "fulfil" (e.g., Johnson, Poythress, Banks); but the fact remains that some of those he cites who allegedly agree with his view (e.g., Murray) in reality have a different meaning for "fulfil" than he does. For example, let us see what Murray actually teaches at that place in his book (*Principles of Conduct*, p.150), to which Bahnsen refers (p.318). Murray says:

> The inclusiveness of Jesus' statement requires us to regard 'the law' as comprising more than those aspects of the law of Moses which have permanent application and sanction. Jesus is saying that he came not to abrogate any part of the Mosaic law. What we call the ritual or ceremonial comes within the scope of his declaration as well as the moral. We ask, of course, how can this be? Did Jesus not come to abrogate the ritual law of the Pentateuch? *He did come to discontinue the observance of the rites and ceremonies of the old economy.* But it is not correct to say that he came to abrogate them. The process of redemptive revelation embraces the Levitical economy of Moses and it is this process of increas-

ing and accumulating disclosure that reaches its culmination and consummation in him who is the image of the invisible God, the effulgence of his glory and the express image of his substance. Hence the Levitical economy must never be viewed in abstraction from the sum total of God's redemptive action and revelation. This is just to say that the ritual ordinances stand in the most intimate organic connection with Christ and his work. In the circumstances of Israel's history they are ectypes of an archetype; *they are adumbrations of an archetypal reality that received its historical accomplishment in the fulness of the time when God sent forth his Son.* Particularly when we think of Jesus' sacrifice of himself upon the cross, and his high-priestly entrance into the holies of the heavenly sanctuary, must we think of the Levitical sacrifice as anticipatory accomplishments of the same great redemptive facts. Jesus himself as the great high priest, *in his finished work and in his continued high-priestly activity, is the permanent and final embodiment of all the truth portrayed in the Levitical ordinances.* Strictly speaking the Levitical ritual did not serve as the pattern for the work of Christ; rather, the high-priestly work of Christ provided the archetype by which the prescriptions of the Levitical law were fashioned and patterned (cf. *Heb.* 9:24-25). *The Levitical were the ectypes and models drawn from the heavenly exemplar. It was for this reason that they possessed meaning and efficacy. And it is for this reason that Jesus could say, even with reference to the ritual ordinances, which as regards observance have been discontinued, 'I came not to abrogate but to fulfil.'*

We have quoted Murray at some length so that the places in the passage which we have italicized may be seen in their context. It should be obvious that Murray puts a different definition to *pleroo* than does Bahnsen. In fact, just because Jesus has fulfilled that in the old economy which was ectypal, far from being "established", it has now achieved its purpose and can therefore be discontinued. While it yet remains to be proved that what applies to Jesus' redemptive work also applies to the discontinuance of the case laws, especially the penal sanctions, we can see why elsewhere Murray maintains that "when there is no scriptural warrant repeated in the New Testament for certain regulations of a preceptive and punitive nature, then they do not bind us today."[1]

The Dutch ethicist, J. Douma, of the Reformed Churches (Liberated) seminary in Kampen, also gives a definition of *pleroo* that agrees with Murray and disagrees with Bahnsen.[2] Again we quote extensively in order to do justice to the context.

2.9 *Fulfilment in Christ* (1). The significance of Christ for our moral reflection is not exhausted by using the example provided by his life. We cannot employ Scripture very well in ethics unless we also know him as the *Fulfiller* of the Old Testament law and prophets. For this fulfilment brought with it a significant alteration, so that we can no longer use the Mosaic law-code, for example, as a guide in the sense outlined in 2.2. Regulations dealing with Israel's sacrificial worship no longer specify our worship. This applies even more to the Mosaic penal code which stipulates capital punishment for more than twenty crimes. Prescriptions in the area of economics (dealing with property, ceasing work during the sabbatical year and the year of jubilee and the like) are nowhere enforced today. But our use of Scripture as a guide would be quite arbitrary unless there were some basis in Scripture itself for viewing these kinds of prescriptions as no longer binding.

[1] This is found in a small monograph by Murray, *The Sabbath Institution* (London: Lord's Day Observance Society, 1953), pp.9-10, and is quoted by Bahnsen in *Theonomy*, p.458. (Murray also makes reference to this point in his *Collected Writings*, Edinburgh: Banner of Truth, vol. 1, pp.211-212). Of course Bahnsen disagrees with Murray and even charges him with inconsistency in the maintenance of this principle. It is interesting that Bahnsen in his later book makes no mention of this disagreement he has with his former teacher. Obviously it is because he now wishes to claim Murray's support for his views which, if the truth be known, Murray would not have agreed with. But to return to Murray's view, does he not state a valid point of exegesis which applies for example even to the Decalogue? Notice how the *Heidelberg Catechism* interprets the Ten Commandments (Lord's Days 34-44), especially the fourth commandment (Q. & A. 103) by which it gives the reader the continuing relevance of the moral aspect while at the same time stripping away old economy accoutrements which no longer apply.

[2] Douma's book in the Dutch language is entitled, *Het Schriftberoep in de Ethiek*, to which I no longer have access. The portions to which I refer come from a nine page document which has been translated by N.D. Kloosterman, which he has entitled, *The Use of Scripture in Ethics*, and which is for use in Mid-America Reformed Seminary, Dyer, Indiana, USA.

Christ has come not to destroy the law or the prophets, but to *fulfil* them, so completely that not one jot or tittle of the law will pass away (*Matt.* 5:17-20). But this word 'fulfil' means something a bit different than 'establish' in the sense of: whatever the law meant for Israel is what it still means for us. For *pleroo* means that this law and these prophets which *are* not full (filled-out) Jesus is going to *make* full or fill them out. And this fulfilling involves a significant alteration. *Because the law was fulfilled in Christ, the Old Testament worship, along with its multitude of prescriptions, has fallen away* [italics added]. Jesus himself relativized the regulations governing ceremonial purity (*Matt.* 15:1-11). Later Peter learned clearly that he was permitted to eat foods earlier forbidden as unclean (*Acts* 10:9-16). With regard to eating and drinking, feasts, new moon or sabbath, all of which served as shadows of the reality of Christ, Christians were supposed to enjoy more freedom than was formerly permitted the Jews (*Col.* 2:16). In connection with the fourth commandment, 'not destroying but fulfilling' means for us that we find the Israelite sabbath in the Christian Sunday.

'Fulfil' means also that Jesus brings the finishing or capstone revelation [italics added]. For example, in the Sermon on the Mount he shows how far-reaching the Old Testament commandments are. If not one jot or tittle of the law will pass away, this means that the law must be taken seriously to its very deepest parts. Jesus didn't abolish the law but made it transparent all the way to its real essence. Not murdering and not committing adultery mean more than the letter of the law indicates. Many jots and tittles of the law would pass away [in that they would be unfulfilled] if one were to violate the command 'Thou shalt not kill' by being bitter against a fellow believer and insulting him by calling him 'dummy' or 'idiot'. Similarly, many jots and tittles would pass away if one were to evaluate divorce, after the instruction of Christ, on the basis of Deuteronomy 24 and not by going back to the situation at the beginning (*Gen.* 2:24, *Matt.* 19:1-9). Similarly, one shortchanges the law in its 'fulfilment' by insisting, as the Judaizers did, on something like bloody circumcision in order to obtain forgiveness of sins (*Gal.* 5:2-6). *The spiritual reading of the Mosaic law*

often renders it impossible to hold to the letter, or merely to the letter, of the law [italics added].[1]

2:10 *Fulfilment in Christ* (2). This fulfilling has consequences not only for what we term 'ceremonial' laws *but also for the 'civil' ordinances belonging to the Mosaic legislation* [italics added]. It is not easy to answer the question as to where the boundary line between 'ceremonial' and 'civil' law lies. Are regulations pertaining to the years of sabbath and jubilee, to the quarantine of lepers, to sowing seed in a field, ceremonial or (also) civil? Identifying what is embraced by the ceremonial element in the Mosaic law-code is not possible. Nor is it necessary. [And then Douma next makes the same point that Kline in his own way makes in his essay, "An Old-New Error"]. *Through Christ's fulfilling of the law an end has come to the exclusivity of Israel as a holy nation and a holy people (Rom. 9:25-26, Gal. 3:29; 6:16, Eph. 2:11-15, Heb. 8:1-6; 11:13-16). Therefore we may say that the ceremonial and civil laws no longer possess juridical authority for us* [italics added]. Calvin (*Institutes* IV, xx, 15f.) says that the freedom is given to all nations to make laws which they deem profitable, as long as they agree with the precept of love.[2] We

---

[1] Gordon in his article (cf. footnote, p.180) points out a fourfold deficiency in Bahnsen's interpretation of *pleroo*. "First, he 'washes out' the prophetic half of the 'law and the prophets', effectively leaving only the 'law' under consideration. Second, he misunderstands the use of *pleroo* in the passage [*Matt.* 5:17-20] to mean 'ratify' rather than 'fulfil'. Third, if he proves his thesis regarding 'exhaustive detail' he proves too much, and would be required to conclude that the Jerusalem Council [*Acts* 15] and the apostle Paul should be called least in the kingdom of heaven [for changing the old economy law regarding circumcision]. Fourth, he fails to appreciate the genuinely temporal character of the parallel temporal clauses, 'until heaven and earth pass away', and 'until all things come to pass'" (pp.28-29).

[2] Calvin's actual statement is, "Therefore, as ceremonial laws could be abrogated while piety remained safe and unharmed, so too, *when these judicial laws were taken away*, the perpetual duties and precepts of love could still remain [italics added]. But if this is true, surely every nation is left free to make such laws as it sees to be profitable for itself. Yet these must be in conformity to that perpetual rule of love [cf. *Rom.*13:4 which might otherwise be interpreted to mean that law-making and law enforcement by the state is merely for the purpose of justice], so that they indeed vary in form but have the same purpose." [Calvin then adds the further significant comment which might well serve as an indictment of some present-day so-called laws]: "For I do not think that those barbarous and savage laws such as gave honour to thieves, permitted promiscuous intercourse, and others both more filthy and more absurd, are to be regarded as laws. For they are abhorrent

may prefer other laws than those in the law of Moses, says Calvin, because they correspond better to the circumstances of time, place and people. He makes the cynical remark that in such a case a nation isn't casting off the Jewish law, since it was never given them anyway (*Institutes* IV, xx, 16f.).[1]

This last observation appears already in the Old Testament. Yahweh gave His law to Israel and not to other nations (Psa. 147:19-20) [italics added]. He placed the Israelite under other commandments than the non-Israelite living among Israel. Foreigners and children of sojourners might be kept as slaves and might remain part of someone's inherited property, something impermissible for Israelite slaves (*Lev.* 25:39-43; 47-49). Interest might not be charged to poor fellow Israelites, but could be charged to foreigners (*Deut.* 23:19-20). Israelites might not eat carrion but sojourners within the gate were permitted to do that; carrion could be sold to foreigners as well (*Deut.* 14:21).

The end of the temple ministry and the decision of the ecclesiastical gathering in Jerusalem 'to lay upon you [Gentiles] no greater burden than these necessary things' (*Acts* 15:28) brought the Christian church, out of inner necessity, to the point of having to distinguish among Mosaic laws between what still needed to be observed and what no longer needed to be followed. Although in the ancient church various distinctions tended toward the triad familiar to us, it was Thomas Aquinas (*Summa Theologiae* II/I, 99.2-4) who crafted the distinction between moral, ceremonial and civil laws.

There is no objection against maintaining this distinction as long as people use it merely as a guideline and avoid the notion that these are watertight compartments [italics added]. We must remember that this distinction never functioned among

---

not only to all justice, but also to all humanity and gentleness" (*Institutes*, IV, xx, 15, pp.1503-1504).

[1] In this connection Gordon's comment is to the point: "How could the Gentiles, described by the apostle Paul as 'outside of the [Mosaic] law' (i.e., *anomos*) possibly be obliged to the law? How could it possibly be meaningful for Paul to distinguish Jews from Gentiles because 'to them belong... the covenants, the giving of the law' (*Rom.* 9:4), if the covenant and its laws oblige non-Jews equally with Jews?" ("Critique of Theonomy: A Taxonomy", p.40).

Israel and (put more strongly) never *could* have functioned. For the Israelite there was across the whole land, with its tabernacle or temple, with its administrative structures and penal codes, only one law. The 'civil' and 'moral' commandments were religious ordinances just as much as the 'ceremonial' commandments. *Israel was a theocracy, in which the 'civil' and 'religious' aspects of life were not distinguished* (pp.2-4) [italics added].

3. Theonomy's attempt to make Moses still binding after all

Douma also has comments to make about the views of Bahnsen, Rushdoony, North, etc. concerning theonomy.

2.11. *Is Moses still binding after all?* An entirely different opinion regarding the validity of the Mosaic law-code is promulgated by the school of Rousas J. Rushdoony, Greg L. Bahnsen, Gary North, and others, who are attracting to the *Christian Reconstruction* movement a significant number of Protestant Christians, especially in the United States. This school believes that the entire Mosaic law-code remains valid for us and should be reinstated in modern civil life. Idolatry, witchcraft, blasphemy, apostasy, adultery, homosexuality and rebellion against parents should be punished today with execution. What Calvin wrote about the freedom of nations to make their own laws is called by Rushdoony 'heretical nonsense'.[1]

The opinions of the school of Rushdoony and his associates serve in a postmillennial context: contemporary society is going to collapse; the human race will perceive that only the return to biblical (Mosaic) law brings rescue. After that a golden age will dawn for the whole world. The new and dominant element in this form of postmillennialism is the plea for the fully integrated reinstatement of the Mosaic law-code. The only exception is the ceremonial laws, which have obtained 'permanent validity and embodiment in Christ.'[2] *This position brings us back beyond the fulfilling of the*

---

[1] *The Institutes of Biblical Law* (Nutley, N.J.: The Craig Press, 1973), p.9.

[2] Bahnsen, *Theonomy in Christian Ethics* (Nutley, N.J.: The Craig Press, 1977), p.207.

law by Christ, and makes of Golgotha a second Sinai and of
Christ a second Moses (p.4) [italics added].

This, however, is neither scripturally valid nor, as Calvin
points out (*Institutes* IV, xx, 16, p.1505), practically feasible. By
way of summary, therefore, the major points which Douma
makes against theonomy and for which he gives abundant
scriptural evidence may be listed as follows:

1. Because the law has been fulfilled in Christ, the worship
of the old economy, together with its many and varied prescriptions, is no longer binding for Christians in this era.

2. As Christ makes clear in the Sermon on the Mount, the
spiritual significance of the Mosaic law transcends its merely
external letter and, in fact, makes it impossible to maintain that
holding to this outward aspect is a fulfilling of its minute "jots and
tittles". This is to say that the intention of Christ's teaching is to
show that fulfilment of the law's "jots and tittles" is beyond man's
ability. Like that of the law as a whole, their purpose is that of a
tutor to lead the sinner to faith in Christ for salvation (*Gal.* 3:24).

3. Since Christ's fulfilling of the law has brought an end to
Old Testament Israel's exclusivity as a holy people and nation,
ceremonial and civil laws which applied to them as a theocracy
no longer possess juridical authority for the present era.

4. The relevance of the already/not yet aspect of the present era

Bahnsen reveals another misunderstanding of a point I made in
my earlier article. There I sought to point out the present
already/not yet character of this age in contrast with the old
economy.[1] The Old Testament prophets, in viewing and delin-
eating the coming messianic age, saw it as an undivided whole,
instituting the grace of salvation but also ushering in divine
eschatological judgment. And the Lord Jesus' forerunner, John
the Baptist, true to the character of an Old Testament prophet,
likewise spoke of grace and judgment in connection with the
Messiah's ministry (cf. *Matt.* 3:1-12). Later, however, after John

[1] *Vox Reformata*, May 1982, p.23.

had been shut up in prison, he began to doubt the judgment aspect of Jesus' ministry; so much so, that he sent some of his disciples to ask of Jesus, "Are you the Coming One, or do we look for another?" (*Matt.* 11:3). In reply, Jesus pointed out the gracious aspect of his ministry (*v.* 5) and invited John to accept this and not be offended because of what he anticipated was not coming to pass according to his Old Testament-oriented expectations (*v.* 6).[1] I then wrote in my earlier article: "John needed to learn that this present age is principally one of grace, with the eschatological judgment put off until Christ comes again. In that very chapter (*Matt.* 11), Christ answers John by pointing to the grace aspects of his ministry (which were such in abundant fulfilment of that which had been announced about him by the prophets of the Old Testament so that no one had an excuse for stumbling in unbelief about him). He then goes on to speak of judgment, calling down "woes" upon Chorazin, Bethsaida and Capernaum, cities in which he had wrought miracles which left their inhabitants without excuse and under an impending judgment far worse than that for Tyre, Sidon, and Sodom (*vv.* 21-24). He likewise makes it apparent that the judgment he is speaking of refers to the time of the great eschatological assize, which will occur at the end of history (cf. *Matt.* 25:31-46), long after these currently flourishing cities will have gone the same way of the flesh as had the formerly great cities of the past he here mentions by name" (p.23).

In assessing my presentation, Bahnsen mistakenly concludes, "Zorn's discussion is completely irrelevant to the issue at hand. Theonomists do not confuse civil punishment with eschatological judgment. It is *rather* Zorn who, by this mistaken use of Matthew

---

[1] Incidentally, it is striking to note that Jesus' disciples, even after his resurrection, still entertained old economy theocratic notions as is evidenced by their question just prior to Jesus' ascension, "Lord, will you at this time restore the kingdom to Israel?" (*Acts* 1:6). And this after the forty days following Jesus' resurrection during which time he had been teaching them about "the things pertaining to the kingdom of God", i.e., the present gospel age. How persistent the mistaken thinking of the disciples was in terms of the old economy's continuance, and how often they needed repeated teaching even up to Pentecost and beyond (cf. *Acts* 10:15; 15:19-21) concerning the differences between the old economy and the new.

11, does so — trying to press a point about *eschatological* judgment from God to refute the theonomic position on *civil* punishment from the magistrates *during this age*" (*No Other Standard*, p.225). Bahnsen's point here, however, is not my point at all, for I make no mention of "civil punishment from the magistrates during this age." Of course I believe in civil punishment by magistrates. Who doesn't? But is that punishment to be the enforcement of the penal sanctions of old economy case laws? *That is the issue.* My mention of the postponement of the eschatological for this age had for its purpose the pointing out of a difference between the old economy and the new, so that what was true of the former does not necessarily apply to the latter.

Bahnsen repeatedly appeals to his critics to indicate how magistrates are to make and enforce laws if the case laws of the old economy no longer apply. Of course they do have their answers, not the least of which is Calvin's[1], but Bahnsen apparently rejects all their answers and even goes on to say, "those who have criticized theonomic ethics... have *no other standard* to offer which can deal with the problems theonomy addresses... If we are not supposed to be governed by God's law, then what *other standard* do the critics seriously set forth? I cannot see that they have offered any credible, biblical alternative whatsoever" (*No Other Standard*, p.270).

5. Divine law in relation to the present era

I am under no illusions whatever that the reply I now seek to give to the above challenge will be satisfactory to the exponents

---

[1] Cf. W. Robert Godfrey's fine chapter (13), "Calvin and Theonomy", in the Westminster Seminary Faculty Symposium, *Theonomy: A Reformed Critique*, William S. Barker & W. Robert Godfrey, eds. (Grand Rapids: Academie Books, 1990). Cf. also my review of this book which appeared in the 1991 issue of *Vox Reformata*, pp.66-69. It is rather striking that Bahnsen has little, if anything, to say about Godfrey's chapter or Calvin's view. In a footnote (24) on p.10 he does, however, claim Calvin, the *Westminster Confession* and the New England Puritans for theonomy, apparently also ignoring two other chapters in the above volume, i.e., Sinclair B. Ferguson's, "An Assembly of Theonomists? The Teaching of the Westminster Divines on the Law of God", and Samuel T. Logan Jr.'s, "New England Puritans and the State", which also effectively counter his claims.

of theonomy. But the following comments are offered in the interests of biblical truth, and will hopefully be in line with Calvin's insights about the relevance of natural law for the civil magistrate in this present era (cf. Kline's advocacy of common grace as the realm in which the civil magistrate operates). By natural law we of course do not mean an autonomous type of law that mankind may to some degree have in common. Rather, we refer to the law of God as it has been written on the hearts of men and which, though obscured by man's sinful depravity, nevertheless remains "the work of the law" (*Rom.* 2:14-15). Of this Calvin remarks in his commentary on Romans:

> We cannot conclude from this passage that there is in men a *full* knowledge of the law, but only that there are some seeds of justice implanted in their nature. This is evidenced by such facts as these, that all the Gentiles alike institute religious rites [even if to idols], make laws to punish adultery, theft, and murder, and commend good faith in commercial transactions and contracts. In this way they prove their knowledge that God is to be worshipped, that adultery, theft, and murder, are evils, and that honesty is to be esteemed.[1]

Calvin admits that men, because of their depravity, do not live up to even that light which the law written in their hearts gives them. In fact, in the state of sin they busily seek to obscure the law in their rebellion against God. But because of God's common grace they do not completely succeed in doing this and this light that remains in them, and to which their consciences testify, makes them responsible to God. Our interest at this point, however, is to notice that Calvin appeals to common grace, by which we mean non-redemptive grace, as the basis for the universal validity of the moral aspect of the law. He says:

> The law of God which we call the moral law [Calvin accepted the threefold division of the law in moral, ceremonial, and judicial categories, though he considered the moral alone as abidingly valid] is nothing else than a testimony of natural law and of that conscience which God has engraved upon

[1] *Calvin's New Testament Commentaries, The Epistles of Paul to the Romans and Thessalonians*, eds., D.W. and T.F. Torrance (Grand Rapids: Eerdmans, 1976), p.48.

the minds of men. Consequently, the entire scheme of this equity of which we are now speaking has been prescribed in it. *Hence, this equity alone must be the goal and rule and limit of all laws* [italics added]. [Then Calvin goes on to add] Whatever laws shall be framed to that rule, directed to that goal, bound by that limit, there is no reason why we should disapprove of them, howsoever they may differ from the Jewish law, or among themselves (*Institutes* IV, xx, 16, p.1504).

Calvin is able to have this regard for natural law because of the threefold use of the law (which is not to be confused with the threefold division of the law). He discusses the former in detail in the *Institutes* II, vii, 1ff. Berkhof defines the threefold use as follows: 1) the *usus politicus* or *civilis*, which refers to the law as an external rule to restrain sin and promote civil obedience, i.e., it is the basis of civil law; 2) the *usus elenchticus* or *pedagogicus*, which refers to the law as that which brings man under the conviction of sin as he becomes increasingly aware of his inability to fulfil its righteous demands. When this takes place the law becomes a tutor to lead the convicted sinner to Christ as the remedy for his need of forgiveness of sin and reconciliation to God; and 3) the *usus didacticus* or *normativus*, which is also referred to as the *tertius usus legis* (or the third use of the law), as a rule of life for believers in gratitude to God for their salvation by grace through union with Christ.[1]

While the second use of the law in large measure presupposes the added light of special revelation, i.e., Scripture (otherwise, how could it be a tutor to lead the convicted sinner *to Christ?*), the third use is wholly dependent on the light of Scripture and only applies to the redeemed community of God's people. Unredeemed sinners neither love God's law nor do they live thankful lives in gratitude to God for the experience of his great salvation in Christ.

The first use, however, would at least in some measure by reason of God's common grace be universally present with fallen

[1] Louis Berkhof, *Systematic Theology* (Edinburgh: The Banner of Truth Trust, 1974 reprint), pp.614-615.

mankind. And it is to this that both Luther and Calvin appeal for the legitimate law-making ability of the civil magistrate according to Romans 13:4 even if it is not God-honouring. Moreover, whether the civil magistrate recognizes it or not, he is still "God's minister", for his office as state governor has been instituted by God. It is, according to Luther in connection with his "two-kingdom-teaching" (*Zweireichelehre*), the kingdom of Christ's left hand.[1]

While in its practical outworking, Luther's teaching seems to have encouraged the development of secular autonomy, with the state increasingly being permitted to go its own way (a case in point would have been Hitler's Nazi state); Calvin had a more biblically balanced view of the relationship between church and state, which Kuyper developed. The church is not just the kingdom of Christ's right hand (the *regnum gratiae* or reign of grace); it also exists within the society governed by the state (the *regnum potentiae* or reign of power). Where possible it is to influence society and the state with a Christian interpretation and application of the law.

In their pagan condition civil magistrates will hardly do an adequate job in promoting justice and providing security for all citizens. While natural law might well go a long way in enabling the state to perform its duties properly according to the divine mandate (whether that is recognized or not), man's fallen condition is constantly present to complicate and corrupt the processes of law-making and law enforcement. For a proper application of the first use of the law would ensure that the rights of all be protected and that retributive justice be enforced where crime has been committed. And where the equity of justice is consistently enforced (the *lex talionis*, i.e., an eye for an eye, etc.), the taking of life, even unborn life, would merit the guilty party's life being forfeited (*Gen.* 9:6). The corruption of man, however, is such that the rights, influence, wealth, etc., of one party is maintained at the expense of the other, with the consequence that injustice rather than justice is done. Examples of injustice

[1] Cf. Chapter 11, p.170, footnote, for quotations from Luther.

can be multiplied. Bahnsen mentions many, e.g., *No Other Standard*, p.186.

But the state's answer to "the Satanic human sacrifices of Santeria,[1] the absurdity of allowing a Hitlerian view of the state, the absurdity of protecting deviant life-styles of abortionists and homosexuals (in the name of privacy-rights)" is not to be the enforcement of the penal sanctions of the Mosaic law-code unless they express the justice of moral law already embodied in natural law. Exponents of Santeria have no more right to take the life of anyone than others have to take their life, even if they do advocate homicide in the name of their religion. As for the so-called rights of homosexuals, does the apostle Paul not say that even natural law condemns their practices, so that they are unjustifiable (*Rom.* 1:26-27)?

The problems of lawlessness in our society today stem not so much from the lack of the enforcement of the penal sanctions of the Mosaic law-code as from the state's lack of a recognition and consistent enforcement of the equities of justice. Here is where God's people, individually and collectively, must fulfil their prophetic role of being a proper leavening influence in society. They have the light of Scripture which informs them of the proper way by which the law is to be applied. With this light, they are by example, vote and office-holding to exert the influence of their proper application of the law. They agree with Calvin:

> For, together with one voice, they [different nations in different times] pronounce punishment against those crimes which God's eternal law has condemned, namely, murder, theft, adultery, and false witness. But they do not agree on the manner of punishment. Nor is this either necessary or expedient. There are countries which, unless they deal cruelly with murderers by way of horrible examples, must immediately perish from slaughters and robberies. There are ages that demand increasingly harsh penalties. If any disturbance occurs in a commonwealth, the evils that usually arise from it must be corrected by new ordinances.

[1] A cult in the United States.

In time of war, in the clatter of arms, all humaneness would disappear unless some uncommon fear of punishment were introduced. In drought, in pestilence, unless greater severity is used, everything will go to ruin. There are nations inclined to a particular vice, unless it be most sharply repressed. How malicious and hateful toward public welfare would a man be who is offended by such diversity, which is perfectly adapted to maintain the observance of *God's law* (*Institutes* IV, xx, 16, p.1505) [italics added].

In this connection Christians might do well to promote the reinstitution of capital punishment for incorrigible offenders, together with making more use of the biblical principle of restitution rather than the alternative of incarceration which, with its overcrowded prisons and failed programmes of rehabilitation, restore the criminal to society where he repeats his crimes against the innocent.

The same principle of natural law should apply even in matters of religion. Theonomists may rail against a position that suggests that the state cannot be trusted to enforce the first table of the Decalogue. For example, Bahnsen not only defends the state's right to execute blasphemers, he considers it an obligation.[1] But Bahnsen's optimistic postmillennial presuppositions govern his position here, namely, states will increasingly become Christian, with the law thereby also being applied in an increasingly theocratic way. Scripture, however, paints a different picture of increasing lawlessness and godlessness for this age, especially as Christ's return draws near.

Scripture describes the end-time state in terms of the supreme dictator who embodies it. He is "the beast" (*Rev.* 13), "the Man of Lawlessness" and "the Antichrist" (*II Thess.* 2). Will such a state correctly enforce the first table of the Decalogue even if it had the competence to do so?

Even before the events of history have advanced to this stage, would it be wise even at the present time to give a state such power? Even in a democracy where majority vote rules, are the laws of the true God honoured? Is it not possible that, before too

[1] Cf. *No Other Standard*, pp.136, 171, 182, 184, 229, 233, 263.

long — with the way events are presently developing — Christians might well be executed for "blasphemy" against a false god, as they are in some Islamic countries today?

A more scriptural position for the state in keeping with the divinely-given mandate as well as with Scripture's eschatology is to let the state see to it that all religions within its boundaries be given the freedom of justice for all, and since God's people know that truth is stronger than error, let the truth of Christianity be permitted freedom of promulgation by the church in the market place of competition for people's minds and hearts. For God's people know first hand the power of the gospel to bring about change in people's hearts and then in the practices of society. This in effect would bring into play the second and third uses of the law, not as something enforced by the state (for the state can just as easily enforce false religion), but as a factor achieved by the leaven of righteousness where the gospel is increasingly believed and its truth is ever more consistently put into practice. This is both the teaching of Scripture and the testimony of history.

XII: THE CHURCH AND SOCIETY

"Beloved, while I was very diligent to write to you concerning our common salvation, I found it necessary to write to you exhorting you to contend earnestly for the faith which was once for all delivered to the saints" (*Jude* 3). By such an exhortation the Word of God would remind the church of one of her primary duties regarding the society in which she finds herself and to whom she is a debtor in the discharge of the ministry of truth (*Rom.* 1:14).

1.   Preserving and propagating redemptive truth

As the church contends for the faith once for all committed to her, she recognizes the twofold task which is hers in this respect. In the first place she is charged with the duty of preserving its truth. In the second place, her contending for that faith will not only be a defensive means of its preservation, but will also be an offensive weapon of its propagation for the benefit of humanity. These are the Lord's purposes for it.

In a way, as some have suggested, the church in the world may be compared with Noah's ark in the flood. For Noah's ark was not only God's means for preserving humanity amid destruction. It was also the means of humanity's later perpetuation as God chose to continue it from the righteous remnant it preserved. So it is also the case with the church, for, as custodian of the truth, she has become the means of humanity's salvation, preservation and fulfilment. But this is so only as long as she clings to the truth and continues to be buoyed up by its power over error. To forsake the truth would be to sink into error which would soon engulf her.

a. *Preserving redemptive truth*

The apostle Paul reminds the church in I Timothy 3:15 that she is the pillar and ground of the truth. To be sure, she is this in her living collective universality, but as Hort points out: "St. Paul's idea is that each living society of Christian men is a pillar and stay of 'the truth' as an object of belief and a guide of life for mankind, each such Christian society bearing its part in sustaining and supporting the one truth common to all."[1] And herein the church's duty in preserving the truth, with its consequent beneficence to mankind, becomes clear. She is to sustain and support the one truth common to her collectively.

This truth, of course, can be nothing other than apostolic truth. Only by means of it is she constituted and identified as the church of Christ, and only as she retains possession of it will she support the truth. But if she is to make it a proper object of belief and a guide of life for mankind, she will have the continuing task of seeking to appropriate the broad reaches of its power, striving to bring to light the hidden depths of its inexhaustible meaning and unfolding the breadth and scope of its application ever more consistently to every area of life's experience. The church does not need more truth, or a different truth. She needs only to understand better and more properly to apply the truth which has been committed to her and of which she is the pillar and stay. For, the church catholic must embody, exemplify and radiate that truth to that part of mankind in which she finds herself.

Furthermore, because the church has become the repository of truth, she only can be the proper interpreter of reality. Reality is reflected in all aspects of God's creation, but without the spectacles of Scripture (to use Calvin's term), reality's true meaning is not discerned. We see this, for example, in the way unbelieving science interprets the facts of the universe, not as a reflection of

---

[1] *The Christian Ecclesia*, p.174.

God's handiwork (*Psa.* 19:1) but in an evolutionistic way that makes mere chance supreme.

The church therefore must endeavour to relate the truth to all reality in such a way that it should be increasingly obvious for all to see that there are no brute facts. All facts, rather, point to their maker and have been created to bring praise and glory to him. As the church increasingly applies the truth to all reality, she also exercises an effective means in preserving truth, not only because truth, like the God from whom it comes, demands all existence for its *Lebensraum* (living-area), but because truth's goal is to overcome error completely in order that it alone may be supreme.

Hence, "The task of giving a Christian interpretation to the present is a special instance of the Christian task of sanctifying the world in the sphere of knowledge. The world must not be allowed to fall prey to false prophecies or to world views which turn on investing some particular sphere of reality with absolute value. It is for us rather to understand each historical present as it comes in the light of what is at the centre of history, Jesus Christ and the salvation he accomplished once for all; we do not interpret revelation by means of historical existence but *historical existence by means of revelation.*"[1] In other words, the truth's best defence is to use it offensively, the goal of which is to bring the knowledge and interpretation of all reality into harmony with its light. Only in this manner can truth be properly preserved and successfully applied, for truth in the redemptive realm demands consistency with it in all the created realm to which it points and from which it adds to the number of its adherents and servants.

b. *Propagating redemptive truth*

This brings us to consider the propagation of redemptive truth, though, as we have just noted, an adequate preservation of the truth will go hand in hand with an active propagation of it. As Christ's last command to his church was that she go forth to make disciples of the nations, so also he gave into her hands

[1] Wendland, *The Kingdom of God and History*, p.191.

the truth by which she could accomplish this mandate, for his church was to teach whatever he had commanded. The apostle Paul, in I Timothy 2:1-4, re-emphasizes Christ's mandate when he teaches the new *ecclesiae* of God that he whom they worship is emphatically the Saviour God who wills that people of all nations, tribes and tongues should be saved and come to the knowledge of the truth.

Aspects of this task which Christ gave his church have become increasingly varied, if not complex, as man's cultural development has grown throughout the Christian era. We shall touch on those aspects in the remaining headings of this section. The church must not forget, indeed she must always keep uppermost in her thinking and activity the fact that she is an evangelist of the gospel whose implications embrace the entire truth of the kingdom of heaven. Ridderbos points this out when he tells us: "Christ's command to preach the gospel to all nations is an organic and natural conclusion to his preaching of the kingdom of heaven. This latter, as a redemptive-historical entity, encompasses the entire administration of fulfilment which involves Jesus' redemptive ministry and all that follows in the history and activity of the world as a consequence. Hence, the church's preaching of this whole gospel is one of the most essential duties that she has to fulfil in the world at this time."[1]

As the church preaches the gospel, she disseminates the truth which not only makes the people of God wise to salvation but also equips them for good works (*II Tim.* 3:15-17). While this is the church's direct activity with respect to the truth committed to her, indirectly she must also seek to subdue, recreate and sustain an environment in harmony with truth's interpretation of it. For in such an environment the truth will be given its most favourable acceptance and application.

2. Nurturing the diversity of gifts

God alone is the giver of every good and perfect gift of which mankind has become the recipient (*James* 1:17). This is true

---

[1] Cf. *The Coming of the Kingdom*, pp.381-382.

alike of church and society. That the church has been made the object of divine favour and munificence, none may question. Her members have been translated from the kingdom of darkness into the kingdom of light by the action of God's grace alone (*Col*. 1:12-14). Her members have been given various gifts and talents according to the grace of God (*Rom*. 12:6-8), for the well-being and edification of the body as a whole (*Eph*. 4:8-16). On the whole structure of this spiritual edifice the grace of God attesting to its master-builder is written large (*Eph*. 2:10, *Heb*. 3:6).

But does God bestow grace on the world at large and even in some measure on the reprobate?[1] This has been questioned and even denied by some whose theological position is governed more by logical and possibly philosophical conclusions than by Scripture. It is true that a clear antithesis between good and bad, righteous and unrighteous, saved and lost, God and the devil must ever be maintained. Moreover, the distinction between the saints and the reprobate is clear and has come about as a result of God's discriminating action by the bestowal of his saving grace upon the former alone. But, while this is Scripture's clear teaching, this does not deny the fact that God also bestows grace on the non-elect.[2]

Clearly, common grace is not to be confused with saving grace. For, while its bestowal by God leaves the reprobate without

[1] John Murray defines common grace as: "every favour of whatever kind or degree, falling short of salvation, which this undeserving and sin-cursed world enjoys at the hand of God", *Collected Writings*, vol. 2 (Edinburgh: Banner of Truth Trust, 1977), p.96.

[2] In 1924, the synod of the Christian Reformed Church officially answered the Revs. Herman Hoeksema and Henry Danhof who vigorously denied the existence of any form of common grace. Synod said: "1) There is, besides the saving grace of God, shown only to those chosen to eternal life, also a certain favour or grace of God which he shows to his creatures in general; 2) this grace includes a restraint of sin in the life of the individual and in society; and 3) this grace enables the unregenerate, though incapable of any saving good, to perform civic good" (my paraphrasing, taken from Cornelius Van Til's *Common Grace* (Philadelphia: The Presbyterian and Reformed Publishing Company, 1954), pp.19-22, where he also gives the full text, including Scripture and confessional references. The Protestant Reformed Church in the United States, originally a group that broke from the Christian Reformed Church in 1924 under the leadership of Hoeksema, continues to deny that common grace is the teaching of Scripture.

excuse for his hard and impenitent heart (*Rom.* 2:5), it never-theless creates the context in which God bestows his saving grace on his elect. Genesis 9:8-17 makes this obvious, for it is an unconditional covenant which God made with the world, and which included man indiscriminately and even the animals.

As a background grace, God accomplishes with it: "the restraint of the operation of sin in man, partly by breaking its power, partly by taming his evil spirit, and partly by domesticat-ing his nation or his family."[1]

This is a necessary function of common grace, for if God did not restrain the workings of man's depravity, it would long ago have led to the total reprobation of the human race, as almost became the case in the antediluvian period. But further, if God by his common grace did not restrain man's depravity, its force would accomplish the complete destruction of man's life, even before birth.

In this connection, therefore, God's fixing of man's average life span at seventy years (*Psa.* 90:10), must be viewed as an action of his common grace by which he says to sin in man's constitution, "Thus far you may go, but no further!" By common grace, there-fore, God creates an environment in which his special grace can come to fruition in the objects of his redeeming love.

Yet by means of common grace, God accomplishes even more. As Van Til puts it: "God's rain and sunshine comes, we know, to his creatures made in his image. It comes upon a sinful human race that they might be saved. It comes to the believers as mercies from a Father's hand. *It comes upon the non-believer that he might crucify to himself the Son of God afresh*"[my italics].[2]

The contents of Van Til's first three sentences are indisputable. In the gifts of common grace God's goodness to man is revealed in the same way that God's grace as embodied in the gospel is revealed to all in its universal proclamation, though not all men are saved. But then, in the sentence italicized, Van Til makes a further poignant observation by linking Hebrews 6:6 (the ultimate

[1] Kuyper, *Calvinism*, p.124.
[2] *Common Grace*, p.95.

renunciation of God's grace by the sinner under the gospel), with his misuse of the gifts of God's common grace and the consequences to which this leads. Just as the rejection of the gospel by the lost is without excuse and becomes to them an aroma of death to death (though even in this God is glorified), so also by the perversion of the gifts of God's common grace they heap on themselves God's just judgment and indignation.

Gifts of common grace, therefore, have their definite place in this world and are to be taken into account by the church, not only as she herself partakes of them "as mercies from a Father's hand", but as they are to be found in society as a whole. But what ministry has the church to perform in the light of these gifts which her Lord bestows on mankind?

a. Gifts of common grace

The church must first of all remember that the cultural mandate of Genesis 1:28 was given to mankind as a whole. Mankind generally, as well as the church specifically, is responsible to God for the way in which this is fulfilled. Men must, therefore, be reminded of their duty and warned of their culpability in the light of their stewardship before God. As their life, their time, their possessions, their talents and their abilities are gifts from God's liberal bounty shown to them, so they should be employed in the service of God, and when they are not, man is left without excuse (*Rom.* 1:19-20) and ripe for judgment and consequent punishment (*Matt.* 25:26-30).

It must be made clear to all that, just as they are responsible for the way in which they hear the gospel, so they are accountable for the way in which they employ the gifts of God's common grace. Just as God's Word never goes forth to return again void of that purpose for which it was sent (*Isa.* 55:11), so neither is God's grace ever bestowed in vain but will also accomplish its purposes of blessing or judgment. God's common grace, like his special grace, leaves the mass of men without excuse in the duty they are to perform for him. Falling short in that duty, as Van Til puts it, they crucify to themselves the Son of God afresh.

In the second place the church must remember that, since all grace from God is good, it is not only to be accounted for, but from it enrichment is also to be received. Gifts of common grace, being an earlier bestowal than special grace, as seen in Genesis 4:20-22, bear testimony to a higher reality that should have been man's to enjoy than that which is now experienced because of nature's corruption by sin. To the unbeliever, they bear testimony to what might have been in the fullest sense life's ennoblement, nature's enrichment and creation's enjoyment, had fellowship with the author of these gifts been maintained or were he still to be sought by them. And it will be a heightened agony of the reprobate in final perdition to have partaken of them in this world, to have participated in their fuller development and expression (though more or less perverted by sinful depravity), to be totally and eternally deprived, not only of God, but also of them.

To the church, however, the gifts of common grace bring comfort and hope: comfort in that they react against the end which the curse's corruption seeks to establish, as though it alone were the final and inexorable conclusion of all creation; hope in that what they already disclose in this life of the higher and ultimate reality can be looked forward to with eagerness and desired to the full with a longing whose intensity deepens as that ultimate reality moves ever closer to her. It is, as Kuyper, Sr., says: "The world of sounds, the world of forms, the world of tints, and the world of poetic ideas, can have no other source than God; and it is our privilege as bearers of his image, to have a perception of this beautiful world, artistically to produce and humanly to enjoy it."[1] And we might add, to be prepared by it for eternal reality.

The church, however, must observe a caution concerning this eternal prospect. She must always remember the distinction that

[1] *Calvinism*, pp.156-157. Kuyper admits his indebtedness to Calvin, of whom with respect to art he says the following: "Calvin esteemed art, in all its ramifications, as a gift of God, or, more especially, as a gift of the Holy Ghost; that he fully grasped the profound effect worked by art upon the life of the emotions; that he appreciated the end for which art had been given, viz., that by it we might glorify God, and ennoble human life, and drink at the fountain of higher pleasures, yes even of common sport; and finally, that so far from considering art as a mere imitation of nature, he attributed to it the noble vocation of disclosing to man a higher reality than was offered to us by this sinful and corrupted world." *Ibid.*, p.153.

exists between the creator and his creation. The latter may point to a larger reality to which the church looks forward and of which she already partly partakes, but none of this is either to be confused or identified with God, lest, in so doing, the second commandment be violated. For this reason religion most pure, and worship most spiritual eschews such outward ornamentation as might fallaciously become associated, if not identified, with the creator. God is a Spirit and those who worship him must do so in spirit and in truth (*John* 4:24). Hence, "It is pure spiritual religion which with one hand deprives the artist of his specifically religious art, but which, with the other, offers him, in exchange, a whole world to be religiously animated."[1]

Gifts of common grace, therefore, as with gifts of special grace, can, positively speaking, only fulfil their proper purposes with the church; for she alone can fully discern their significance, appreciate their value and contribute to their understanding and development. But negatively speaking, they also fulfil their purpose with the reprobate, in whose hands they are exploited as their distorted views, wrong values and misdirected goals see fit.

It is a sad truth but undeniable fact that in too many instances the field of common grace's development has by the default of believers fallen to unbelievers. It is not the church's business, collectively speaking, to invade the realms of science, art, commerce, etc., and thereby both to dissipate those energies which she should preserve for her high calling in gospel employ (*Luke* 9:60), and to subject herself to the dangers of idolatry. But her members, considered as individuals, are as fully charged with the fulfilment of the cultural mandate as anyone else. It is rather sad, therefore, to see worldlings now, like the Cainites long ago (*Gen.* 4:20-22), making the most significant advances in the realms of common grace in spite of the error of their aims and intentions. May it not be due to the fact that members of the holy circle have to their shame not yet grasped the truth of their Lord's statement that, "The children of this world are in their generation wiser than the children of light"? (*Luke* 16:8).

---

[1] *Calvinism*, p.159 (taken from Von Hartmann).

b. *Maximizing the gifts of common grace*

The church in her individual members must address herself to the task of maximizing the gifts of common grace as far as possible, in order to serve the kingdom of God and fulfil every purpose of God for her. In so doing, the church will, firstly, manifest the kingdom of God on earth. For, "Whenever one of these spheres [science, art, commerce, industry] comes under the controlling influence of the principle of the divine supremacy and glory, and this outwardly reveals itself, there we can truly say that the kingdom of God has become manifest."[1] This is simply to say that the church, besides being a manifestation of the kingdom herself, is also to manifest it in every part of the society in which she moves. Hence the truth of Vos's comment: "While it is proper to separate between the visible church and such things as the Christian state, Christian art, Christian science, etc., these things, if they truly belong to the kingdom of God, grow up out of the regenerated life of the invisible church."[2]

However, instead of suggesting with Vos that these things proceed from the church's, corporate capacity, we would prefer to say that they proceed from the church through her individual members. Perhaps Vos uses "invisible" in this indefinite sense, for it is hard to imagine how the invisible church might otherwise make her impact felt. The Holy Spirit within her fulfils his variegated activity by embodiment in her visible members.

Secondly, by maximizing the gifts of common grace, the church through her individual members will already be bringing to fruition that task which it will be her occupation to discharge for all eternity, namely, to bring all into the sphere of her sovereign Lord's dominion, not only that she may declare his glory, but that his will may be done perfectly. "There must be a *Science* which will not rest until it has thought out the entire cosmos; a *Religion* which cannot sit still until she has permeated every sphere of human life; and so also there must be an *Art* which,

[1] Vos, *The Kingdom and the Church*, pp.87-88.
[2] *Ibid.*, p.89.

despising no single department of life adopts into her splendid world, the whole of human life..."[1]

c. Cultivating special gifts of grace

Where the church has a task to perform in society with respect to the gifts of common grace, she must also remember that she has a duty to perform with respect to herself in the cultivation of those special gifts of grace which have been given her by her ascended Lord. For those gifts are for the perfecting of the saints and building up of the body of Christ until it reaches the stature of his fulness (*Eph.* 4:11-13). This brings us to the consideration of the present state of the visible church with all its division, disunity and disarray. Can the church, in these circumstances, truly cultivate her special gifts of grace, or is she not bound to be hampered by such undeniable disorganization and disorder?

Proponents of the modern ecumenical movement would answer this question in the affirmative and advocate the speedy organic union of the visible body of Christ sundered in "sinful disunity", and thereby supposedly make true the prayer of Christ for his church as found in John 17:11, "That they may be one as we are". However, several things must first be considered in this connection before we may reach a final decision in this matter.

In the first place, it is not diversity that hinders the proper operation of the church organism but division. After all, life flows out from Christ through his body to all her members. Therefore, the unity of the body of Christ is threatened not by diversity, but by division. That is to say, from the very nature of the church's description as a body, we would properly infer that there is diversity in the function among the differing members. The eye differs from the ear and the hand from the foot, but they all derive their life from the one body to which their respective functions contribute. But if division through amputation takes place, their effectiveness is destroyed. In the same way, the varied communions of the body of Christ, like her individual members, have

---

[1] Kuyper, Sr., *Calvinism*, p.163.

diversified gifts in the discharge of the church's task in reaching all classes of men in the society to which she is to go. And just as the foot might fail and the hand succeed, so also one communion or denomination might fail where another might succeed in the same given situation.

This does not justify the different existing denominations in the Christian body, for division as it exists today in our imperfect world is the result of sin. Here, however, we simply note the fact that, despite the presence of divisions, the Lord does use the differing denominations to accomplish his sovereign purpose in the spread of the gospel for the gathering and perfecting of his people.

Therefore, as we recognize that the body needs many members to perform its task properly, we must not stereotype the sovereign operations of the Spirit, or the particular gifts he bestows, into a unitary form or particular mould or arbitrary conception of what we might regard as the unity of the body — as long as the life of Christ is manifested. Diversity, therefore, is not division, as long as those members abide in their head and bring forth fruits to the good of the body as a whole.

In the second place, we must remember that true organic unity in the body of Christ is itself a concept which is contingent on the purity and persuasion of those making up that union. If the schism of heresy or the sin of unfaithfulness to the head is not properly dealt with by means of the disciplinary measures committed to that body, then a de facto division exists even though visible unity may still be present. The clear duty of the church in this instance would be to create visible disunity by cutting off the gangrenous infection rather than overlook its harmfulness to the whole organism, or even seek further forms of union by ingrafting bodies as foreign to her as the present malignant part.

This leads us to the third consideration which is that of asking whether the organic union of the body of Christ is in every case a desirable or even correct thing? We have seen how the above two factors already lend weight to a negative conclusion to this question. To this must also be added the consideration of creedal differences whose resolve for the sake of organic union could come only at the expense of spirituality or the convictions of conscience.

As Kuyper puts it: "Do I mean that all believing Protestants should subscribe, the sooner the better, to the Reformed symbols, and thus all ecclesiastical multiformity be swallowed up in the unity of the Reformed church organization? I am far from cherishing so crude, so ignorant, so unhistorical a desire... The Calvinistic confession is so deeply religious, so highly spiritual that, excepting always periods of profound religious commotion, it will never be realized by the large masses, but will impress with a sense of its inevitability only a relatively small circle. Furthermore, our inborn one-sidedness will always necessarily lead to the manifestation of the church of Christ in many forms."[1] Kuyper has here given objections to organic union that are based on a realistic appraisal of the de facto situation in the church. However, should it not be argued against Kuyper that, in principle, the church should be as highly spiritual and as deeply religious as the best of her creeds? And as for one-sidedness, the church's aim must ever be to grow into the fulness of Christ. But in defence of Kuyper, it may seriously be questioned whether the consistent application of principle here would not evince a serious miscalculation of human nature's basic depravity, as well as be a virtual denial of the necessity for the Spirit (not human organization) to lead the church to the proper expression of her unity consistent with her creedal statements of scriptural truth. If this be the case, it should also be recognized that organic union at the expense of scriptural truth would merely result in hurt to the purity of the visible church and the power of her witness, if it would not also impede the proper use of the diversity of her gifts for the benefit of the body of Christ as a whole.

This is not to advocate the pluriform concept of the church as over against her uniformity. The church of Christ is one. And in many places of her communion such breaches exist as to seriously impair the strength of her witness to the world and the power of her inner growth to the measure of her Lord's

[1] Kuyper, Sr., *Calvinism*, pp.191-192.

stature. To the repair of such breaches she should address herself posthaste, lest she degenerate into a landmark of sin's ruin, rather than grow into a fruit of divine grace.

Yet the church militant is not the church triumphant. The latter will be complete, one, total. She will also possess the perfection of eternity. However, though the church militant is technically not of this world, she shares in its imperfections insofar as her present state is imperfect. This does not excuse her sins and failings. Rather, it should spur her on to realize, as much as possible, that which is already true of her in principle. But her principle of unity can never be used to obscure those other principles of equal importance; namely, the maintenance of her purity in a world that constantly seeks to corrupt her, and the putting to full use of her power for propagation and sanctification expressed through her many diverse gifts.

The uniformity of the church visible is therefore at best only relative within the concept of pluriformity as long as she exists in this age and partakes of its imperfections. But her goal should be the realization of the former as principle, as over against the latter as fact. In keeping with this, she should also remember to contend for soundness rather than size, transformation rather than conformity and gifted diversity without needless division.

To conclude with the words of Kuyper speaking of the visible church that is most consistent with these principles: "Albeit the church reformed in bone and marrow may be small and few in numbers, as churches they will always prove indispensable for Calvinism; and here also the smallness of the seed need not disturb us, if only that seed be sound and whole, instinct with generative and irrepressible life."[1]

3. Transforming society

In the nineteenth century, the influential German theologian, Albrecht Ritschl, popularized the concept that the kingdom of God was simply a realm of social ethics. Linton tells us that: "For Ritschl, the kingdom of God was little more than an ethical

---

[1] *Ibid.*, p.195.

kingdom of personalities... The church on the other hand was a religious community. Hence, the kingdom of God was to be thought of as the broader concept of the total moral-spiritual values; the church on the other hand is the narrower concept of religious expression."[1] One wonders, however, how Ritschl could come to such a conclusion from the New Testament data. For as Filson has pointed out: "...the New Testament disappoints those who are looking for a vital social message. It did not anticipate a steady development which will gradually realize a perfect human society... Moreover, the New Testament has no detailed plan for social reform or revolution."[2]

This is quite a disenchantment from the position Ritschl popularized and which became identified with older theological liberalism. What then does the New Testament say about social transformation? "It all centred in and derived from the gospel message and the life of faith. The basic need of all men was spiritual; therefore they needed first of all to hear the gospel and believe. Conversion and spiritual renewal were the hope of the world and of society as well as of individuals."[3] Wendland adds: "Actually, Jesus spoke nowhere of the regeneration of the life of the common people, or of human society, or of the state powers of this aeon."[4]

The hope of this age as well as for the institutions which are to be found in it lies not so much in their reformation as in their regeneration or transformation by the new life of the age to come. Christ, and the New Testament after him, did not major on minors or seek to patch up the old garment by tearing a piece from the new (*Luke* 5:36). What this old world needs, he taught, is the wine of the new age, contained in the new wineskins of the final order. Improvement of the present social orders, therefore, is only relative, depending on how much of the new

---

[1] *Das Problem*, pp.120-121.

[2] *Jesus Christ the Risen Lord*, p.249.

[3] *Ibid.*, p.250.

[4] Quoted by Braun, *Neues Licht*, p.102 (footnote).

life transfuses them through the individual transformed lives which constitute them.

The church's task with respect to society, therefore, must principally be that of its spiritual renewal through repentance and the obedience of faith. It is only as God's sovereignty is acknowledged and his grace and mercy received in Christ Jesus that problems arising in society from its soul-sickness caused by sin and separation from God will find resolve. "On the one hand, his [Jesus'] doctrine of the kingdom was founded on such a profound and broad conviction of the absolute supremacy of God in all things, that he could not but look upon every normal and legitimate province of human life as intended to form part of God's kingdom. On the other hand, it was not his intention that this result should be reached by making human life in all its spheres subject to the visible church."[1]

As the church puts into action this programme with basically spiritual emphasis, changes in the temporal realm which are not under the church's jurisdiction will nevertheless occur, as Vos suggests. Some specific forms this process of christianization takes are suggested by Filson: "Just as there was no political revolt, but rather prayer for all in authority (*I Tim.* 2:1-12), so also there was no antislavery agitation (*Col.* 3:22-25). Nor was there a compulsory share-the-wealth programme; even in Jerusalem, in the early days of the church, the sharing was voluntary (*Acts* 5:4). There was no class war; men of every kind and class lived together in the church (*Gal.* 3:28, *Col.* 3:11). The church had no programme of political action to alter the form of society... In essence the programme of the church disregarded the social divisions of society; it made the church a home for all classes; its democratic basis was a common repentance, a common faith, a common worship and fellowship, and mutual love."[2]

The church as the society of God filled with his life, subject to his sovereignty and obedient to his gospel, will effect such a transformation of society as the leaven of her truth and life

---

[1] Vos, *The Kingdom and the Church*, p.88.
[2] *Jesus Christ the Risen Lord*, pp.250, 253.

actively permeates. She cannot make society the church, for this would be to deny the existence of the kingdom of darkness within society. But the church can continually contribute to society's christianization in that the good she possesses will gain relative ascendancy over the evil in society as it will in the church absolutely.

This brings us to consider the dangers of which the church must always be aware. In the first place, if the church seeks constantly to christianize society, she must constantly recognize that society is ever out to secularize her. Filson suggests in what way the church from its earliest existence encountered the danger of secularization: "They [Christians] had to maintain a delicate balance between friendship and contact with all kinds of people on the one hand, and separation from clearly pagan and cheap aspects of social life on the other... They were contributing to social change by the vitality of their faith, their wholesome worship and fellowship, and their moral life. But it was a slow and indirect method of change; it offered no formal programme for direct action."[1]

In the execution of this often painfully slow programme, the church might at times succumb to the temptation of compromise and worldliness. But where this would occur, she would not then infuse society with the clear stream of true Christianity. Rather, she would only allow the evil of the world to pollute her. Of this danger she must ever be aware, and must avoid it at all costs and at all times; for compromise and worldliness are subtle and intoxicating temptations to her as a supposed means of fulfilling her task in the world.

But there is an even more insidious danger which the church encounters in a world of depraved humanity making up fallen society. This is for the world to adopt the values of the church, call them its own and thereby render the church in its estimation superfluous. It is the mystery of iniquity at work, continually becoming more complex in the deception of error by its admixture

[1] *Ibid.*, pp.255-256.

with truth, or borrowing from the church's truth a pattern from which to forge the imitations of pseudo-truth.

In other words, the world, by diabolically cunning imitations, seeks to become like the church. And if the church fails to discern this prostitution of her absolute spiritual values, or fails to oppose this secularization of the spiritual, then her defeat is imminent; for she has not christianized society. Society will have taken from her her distinctive values (gospel, truth, righteousness, etc.), made them its own by secularization and thereafter proceeded to dismiss the church as no longer relevant.

Wendland points out how this peril manifests itself in history: "From the theological point of view it is of the utmost importance to note that each advance in man's rule of the world brings with it a fresh form of the demonic; thus the age of modern science brings the demonic in the form of a denial of God on the grounds of reason; the age of technical improvement, the degradation of man to a slave or to a function within a system of machine-production; the capitalistic intoxication of an absolutely limitless expansion of production and profit produces the worship of mammon: the conquest of space and time by radio and air transport, man's enslavement to speed and an imperialistic desire to expand."[1]

In this statement we are furnished with several examples of society's secularization of the church's values by making them its own. The church teaches that science should interpret this world to God's glory. Society, recognizing the value of science, adopts it to set itself up as God by means of its own interpretation and determination of reality. Technical improvement should give man more liberty to glorify God. Instead, society perverts it to reduce man to greater slavery in seeking its own selfish goals. The church teaches that private property is the trust of a man's stewardship before God. Society makes it a means of power and exploitation of fellow-man.

And so it continues: "Every Christian development breaks up again and must be won afresh; the secular forces constantly break through such Christian achievements. The *advancing,*

---

[1] *The Kingdom of God and History*, p.162.

world-influencing church becomes once more a church *rejected by the world*."[1] Against these forms of secularism, therefore, the church must ever be on guard. For the world will try to secularize the church and reduce her to its level. Then, to the extent that it successfully does so, the reproach of the cross the church preaches will have ceased. But in conjunction with this attempt, the world will also seek to secularize the church's values. And in this, by increasing cunning and clever imitation, distortion or perversion, the world will be increasingly successful (*II Thess.* 2:7-8).

The church must, therefore, ever be awake to the uniqueness of her nature, her message and her mission. She will seek in measure to make society like herself. But so long as this present age endures, the antithesis between her and it will remain. Society, it is true, will seek to blur if not erase it, either by making the church like itself or itself like the church. And when it succeeds in almost total measure, as it will near the end, then its final destruction under God's judgment at Christ's return will be imminent.

Society's hope, consequently, which is in closest association with the church's task within it, is not conformity but transformation. In the final and absolute sense, this will only be accomplished at the return of the Lord in glory. In the meantime the church, resisting both the temptation to conform to it or the delusion of having it conform to her, will seek its transformation, though ever aware that her best results can only remain relative.

Her task, however, is constantly to seek society's transformation, for while she lives in the present hope of the world's transformation, she must be engaged in that pursuit which at present not only contributes to the final form that will be hers, but also fashions her environment as much as possible to its final form as well. But the church must assess the position of her situation afresh lest in delusion her optimism leads to the world's conquest of her, or her pessimism debilitate her function as the *eschaton* whose goal is to inherit all things in joint heirship with her Saviour God. To this end, she is ever to seek to prepare herself

[1] *Ibid.*, p.189.

and the world for the last hour. "In spite of its transitory nature this vocation to the world and to historical work is incumbent on us because the world is and remains God's, as will be anew attested and confirmed by him at the coming of his kingdom, and because secular history is being guided towards the coming of God's kingdom in its perfection."[1]

4. Bearing witness to and directing toward the true utopian goal

Little more remains than to bring our subject to its appropriate conclusion. This can now be done. For as we have seen, the church by the very fact that she exists as an intrusion of the final order into this present dispensation bears witness to what man's utopian goal should be and directs him to it. Man's chief end, after all, is to glorify God and to enjoy him forever. And only as the church is heard and heeded will this goal be attained. Man may not hear the church, or he may refuse to heed her and thereby seek to create a utopia by which to make a name for himself. But all his efforts are doomed to failure and will come to nought in the same way that the tower of Babel became a standing landmark to man's sinful folly as he at that time refused to hear or heed the voice of God.

Wendland, therefore, makes an accurate judgment concerning this vain search of man for utopia apart from God when he says: "This false faith in utopia springs out of the passionate longing in man, which nothing can stifle, *for a new creation, a restoration of human nature.* He can neither live nor think without the quest for completion and perfection. Would that man could understand this! For in his very faith in these utopias man bears witness against himself that he has sinned and fallen away from God."[2]

Man wants a utopia. In fact, he is incomplete without one. And the marrow of his being still continues to cry out to him that this is so. But man in sin does not want the only utopia

[1] *Ibid.*, p.186.
[2] *Ibid.*, p.171.

which will ever be, the utopia of God. From this he already turned away in the garden of Eden. And when he turned away, he turned, not to another or a different utopia, but to destruction. From this condition he needs to be rescued. From this delusion he needs to be disabused. God alone is able to perform this. And he will in Christ. Christ alone is the hope of the world and his kingdom alone is the true utopia. May the church, therefore, understand her task and be diligently about the business of her head and king.

"The fact that the church is there, in the midst of time and history, is what alters and continues to alter the world and history, in so far as the church is faithful to its charge."[1] The church, for the sake of her Lord and the realization of her being and existence in this present age, cannot afford to be complacent about her witness or indifferent to her ultimate goal. For if she is complacent about her witness, then she has ceased to be the voice of her Lord and herald of his truth. And if she is indifferent to her ultimate goal, she has not only become too much a part of this temporal world, but she belies that eschatological destiny toward which all is inexorably moving, namely, God's ultimate sovereignty over all created habitation, which is to be as complete as the way in which the waters now cover the sea.

"Only the church as it waits in hope understands that any influence which Christianity exerts on various ages or on historical institutions must somehow serve to *prepare the world for its last hour,* for the coming of God's ultimate sovereignty."[2] She cannot do this perfectly, completely, finally, or alone without her Lord's help. But that she can do so to any appreciable degree is because of what her Lord has chosen to accomplish through her as his body which is presently growing unto his fulness.

It is therefore true: "Jesus Christ gave men a social hope for this world and for the world to come, partial hope for this age of history and a perfect hope for history beyond history. The kingdom of God, i.e., the rule of God, is being realized in measure

[1] *Ibid.*, p.188.
[2] *Ibid.*, p.189.

now and could be realized far more; but it is Christian realism to admit that it can never be fully in space and time as we mortals know them."[1]

So the church must continue to pray, "Thy kingdom come." But the church also realizes that the kingdom is already in her midst. Vos concludes his book with a statement which will also do duty here: "The thought of the kingdom of God implies the subjection of the entire range of human life in all its forms and spheres to the ends of religion. The kingdom reminds us of the *absoluteness, the pervasiveness, the unrestricted dominion,* which of right belong to all true religion. It proclaims that religion, and religion alone, can act as the *supreme unifying, centralizing factor* in the life of man, as that which binds all together and perfects all by leading it to its final goal in the service of God (*Matt.* 5:48)."[2]

[1] Frank Wilson Price, *Marx Meets Christ* (Philadelphia: Westminster Press, 1957), p.78.

[2] *The Kingdom and the Church*, p.103.

BIBLIOGRAPHY

Aristotle, *The Nicomachean Ethics*, (The Loeb Classical Library), Cambridge: Harvard University Press, 1947.

Allis, Oswald T., *Prophecy and the Church*, Philadelphia: Presbyterian and Reformed, 1947.

Atkins, Gaius Glenn, and Frederick L. Fagley, *History of American Congregationalism*, Boston and Chicago: Pilgrim Press, 1942.

Bahnsen, Greg L., *Theonomy in Christian Ethics*, Nutley (USA): Craig Press, 1977.

————, *No Other Standard: Theonomy and Its Critics*, Tyler (USA): Institute for Christian Economics, 1991.

Bannerman, D. Douglas, *The Scripture Doctrine of the Church*, Grand Rapids: Eerdmans, 1955.

Barker, William S. and W. Robert Godfrey, eds., *Theonomy: A Reformed Critique*, Grand Rapids: Academie Books, 1990.

Berkhof, Hendrikus, *Christ the Meaning of History*, Grand Rapids: Baker Book House, 1979.

Berkhof, Louis, *Systematic Theology*, Edinburgh: Banner of Truth Trust, 1974 (reprint).

Berkouwer, G.C., *The Church*, Grand Rapids: Eerdmans, 1976.

Boettner, Loraine, *The Millennium*, Phillipsburg, N.J.: Presbyterian and Reformed, 1958.

Bowman, John Wick, *The Drama of the Book of Revelation*, Philadelphia: Westminster Press, 1955.

————, *The Intention of Jesus*, Philadelphia: Westminster Press, 1943.

Braun, F.M., *Neues Licht auf die Kirche*, Einsiedeln/Köln: Verlagsanstalt Benziger, 1946.

Bright, John, *The Kingdom of God*, New York/Nashville: Abingdon/Cokesbury Press, 1953.

Broadus, John A., *Commentary on the Gospel of Matthew*, Philadelphia: American Baptist Publication Society, 1886.

Bruce, F.F., *Commentary on the Book of Acts*, Grand Rapids: Eerdmans, 1954.

Calvin, John, *Institutes of the Christian Religion*, J.T. McNeill, ed., Philadelphia: Westminster Press, 1960.

Cameron, Viola M., *God's Plan and Man's Destiny*, Philadelphia: Presbyterian and Reformed, 1955.

Campbell, Roderick, *Israel and the New Covenant*, Philadelphia, Presbyterian and Reformed, 1954.

Carson, D.A., ed., *The Church in the Bible and the World*, Grand Rapids: Baker Book House, 1987.

Carson, D.A. and John D. Woodbridge, eds., *Scripture and Truth*, Grand Rapids: The Zondervan Corporation, 1983.

Chantry, Walter J., *God's Righteous Kingdom*, Edinburgh: Banner of Truth, 1980.

Clouse, Robert G., *The Meaning of the Millennium: Four Views*, Downers Grove: InterVarsity Press, 1979.

Conn, Harvie M., ed., *Theological Perspectives on Church Growth*, Phillipsburg, N.J.: Presbyterian and Reformed, 1976.

Cullmann, Oscar, "Königsherrschaft Christi und Kirche im Neuen Testament," *Theologischen Studien*, herausgegeben von Karl Barth, Heft 10. Zollikon-Zurich: Evangelischer Verlag, 1941.

———, *Der Staat im Neuen Testament*, Tubingen: J.C.B. Mohr, 1956.

———, *The State in the New Testament*, New York: Charles Scribner's Sons, 1956.

Davis, John J., *Christ's Victorious Kingdom*, Grand Rapids: Baker Book House, 1986.

DeJong, P.Y., *The Church's Witness to the World*, 2 Vols., Pella (USA): Pella Publishing Co., 1960.

Delitzsch, Franz, *Biblical Commentary on the Prophecies of Isaiah*, 2 volumes (*Keil and Delitzsch Series*), Grand Rapids: Eerdmans, 1954.

Dijk, K., *Het Einde der Eeuwen*, Kampen: J.H. Kok, 1952.

———, *De Toekomst van Christus*, Kampen: J.H. Kok, 1953.

Filson, Floyd V., *Jesus Christ the Risen Lord*, New York-Nashville: Abingdon Press, 1956.

Flew, R. Newton, *Jesus and His Church*, London: Epworth Press, 1938.

Geldenhuys, Norval, *Commentary on the Gospel of Luke*, Grand Rapids: Eerdmans, 1952.

Goldsworthy, Graeme, *Gospel and Kingdom*, Exeter: Paternoster, 1981.

Gottschick, J., "Kingdom of God," *The New Schaff-Herzog Encyclopedia*, Vol.VI, Grand Rapids: Baker Book House, 1953.

Hendriksen, William, *Exposition of the Pastoral Epistles*, (N.T.C.), Grand Rapids: Baker Book House, 1957.

Hodge, Charles, *Commentary on the Epistle to the Romans*, Grand Rapids: Eerdmans, 1950.

Hort, F.J.A., *The Christian Ecclesia*, London: MacMillan, 1900.

Hughes, Archibald, *A New Heaven and a New Earth*, Philadelphia: Presbyterian and Reformed, 1958.

Jamieson, Fausset, and Brown, *Commentary on the Whole Bible* (one volume), Grand Rapids: Zondervan Publishing House, n.d.,(eighth edition).

Jenkins, Daniel, *The Strangeness of the Church*, Garden City, New York: Doubleday and Co., 1955.

Keil, C.F., *The Minor Prophets*, 2 Vols., (Keil and Delitzsch, *Commentary on the Old Testament*), Grand Rapids: Eerdmans, 1954.

Kromminga, D.H., *The Millennium*, Grand Rapids: Eerdmans, 1948.

Kueng, Hans, *The Church*, Garden City, New York: Image Books, 1967.

Kuiper, R.B., *The Glorius Body of Christ*, Grand Rapids: Eerdmans, 1966.

Kuyper, Abraham, Sr., *Calvinism*, Grand Rapids; Eerdmans, 1943.

Kuyper, Abraham, Jr., *Van het Koninkrijk der Hemelen*, Kampen: J.H. Kok, 1932.

Ladd, George E., *A Theology of the New Testament*, Grand Rapids: Eerdmans, 1974.

Leith, John H., *Creeds of the Churches* (third edition), Louisville: John Knox Press, 1982.

Lightfoot, J.B., *Saint Paul's Epistle to the Colossians and to Philemon*, Grand Rapids: Zondervan Publishing House, n.d., (reprint of 1879 edition).

Linton, Olof, *Das Problem der Urkirche in der neueren Forschung*, Uppsala, 1932.

Luther, Martin, "Predigt auf das Fest der heiligen Engel," *Sämmtliche Schriften*, Vol.X, St. Louis: Concordia Publishing House, 1885, pp.1066-1089.

Mayor, J.B., *The Epistle of St. James*, London: MacMillan, 1897.

Michaelis, D. Wilhelm, *Reich Gottes und Geist Gottes nach dem Neuen Testament*, Basel: Druck und Verlag von F. Reinhardt, 1930.

Milligan, George, *St. Paul's Epistles to the Thessalonians*, London: MacMillan, 1908.

Minear, Paul S., *The Kingdom and the Power*, Philadelphia: Westminster Press, 1950.

———, *Images of the Church in the New Testament*, Philadelphia: Westminster Press, 1960.

Moltmann, J., *The Church in the Power of the Spirit*, New York: Harper & Row, 1977.

Montgomery, John Warwick, *God's Inerrant Word*, Minneapolis: Bethany Fellowship, Inc., 1973.

Murray, John, *Collected Writings*, Vol.2, Edinburgh: Banner of Truth Trust, 1977.

Nygren, Anders, *Christ and His Church*, Philadelphia: Westminster Press, 1956.

Plummer, Alfred, *A Critical and Exegetical Commentary on the Gospel According to St. Luke*, (I.C.C. Series), 4th edition, Edinburgh: T. & T. Clark, 1913.

Prenter, Regin, "Die Systematische Theologie und das Problem der Bibelauslegung," *Theologische Literaturzeitung*, Halle/Berlin, October, 1956.

Price, Frank Wilson, *Marx Meets Christ*, Philadelphia: Westminster Press, 1957.

Ridderbos, Herman N., *The Coming of the Kingdom*, Philadelphia: Presbyterian and Reformed, 1962.

Salmond, S.D.F., *The Epistle to the Ephesians*, (E.G.T. Series), Vol.III, Grand Rapids: Eerdmans, 1951.

Sauer, Erich, *From Eternity to Eternity*, Grand Rapids: Eerdmans, 1954.

Schmidt, K.L., "Basileia," *Theologisches Wörterbuch zum Neuen Testament*, Band I, Gerhard Kittel ed., Stuttgart: Verlag von W. Kohlhammer, 1933.

Swete, H.B., *The Apocalypse of St. John*, London: MacMillan, 1911.

Van Til, Cornelius, *Common Grace*, Philadelphia: Presbyterian and Reformed, 1954.

Vos, G., *The Kingdom and the Church*, Grand Rapids: Eerdmans, 1951.

————, *The Pauline Eschatology*, Grand Rapids: Eerdmans, 1952.

Wendland, H.D., "The Kingdom of God and History," *The Kingdom of God and History: A Symposium*, Chicago/New York: Willet, Clark and Co., 1935.

Westcott, B.F., *The Epistle to the Hebrews*, Grand Rapids: Eerdmans, 1952.

————, *The Gospel According to John*, Grand Rapids: Eerdmans, 1954.

Westminster Theological Seminary Faculty, *The Infallible Word*, Philadelphia: Presbyterian Guardian Publishing Corporation, 1946.

Wilkinson, T.L., *The Westminster Confession Now*, Melbourne, 1992, (available from the author).

INDEX OF AUTHORS

INDEX OF SELECTED SUBJECTS AND TITLES
(Main themes can be readily traced by the Contents pages)

INDEX OF SCRIPTURE REFERENCES

CHRIST TRIUMPHANT

[237]

CHRIST TRIUMPHANT